970.1 White, Jon Manchip
W

Everyday life of the
North American
Indian

23524

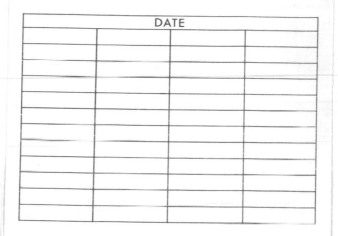

Everyday Life of the
NORTH AMERICAN INDIAN

The face of the American Indian.

Everyday Life of the
NORTH AMERICAN INDIAN

by

JON MANCHIP WHITE

HOLMES & MEIER PUBLISHERS, INC.

New York

First published in the United States of America 1979 by
HOLMES & MEIER PUBLISHERS, INC.
30 Irving Place, New York, N.Y. 10003

Library of Congress Cataloging in Publication Data
White, Jon Manchip.
  Everyday life of the North American Indian.
  1. Indians of North America—Social life and customs. I. Title.
E98.S7W48 1979   970′.004′97   79–84
ISBN 0-8419-0488-X

PRINTED IN GREAT BRITAIN

To My Wife

Ten Years on the Rio Grande

Contents

List of Illustrations

LIST OF ILLUSTRATIONS

Maps & Figures

Acknowledgments

The Author and Publishers wish to thank the following for their kind permission to reproduce the illustrations in this book: the Arizona State Museum, for figs 33, 75; figs 2, 3, 4, 5, 6, 20, 21, 22, 29, 50, 56, 63, 64, 76, 77, 78, 82, 85, 88 (all Photos by Helga Teiwes); fig. 9 (Photo by C. M. Wood); figs 80 and 83 (Photos by Tad Nichols); and figs 87 and 90 (Photos by L. F. H. Lowe); the British Museum, for figs 34 and 68; Cincinnatti Art Museum, for fig. 60; The Exhibit Museum, University of Michigan, for figs 7, 10, 13, 14, 32, 35, 37, 43, 44, 45; the Mansell Collection, for the frontispiece, and figs 25, 26, 36, 53, 54, 58, 62, 69, 73, 74, 91, 93, 97; Milwaukee Public Museum, for figs 11 and 12; the Northern Natural Gas Company Collection, Joselyn Art Museum, Omaha, Nebraska, for fig. 102; the Smithsonian Institution National Anthropological Archives, Bureau of American Ethnology Collection, for figs 27, 28, 70 and 104; Western Americana Picture Library, for figs 1, 8, 15, 16, 17, 18, 23, 24, 30, 31, 38, 39, 40, 41, 42, 46, 47, 48, 49, 51, 52, 55, 57, 59, 61, 65, 66, 67, 71, 72, 79, 81, 84, 86, 89, 92, 94, 95, 96, 98, 99, 100, 101, 103, 105, 106; and the Zoological Society of London, for figs 19 (a)–(e). The maps and figures were specially drawn by Alan R. Gunston. LSIA.

1
The Spirits
of The Ancestors

The Conestoga wagons creak and lumber across the prairie, their canvas flapping like a convoy of little ships labouring across an enormous empty ocean. The sun is just passing its zenith and beats down pitilessly. The trail-boss and his outriders urge on the teams of tired mules and their drivers; they must make the waterhole marked on their makeshift maps by nightfall. Suddenly the trail-boss stiffens in his saddle. He lifts his hand to his dust-streaked face and peers under it at the distant horizon. Where the edge of the vast plain meets the sky he can see a brown plume coiling into the air. Could that dim smudge be anything more than an ordinary dust-devil? No: this is Indian country. A moment later his ears catch the drumming of hoofs and the yelling of war-cries. Quickly he orders the toiling wagons to swing inwards and laager into a tight circle. Men leap out and pull down packing-casks, chests, trunks, even pieces of furniture, thrusting them beneath the wagons and into the gaps between to serve as a barricade. Winchesters and Navy Colts are snatched from their holsters and boxes of ammunition are broken open. The women crouch beside their menfolk, loading the spare weapons or huddling protectively above the children. None too soon. The first wild wave of horsemen is already breaking against the flimsy barrier. The men lying behind the upturned armchairs and chests of china and water-barrels fire into a blur of half-naked bodies daubed with paint and feathers. The air is filled with savage yells, with the crack of guns, with the reek of blood and sweat and gunpowder. Again and again the attackers return to the charge, leaving their dead draped across the barricade and the upturned shafts of the wagons. Finally they fall back on their traditional tactic of riding full tilt around the besieged band, yelping and yippying, guiding their bedizened steeds with their knees, twisting sideways to loose off their arrows and fire the rifles stolen from the victims of earlier massacres or sold to them by renegade white traders. The defenders squint grimly down the scorching

13

barrels of their guns and pour fire into the maddened mass of the savages as they pound by, the manes and tails of their mounts and their own plaited locks and headdresses streaming out behind them. Bullets thud into bodies. Redskins topple to the ground to be trampled by their own comrades as they whirl past in a vortex of dust. The trail-boss is hit. His

1 *Indians attacking a wagon train. After a painting by Frederic Remington.*

second-in-command snatches up his rifle and takes command. There can be no surrender, for the white men know that they can expect no quarter. They will be scalped, their wives and daughters will be seized as slaves and squaws, their children will be brought up in Indian ways. And now the arrows ripping into the wagons are tipped with fire and the tindery canvas burns with an oily flame. There is no alternative but to fight to the last, to sell their lives dearly . . .

Such is the portrait of American Indian activity with which we are familiar from watching a thousand movies. It is exciting and entertaining. But is it true? Does it really correspond to historical facts?

The answer is – a little . . . but not much. Yet the Hollywood stereotype, invented for the purpose of spinning a good story, has gone deep, and has done a great deal of damage. Many millions of people all over the world, even in the United States and Canada, know almost nothing about the American Indian apart from the crude picture built up in their minds by the cinema and television. The visual medium is potent: in irresponsible hands it can be dangerously misleading. Overexposure to cheap, run-of-the-mill 'Cowboy-and-Indian' films and pulp-novels has implanted a false image of the American Indian – as well as a false image of the American cowboy.

It must also be admitted that the American Indian has contributed generously to his own misleading stereotype. For example, he was deeply impressed by the showy caricature of himself portrayed in the show-ring, during the last century, by the Wild West circuses of such entrepreneurs as William F. (Buffalo Bill) Cody and William (Pawnee Bill) Lillie – though the Wild West Show had been started, in all good faith, as early as 1837, when George Catlin, the great artist and traveller, displayed his 'Indian Gallery'. At one stage there were over 50 such 'Indian Shows' going the rounds. The genuine Indian could not resist the showy and largely fake regalia of the stage Indian. He added the latter's plumes, spangles and sequins to his own costume, making it glamorous but spurious. Thus the Indian himself bears, ironically enough, much of the responsibility for his own 'Hollywoodization'.

Misconceptions about Indians

Let us briefly consider a few distortions about the life of the American Indian which were implied by our opening scene.

First – and for this we can hardly blame the film-writer – the very words *Indian* and *Redskin* are inaccurate. The American Indian, as we shall see in a moment, is of Asiatic and Mongolian origin: but he has no connexion whatever with the Indian of the Asian sub-continent. The mistake occurred when Columbus first reached the shores of the New World in October, 1492. When he sighted the Island of San Salvador (modern Watling Island), he thought he had reached 'the Indies', as the Far East was then called, and that he was looking at the coast of Japan. The existence of an entire continent blocking off Europe from the Indies came as a complete surprise to the explorers of that day. As for the word *Redskin*, it came into service because for some reason the first Frenchman to reach America in the middle of the sixteenth century called the native Americans *peaux rouges*. The French pride themselves on their precise use of language: but here they were inaccurate. None of the American Indians were or are red-skinned, but were either a light or a dark brown, or as fair as any Frenchman.

However, the two major misconceptions conveyed by our introductory scene are that (1) the American Indians were by nature bloodthirsty, and that (2) they were exclusively a race of horsemen. Moreover the Indians in

15

Hollywood films appear to inhabit only the deserts and mountains of the Southwest, or occasionally the northern plains, and only seldom the other three-quarters of the country where they were actually more numerous. The Southwest – West Texas, New Mexico, Arizona, Southern Utah and Southern Colorado – is pictorially spectacular, and makes a strong appeal to the film-director; and the Southwest also contained three of the most famous tribes: Navajo, Apache and Comanche. These tribes were certainly mounted: yet even so the popular notion of their behaviour is erroneous, since only the Comanche were truly a horse-orientated people of the type depicted in the movies. The Apache were poor horsemen, liking to eat horses as much as to ride them, and they usually fought on foot. As for the Navajo, they were generally a pacific people, especially when compared with the Apache and Comanche; they were herdsmen and pastoralists, employing their shaggy ponies less for warfare than for tending their sheep and cattle. In any case, the Navajo, Apache and Comanche were only three of more than 600 tribes that are believed to have existed during historic times, so the emphasis on them by novelists and film-writers is lamentably lopsided. As the following pages will show, the majority of Indian tribes did not live in desert conditions, and were not primarily, if at all, horsemen. The horse itself became a factor in Indian life only a century or two before the native mode of life was extinguished by the white man: for more than 20,000 years, the Indian had survived and prospered without the horse.

Even on the eve of the European onslaught, most Indians were hunters, agriculturists, food-gatherers or fishermen, living peacefully in a humdrum and unassertive fashion. Far from being shiftless nomads, most of them were settled on their own fairly well defined territories, or were actually sedentary farmers or fisherfolk. True, many tribes possessed a martial tradition, but since most peoples were small, and split further into individual bands, and because of the constant necessity of securing food, their combats were not so much all-out wars as random brushes and skirmishes. It was the white man, with his organized armies, his advanced weapons, his love of conquest, who taught the Indian the business of ruthless and unrestricted warfare, forcing him onto the defensive, making him wage a gallant but hopeless battle against tremendous odds, in an effort to preserve his property and his identity. The real aggressiveness was demonstrated by the white man, not the Indian, dropping back steadily from the East towards the West, where he was finally swallowed up in the setting sun. The majority of the massacres were perpetrated by the white man on the Indian, not vice versa: and indeed the story of how the Indian was cheated, dispossessed and largely exterminated by the advancing European is a saddening and shocking one.

16

We shall be taking a closer look at Indian warfare in a later chapter; here we are only noting that the popular impression of the Indian would appear to be that of a footloose and bellicose race, primarily confined to the Western plains or the arid Southwest. For this the modern Hollywood screenwriter and the writer of Westerns is largely to blame, although several important American novelists, such as Willa Cather, set their work in the Southwest for artistically valid reasons. The writers of earlier days, however, Fennimore Cooper or Owen Wister, set their 'Westerns' in the East: but in our own century the Indian has somehow become consigned to the same vague westerly Never-Never-Land as the American cowboy, the American pioneer, and the American cavalry.

In western fiction, the Indian has usually been cast in the role of a permanent antagonist of the white man. Such was by no means always the case. For example, when the wagon-train described in our opening paragraph rolled across the prairie, it would probably have been helped rather than hindered by the local Indians. Thousands of white travellers were succoured by friendly Indians in the wastes of North America, and provided with food, drink, shelter, and guides. The initial reception accorded by the Indian to the white interloper was almost always amicable. The Indian was intrigued by the newcomer, by his appearance, dress, technology and religion. He assumed that the continent was big enough to accommodate both of them – as, at the beginning, it was. He had no idea that the numbers of the white man on the eastern seaboard would swell in such a monstrous fashion and so rapidly become a threat. It took him a long time to realize that the wagon-trails and stage-coach lines and railway networks pushing onto his ranges were fetters that would imprison him. But then he saw that the passengers in those wagons and railway-trains were not neighbourly and co-operative folk, but miners, soldiers, merchants and sod-busters who would obliterate him and rape the hills, rivers, meadows and woods that had been his home for more moons than the gods themselves could count.

The trouble was that there could never really be a compromise between the Indian and the white man. The confrontation was bound to be deadly and to end in ruin for the Indian. The difference between the two modes of life was absolute. The Indian life was too bizarre, too frightening, too unpredictable to the white man: and where there is fear, there is hate. Then, too, the American Indian, like his Mexican counterpart in the time of Cortés and Pizarro, had the misfortune to encounter the European – Spaniard, Frenchman or Englishman – at a time when those nations were passing through a particularly vital and imperialistic phase of their history, reinforced in the case of independent America by the iron

17

dynamism of the Industrial Revolution. After the Texans had established their republic in 1836, after Mexico had been thoroughly defeated and dismembered in 1848, after the Civil War had been cleared out of the way and President MacKinley had declared America's 'Manifest Destiny', there was no longer any place in the American scheme of things for America's 'savage', 'backward' and 'uncivilized' indigenous occupants. They had to go – and go they did.

They were thoroughly disposed of. The end of Indian resistance was signalled by the murder by the Seventh Cavalry of over 300 men, women and children of the Sioux nation at Wounded Knee, South Dakota, on 29 December 1890. By that time the American Indian population, which had never been large, had been cut in half by massacre, forced marches, forced removals, imprisonment, disease, and deliberate starvation; later it would be worn down further by alcoholism and loss of the will to live. By the end of the nineteenth century nobody, American or European, could have been blamed for assuming that it was not merely a case of 'The Last of the Mohicans' but of 'The Last of the American Indian'. Indeed, there are probably many people in the world today who would be surprised to learn that the American Indian is not actually extinct, like other peoples who have succumbed beneath the weight of the invading white culture. The names of many celebrated tribes have vanished from the map. Of the 600 tribes known to have been in existence in 1800, only about 250 have survived into the twentieth century, most of them in small numbers.

If many people may be forgiven for assuming that the American Indian no longer enjoys a distinct existence, there are probably even more who lack any knowledge of his life up to the moment when destiny brought him into contact with the European. In fact, during the last half-century the Indian population of America has shown an astonishing resilience, and the Indian birth-rate is more than double that of other segments of American society. Slowly, in the face of sickness, poverty and unemployment, the Indian nation is on the way to regaining something like its original level of perhaps a million souls. And just as the Indian – tough, courageous, a survivor – possesses a future, so also he possesses a past. His lineage is ancient, complex, and impressive, giving the lie to those of his enemies who found it convenient to dismiss him as a simple 'primitive' or an uncouth 'savage'. His ancestors can be traced back not for a few generations, or even a few centuries, but for a period of between 20,000 and 30,000 years: as long a pedigree as that of the Europeans. Just as archaeologists are beginning to fill in the gaps in African prehistory, so that a new and unexpected portrait of that continent is emerging, so the gaps in North American prehistory are being similarly dealt with. As in the case of Africa, the life of prehistoric

America before the arrival of Columbus is turning out to be wonderfully rich and varied.

Origins and settlement

Where did he come from, the North American Indian? We must make some attempt to answer this question if we are to appreciate what Indian life was like at its proud peak.

Even to grasp the character of a modern nation-state, in which life changes with bewildering rapidity, requires a knowledge of the influences and forces that have moulded it. Communities, like individuals, are the product of their past, even though they may ignore or belittle it. One of the difficulties of writing about the American Indian is that the citizens of the United States, and even of Canada, have little interest in the distant past. The average American takes it for granted that the annals of his country started in 1776. The Colonial Period, stretching back more than two centuries earlier, is misty and insubstantial; and what happened in the ages before that is a complete blur. Nonetheless, the story of the Indian is as integral a part of the history of America as the story of the European. Indeed, it is possible that the modern American might feel more at home in today's world if he could comprehend something of the Indian and Colonial epochs, and regard them not as ephemeral or irrelevant but as the sheet-anchor of his country's history. Such an attitude would help to assuage that sense of newness, of being a *parvenu* on the world stage, that often oppresses him. Thirty thousand years, as we have said, is an impressive span.

Be that as it may, the original Americans, unlike the later mass of Europeans, came not from the East but from the Northwest. Three hundred centuries ago the face of North America was very different from what it is now. Its whole upper half was in the grip of the final stage of the Great Ice Age. The fourth and last invasion of the polar ice-cap, called by geologists the Wisconsin Glaciation (corresponding to the Würm Glaciation in Europe) clamped a tight white seal over three-quarters of Canada, reaching southwards to engulf the Great Lakes. As the ice-cap advanced, the wildlife of North America was driven southwards onto the warm, moist, tree-laden, succulent ranges that extended over the entire area of the United States – ranges fed by the plentiful rains created by the thermal conditions at the edge of the ice-pack. This wildlife was magnificently abundant. It included not only animals with which we are acquainted today, such as the elk, moose, caribou, deer and peccary, but the mammoth, the mastodon, the camel, the tapir, the weird and ungainly giant sloth who walked on the backs of his hands, the musk-ox, and the huge long-horned bison. There

19

was even a species of horse – for the horse had once existed and had either been killed off or had died out in North America ages before it was re-introduced by the Spaniards.

These were huge animals, packed with meat, plentifully supplied with the bone, hide and sinew on which early man relied for his clothing, tents, and a hundred other items. It was natural that, when the bands of hunters who were already wandering the wastes of Siberia should have got wind of this rich quarry, they determined to seek it out. But how, in view of the barrier of ice that everywhere existed, could they reach it?

The first part of their trek, they found, was easy enough. A convenient ice-free corridor led them to the northeast corner of the Asian continent, where they discovered a wide, dry strip of tundra extending in the form of an isthmus across what are now the Bering Straits. The Straits today are only sixty miles wide, and can easily be traversed by the Eskimos in their skin boats; but then, when the sea-level had dropped an extra 200 feet because so much of the Arctic Ocean had been locked up as ice, crossing the wind-swept land-bridge represented little more than an easy stroll for such hardy folk.

It was when they reached Alaska that their troubles began. Except on three or four occasions during the Wisconsin Glaciation, the ice-sheets that separated the arctic regions from the beckoning paradise to the south were frozen solid. It was during those rare intervals, when a valley in the icefield opened, that the more daring spirits ventured into the heart of the unknown continent. With the Rockies Glacier enveloping the west coast of Canada to their right, and the Laurentide Glacier mantling central and eastern Canada to their left, they journeyed southwards, keeping to the line of what was to be the Mackenzie River and hugging the eastern slopes of the Rocky Mountains, which were already the backbone of the Americas. Eventually they emerged on to the lush grasslands of Montana. There, clear of the gloomy fastnesses of the glaciers, they were free to choose the direction in which they would next advance. Some of them chose the forested country to the east; others moved west to the Pacific coast; and the remainder continued southwards, through Wyoming and Colorado, until they came to the lands now occupied by Arizona and New Mexico. Nor did they necessarily halt there. Some of the more daring hunters pressed down through Mexico and Central America into South America, until after many centuries they reached Chile and the Argentine and could go no further. There is an interesting parallel here with Africa, for it took the northerly tribes of that continent many millennia to filter as far as the Cape of Good Hope, and indeed they only got there shortly after the Dutch colonists had already established themselves there by sea. Oddly enough, it was only to

20

be in Central America, with the advent of the Olmecs, Mayans, Toltecs, Zapotecs and Aztecs, and in South America with the rise of the Incas, that the New World would sprout any higher civilizations before Columbus. And we shall be constantly reminded throughout this book that Mexico, in particular, constitutes an intimate extension of the area we are studying, and that certain events that happened there had repercussions that determined the development of culture in the lands to the north.

It is possible, of course, that the earliest hunters reached Canada and America by some other means than the Alaskan route, or, as in the case of the Aleuts and certain Eskimo groups, by island-hopping along the Aleutians. It would be foolish to be too dogmatic, in the imperfect state of our present knowledge. The splendid seamen of Polynesia may have made a sporadic landfall in South America, while about 1000 years ago small numbers of Vikings, perhaps led by Leif Erickson himself, may have founded a settlement at L'Anse aux Meadows on the Great Northern Peninsula in Newfoundland. But the bulk of the first waves of American immigrants certainly travelled south from the Yukon, in the manner indicated. There appear to have been two main groups, the earliest one leaving Siberia at a time when the typical languages of the area had taken full form, the second several millennia later. The date for the original settlement is definitely earlier than 10,000 B.C., and may eventually prove to be as early as 50,000–40,000 B.C. As for the second and more populous wave, it must have arrived prior to 9000–8000 B.C., since it was at that time that the Alaskan land-bridge, affected by the drastic climatic change that accompanied the end of the Ice Age, broke up and sank beneath the sea.

The evidence of physical anthropology and blood-typing strongly suggests that the characteristics of the modern Indians take their origin from the Classic Mongoloid peoples of Siberia and Upper Canada. These peoples, like the Indians, have brown eyes, straight black hair, very little beard or body hair, a broad nose with a low bridge, slanting eyes with a typical inner fold to the eyelid, and a blood-group high in type B. Unfortunately, there is an almost total lack of the fossil material that would tell us what these original Americans actually looked like. From the town of Midland in Texas came 'Midland Man', in reality the bones of a young woman who died between 10,000 and 15,000 years ago, and from Mexico City came the controversial remains of 'Tepexpan Man', who might have been about the same age. Other human fossils that may be about 10,000–15,000 years old have been unearthed at one time or another in Minnesota, Mississippi, Florida, Colorado, Alberta, and from no fewer than five different sites in California (Arlington Beach, Luguna Beach, Los Angeles, Rancho La Brea, and San Diego). A most promising find hailed

21

from the Marmes site in Washington State, where the remains of three skulls that could be dated between 11,000 and 8000 B.C. were unearthed. To make the discovery more exciting, the bones were accompanied by a bone spearpoint and a bone needle, and for a time it seemed that science had stumbled on the relics of a rich aboriginal culture. Unfortunately, the American Army Corps of Engineers saw fit to build a dam on the site, and the Marmes Rockshelter, which might have yielded priceless information, now lies beneath 40 feet of water.

It is not surprising that in countries as large and underpopulated as the United States and Canada it should be difficult to locate and excavate human fossils; even in Europe there is a dearth of such material. However, if the physical remnants of these ancient hunters are scarce, there is a relative abundance of the spearpoints with which they hunted their game and which, since hunting was their ceaseless, day-long, life-long occupation, they manufactured by the million. These spearpoints, which are not anonymous and friable like bone, can yield a fair picture, when plotted on a map, of the range and distribution of the main hunting groups. There appear to have been three of these groups, though whether they represent successive phases of the same hunting tradition, or three distinct peoples who may or may not have associated with one another, it is impossible at present to determine.

The older of the three would appear to be the *Clovis culture*, named after the town in New Mexico close to which implements of a distinctive type were first found (see Figure 1). The Clovis huntsmen were certainly pursuing large game animals in the American Southwest as early as 10,000 B.C., particularly the mammoth, and also the extinct giant bison, *Bison antiquus*. These mammoth hunters may have been the cousins or even the elder brothers of the hunters whose remains have been found in the Sandía Cave at Albuquerque, New Mexico. The Clovis culture – sometimes called the *Llano culture* – is famous for its exquisite spearpoints, with a characteristic fluting or channelling at the base to facilitate insertion into a cleft in a wooden shaft.

The same feature, a deep groove now extending the whole length of the point, occurs in the flintwork of the hunting complex that began to overlap with the Clovis culture about 9000 B.C., after the passage of another thousand years. These were the people of the *Folsom culture*, named after yet another town in the American Southwest – though we must emphasize that, even if the Southwest was prime hunting country, Clovis points in particular are scattered throughout the whole of North America. However, a distinct variety of the Folsom point, the Plainview point, named after a town in Texas, shows that definite sub-divisions of the principal hunting

22

peoples were beginning to emerge. Such was definitely the case with the
third element in this earliest period, the group of cultures summed up by the
general label of the *Plano culture*, recognizable from about 7000 B.C. onwards.
The term embraces a series of cultures scattered across America and once
more designated by an individual form of spearpoint, the chief tool in the

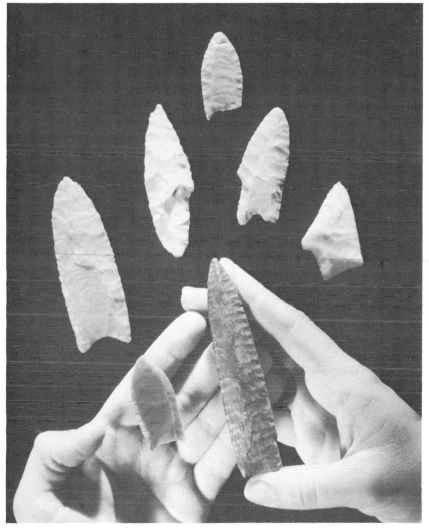

2 *Early projectile-points from the Southwest.*
(Top: Folsom, Sandía, Folsom, Gypsum Cave (2);
Bottom: Folsom, Yuma.)

23

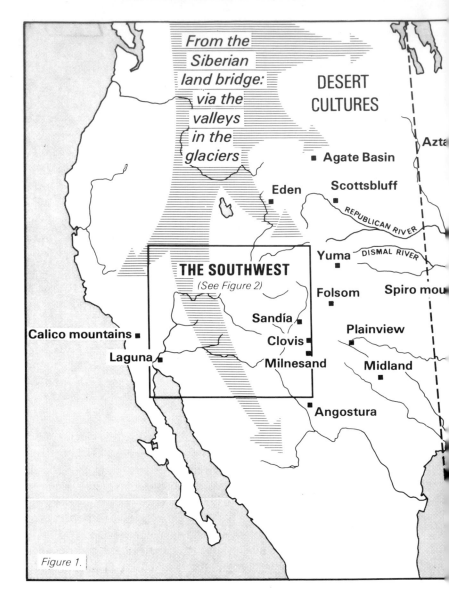

From the Siberian land bridge: via the valleys in the glaciers

DESERT CULTURES

Azt⸱

■ Agate Basin

Eden
■

Scottsbluff
■

REPUBLICAN RIVER

THE SOUTHWEST
(See Figure 2)

Yuma
■

DISMAL RIVER

Folsom
■

Spiro mou⸱

Sandía ⸱
■

Clovis ■

Plainview
■

Calico mountains ■

Milnesand

Midland
■

Laguna ⸱
■

■ Angostura

Figure 1.

24

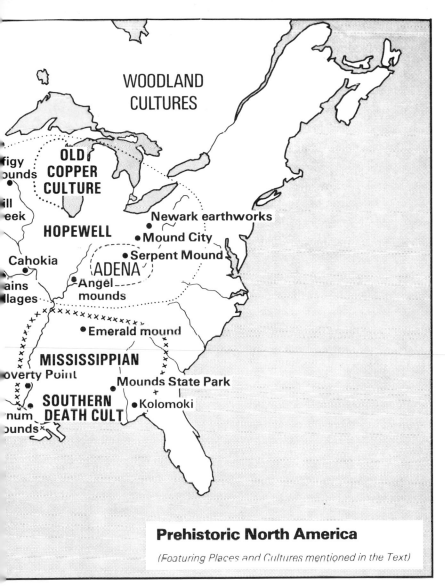

WOODLAND
CULTURES

figy
ounds

OLD
COPPER
CULTURE

ill
eek

Newark earthworks

HOPEWELL

Mound City

Cahokia

Serpent Mound

ADENA

ains
lages

Angel
mounds

x×xxxxxxxxxxxxxxx

Emerald mound

MISSISSIPPIAN

overty Point

Mounds State Park

SOUTHERN
DEATH CULT

num
ounds

Kolomoki

Prehistoric North America

(Featuring Places and Cultures mentioned in the Text)

prehistoric arsenal: *Scottsbluff*, *Angostura*, *Eden*, *Milnesand*, *Agate Basin*, and others. The Plano hunters fashioned a long narrow point, sometimes referred to as 'leaf-shaped', or 'lanceolate-shaped'.

Nevertheless, it should not be assumed that the spearpoint was the only artifact manufactured by these ancient peoples. In addition to points, they made choppers, knives, scrapers, and other stone implements, also needles, borers and smoothers of bone. They also certainly knew the use of fire, a discovery which is known to have occurred independently in several localities throughout the world in the Old Stone Age. The existence of stone palettes suggests that they were familiar with painting and other artistic procedures, though nothing comparable to the rich heritage of sculptures and murals of the Old Stone Age in the Old World has survived. No doubt, like their counterparts in Europe and elsewhere, they were skilled workers in wood and leather and in other perishable materials; and like their Indian descendants they may even have lived in tents and wooden houses, as well as in the recesses of caves and beneath overhanging cliffs. Unfortunately, the processes of time have destroyed the more ephemeral handiwork of the inhabitants of such a remote epoch.

Clovis – Folsom – Plano. This represents the sequence of events in what is called the *Paleo-Indian* (i.e. 'Dawn of the Indian') or *Lithic* (i.e. 'Stone-using') period. This era comprises an immense stretch of time, which may ultimately be seen, as we have suggested, to reach back 50,000 years, and which is commonly taken to have ended about 8000–7000 B.C. Although the typical spearpoints of the three cultures are found all over North America, they do not occur in exactly the same form in Central or South America; yet the colonization of the southern continent must have been effected by bands of hunters dribbling south at the average rate of only a kilometre or two a year. At any rate, by about 8000 B.C. Lithic-type cultures had lodged themselves as far away as the southernmost tip of Argentina – which in turn suggests that the present cultures in Canada and the United States must have been soundly established at least some tens of thousands of years earlier.

Those hardy souls who entered Central and South America no doubt avoided the matted, fever-ridden jungles, and clung to the high, dry, healthy slopes of the cordilleras. In North America, on the other hand, many hunting bands seem to have deliberately settled beside lakes and marshes, once extensive but mostly dried up long ago and now discernible only to the eye of the expert. Here the great animals which preceded man across the Arctic land-bridge, whose spoor he followed, came to drink and disport themselves.

We shall be describing the more sophisticated techniques of the Indian and Paleo-Indian huntsmen later: but two major methods of hunting were widespread as early as 10,000 B.C., and one of them persisted almost into our own time. The first was the systematic tracking and cornering of the mammoth, mastodon and other giant quarry by bands of Clovis hunters, who then darted in to deliver mortal wounds with their puny spears. The animals were brought to bay on a lakeshore, or at the end of a rocky canyon,

3 *Clovis huntsmen trap a mammoth at the end of a canyon.*

and many spearpoints have been found actually embedded in the bones of such prehistoric prey. Later, the bands that spread across America in pursuit of game refined the same technique to kill the last of the remaining big-game animals, the bison.* The early hunters devised regular 'buffalo jumps', sometimes using the same location over and over again. Hundreds of these primitive 'jumps' have been found, some of them clearly used for

---

*The words 'bison' and 'buffalo' are used interchangeably by Americans to denote the same animal. 'Bison' is technically correct, since the Latin generic term for the North American animal is *Bison*; whereas the 'buffalo', for which the generic term is *Bubalus*, is a distinctly different creature, native to Africa and India. However, we will revert for the rest of this book to 'buffalo', since it has long since passed into general use.

many centuries. They consisted of a slope leading gradually and deceptively to the edge of a sheer drop, the fall from which was high enough to kill or maim the animal. Boulders or piles of stones were arranged in such a way as to lead a herd of buffalo into a funnel from which it was impossible to turn and escape. Men would hide behind the boulders and leap out, shouting and waving weapons, until the animals panicked and stampeded. It was not difficult to drive buffalo since, though dangerous at close quarters, they were stupid animals, with weak eyesight and a poor sense of smell. Once the unfortunate creatures had fallen to their deaths, the choicest parts, such as the tongue and intestines, were cooked and eaten on the spot, and the carcases stripped of their hides and other useful portions.

By about 5000 B.C. the northern glaciers were in full retreat, and the climate of America was undergoing a drastic change. The plains and the fertile Southwest were drying up, becoming so desert-like that even the buffalo, the last survivor of prehistoric times, began to dwindle and did not flourish again for centuries to come. Man could no longer rely on a supply of large animals for subsistence, and had to seek out other resources. It was here that he showed his marvellous capacity for improvising and coping with radically different conditions.

Already, as early as 8000 B.C., a new phase of cultural activity had started to manifest itself. This, coinciding with the later phases of the Lithic culture and eventually superseding it, is called by archaeologists the *Archaic period*, and is considered to have lasted until about 1500–1000 B.C. All such dates, of course, are only approximate, and are offered in a tentative way: no early community said to itself: 'Well, here we are at 8000 B.C., and the Paleo-Indian period shows signs of coming to an end, so we ought to be thinking about how to meet the challenge of the Archaic'. The fact is that some communities never developed more than a rudimentary technology, while others, more favoured by physical circumstances or producing gifted individuals, broke through to a higher level of material existence.

To supplement their original tool-kit of stone and bone certain societies, distributed across the whole face of North America, began to make items which we increasingly associate with the full flowering of Indian life: pottery, basketwork, fur clothing, beadwork, sandals, moccasins, musical instruments, and a mass of other objects. Amazingly, about 3000 B.C., in Wisconsin, Minnesota, and Michigan, an Archaic Indian people actually learned to use copper. This was at a date as early as any people were using metal in Europe or Asia. They did not know how to smelt it, or harden it, and used it in its raw state; nevertheless they extracted it, hammered it into sheets, and manipulated it to make axes, knives, harpoons, spear and arrow points, ornaments, and fishhooks.

It seems clear, in short, that some extensive settling-down or shaking-down process was taking place all over North America. It had taken 10,000–20,000 years or more for its population to grow from a few hundred Asian nomads to the thousands or tens of thousands of native Americans. The arduous existence of the earliest huntsmen – trudging after the herds, month in and month out, in season and out of season – had not been conducive to a growth in numbers. Infant mortality must have been high even by primitive standards, and the expectation of life correspondingly low; nor do people leading such a life welcome an increase in their numbers, for if more people mean more warriors and huntsmen, they also mean more mouths to feed. Moreover, we must remember that hunting itself, in those days before fire-arms, was a very dangerous pursuit; the early hunters despatched gigantic tusked animals with little more than their bare hands, or engaged in long and punishing steeple-chases after the deer and antelope.

Slowly, men and women learned from the accumulated experience of the procession of the generations. As their skills became sharper, life became easier – even if only marginally so – and there was a little more leisure in which to invent and improve such essentially spare-time pursuits as pottery, weaving, dancing, and making music. Even as the larger and meatier animals were disappearing, people were becoming more adept at catching smaller ones, and were stocking the larder with other foodstuffs. Then, just as the new leisure furnished the luxury of indulging in slightly larger families, so the growing tribes started to develop a territorial sense. In a continent the size of America, a few tens of thousands, or even hundreds of thousands, would not make for overcrowding. Nevertheless, they would have to take increasing care not to poach on what they were beginning to recognize as other people's preserves, any more than they would want their neighbours to encroach on theirs. The Indian never became possessive in the obsessional way of his white enemy, and, except for a few tribes, he would always be wedded to some sort of wandering life: but, as the Archaic era progressed, a definite feeling of ordering and patterning became apparent, and must have been obvious even to the freer spirits who roamed the great ranges.

Archaeologists, while glancing briefly at the inhospitable Arctic region, customarily divide the Archaic period into two grand halves: the *Eastern Archaic* and, in the West, the *Desert Culture*. In fact, no less than five distinct culture-areas, which would provide the groundplan for the history of the American Indian until the present century, were already beginning to emerge. These were: The Southwest; the Eastern Forest or Woodland, comprising the regions of the Lakes, the Northeast and the Southeast; the

Plains and Prairies; California and its Basin; and the Northwest and the Plateau. We shall devote a paragraph to each of these areas in turn: since, if the American Indian never achieved the high civilization of his relations in Central and South America, during the Archaic period he enjoyed his own Golden Age. When we think of the Indian today, we visualize him as he appeared during the course of the past three centuries – the centuries when he came into contact with the white man. Actually, these are the very centuries of his decadence and degradation. It was in the preceding 3000 years that he was at his peak. And in none of his many forms was he more individual and impressive than in that most venerable of American regions: the Southwest.

The Southwest

We have seen that, in the days when the eastern slopes of the Rockies were the ladder by which the Mongoloid immigrants descended into the heart of the continent, the climate of the Southwest was moist and fertile. It lay directly on the southerly route of the newcomers and was a feeding-ground where large animals clustered thickly. The two earliest identifiable American cultures take their names from places in the Southwest: and in the Archaic period, when a drastic change in the climate had reduced the area to aridity, its inhabitants exercised a remarkable degree of ingenuity and managed to maintain their cultural lead.

The *Cochise people*, who lived in southern Arizona, take their name from a famous Apache chieftain – a compliment which the Apache, who, unlike the Cochise people, were wanderers, and barbarous in comparison with most Indian tribes, scarcely deserved (see Figure 2). The Cochise people were an offshoot of the Clovis huntsmen; but very early, perhaps about 9000–8000 B.C., they settled on territory near the modern town of Douglas. In the early phases of their culture, called the Sulphur Springs and Chiricahua phases, they followed the same existence as their Clovis cousins, hunting and collecting roots, tubers, nuts and berries. It was in the third, or San Pedro phase, that two crucial events occurred: they began to make pottery, and they became the first North American farmers, by starting to cultivate maize. Pottery and agriculture were arts which they learned from tribes to the south, in modern Mexico – another reminder that Mexico, then as now, possessed intimate links with its neighbour to the north. It may have been a group of actual Mexican immigrants, moving northwards in the course of one of those swirling folk-movements that occurred throughout Indian history, who taught the Cochise people these skills. There seem to have been several separate developments of agriculture in the Americas in pre-European times. The cultivation of

30

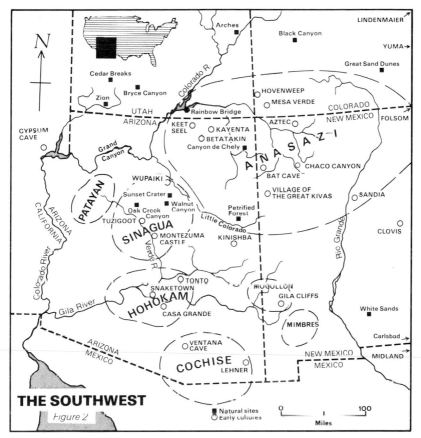

THE SOUTHWEST

Figure 2

■ Natural sites
○ Early cultures

0   100

Miles

tubers appears to have taken place in Venezuela, the cultivation of the potato in the high Andes, and the cultivation of the manioc root in the tropical forests. But it was in the Tehuacán valley in southeastern Mexico, and in another valley to the north of it, that the most significant developments took place. Here, between 5000 and 2500 B.C., several varieties of maize, beans, squash, cotton, peppers, tobacco, pumpkins and other vines were developed; and between 2500 and 1500 B.C. pottery appeared.

The Cochise people began to practise these life-enhancing innovations as early as 5000 B.C., sharing them and to some extent handing them on to a later people called the *Hohokam*, who seem to have come out from Mexico about 500 B.C. and who flourished until about A.D. 1400. The name Hohokam is a word in the language of the Pima Indians, who are their direct descendants, and means 'Those Who Have Gone Before'. It is a term

31

of respect – as well it might be, in view of the achievements of the people to whom it is applied. On the Salt and Gila rivers, south of present-day Phoenix, the Hohokam constructed a network of canals, sometimes 30 feet wide and ten feet deep, that stretched across the plain for an aggregate distance of 150 miles. There, in a series of interlinked settlements, they progressed through a series of four well-defined phases – Pioneer, Colonial, Sedentary, and Classic – in which the individual settlements may have contained at their peak as many as 5000 houses. They were assiduous cultivators, living in roofed, rectangular houses with walls of reeds, and cooking in the typical fire pit which one can still see being used on the Pima Indian reservation. In addition to beautifully decorated pottery, they made elegant jewelry from shell, turquoise and other materials, as well as mirrors inlaid with pieces of iron pyrites. They built ball-courts for the energetic ball-game which was a passion with their Mexican relations, the Toltecs and Mayas. We are fortunate in that there still stands one of the striking buildings constructed during their Classic phase by a sub-group called the Salado people, who had come to settle peaceably among them. This building, which is situated south of Phoenix and is called the Casa Grande,

4 *The Casa Grande, near Phoenix, Arizona: a dwelling-house of the Salado-Hohokam people* (A.D. *1350–1450*).

is of adobe, and although it has been beaten down by the wind and sun, it is still four storeys high, with walls four feet thick – a prehistoric block of flats, perhaps. Not only do the Hohokam appear to have been tolerant of strangers, but seem to have given rise to other tranquil farming peoples who left the Salt-Gila centre, perhaps because of overcrowding, to relocate themselves a relatively short journey away. These were the farmers of the Patayan and Sinagua cultures to the north, and of the Mogollon and Mimbres cultures to the east. Even today the Indians who are almost indisputably the direct descendants of the Hohokam – Pima, Papago, Maricopa, Walapai, Yavapai and Havasupai – remain mild-mannered farmers.

The Hohokam can claim to be the earliest American people to achieve major status in the archaeological textbooks. However, only five centuries after they began to cut their first canals – a short time, prehistorically speaking – a people whose remains have proved equally impressive launched out on their own career in another quarter of the Southwest. 350 miles to the northeast, in what is now the Four Corners area, where New Mexico, Colorado, Utah and Arizona meet at a single point, the *Anasazi* people were seeking out caves and rock shelters to be their homes. The word Anasazi is Navajo for 'The Old Ones' – though the Navajo themselves were not related to the Anasazi, only wandering down from the north long afterwards to occupy the deserted territory once occupied by the people who had constructed awesome and mysterious monuments only to vanish as mysteriously. Today, each summer, hundreds of thousands of tourists drive to the national parks of the Southwest to marvel at their handiwork.

Right from the start, in what is called the Basketmaker period, lasting roughly from A.D. 1 to A.D. 750, the Anasazi were notably adroit. There is no clue as to their origin, though like the Hohokam they must have had Clovis-Folsom blood. Unlike the Hohokam, they avoided the open landscape and had an obsession for clinging to cliffs and tucking themselves away in inaccessible canyons. Even later, when they ventured a little way into the valley to build their huge communal dwelling-houses, they still clung to the comforting shadow of the rock face. They were evidently by nature shy and reclusive but withal industrious and talented.

At first they lived in rock overhangs, or in deep circular holes in the ground entered by a ladder from a hole in the roof. These were the prototypes of the subterranean edifices called *kivas* which will be described in the chapter on religion. We know a great deal about the Anasazi because, whereas the Hohokam cremated their dead and put the ashes in urns, the Anasazi buried their dead in caves, either in small groups or in regular cemeteries of 20 or more. Here, in the high dry air, as in the hot sands of

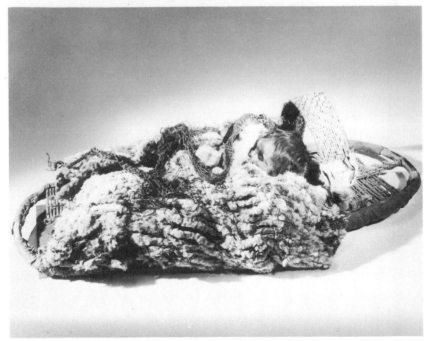

5 *A sandal of the Basketmaker people* (A.D. *200–700*), *woven from yucca and milkweed fibres*.

Ancient Egypt, the remains were perfectly preserved and mummified. Thus we know that the Basketmakers were small, slender, reddish-skinned, with thick coarse black hair, dark eyes, and little facial or body hair. The men wore their hair in three braids, and though the long tresses of the women were sheared off after death, to yield materials for weaving, their cactus combs and bone and shell ornaments indicate that their hair styles were elaborate. Although both sexes wore only a flimsy wool fibre apron around the loins, they protected themselves in those cold altitudes with cloaks of bear, rabbit or deerskin, or woven entirely of hair and fibre. They were cunning weavers, fashioning not merely cloaks and sandals, but baskets so closely-meshed that they could be used for cooking and carrying water, while others served as containers for the corn, squash, beans, cotton, acorns, nuts, seeds and berries which formed their diet. Mostly they lived by hunting – not merely whatever large game they could find, but rabbits, prairie dogs, gophers, rats and mice. These they hunted with spears and spear-throwers, bows and arrows, and clubs, or trapped with snares and finely woven nets. In addition to the turkey – a native American bird – they had domesticated the dog, an invaluable aid in guarding, hunting, and giving warning of danger. They had several kinds of dogs, and their favourite animals were entombed with their masters, to accompany and assist them in the next world.

About A.D. 750, the Basketmakers became more ambitious. They began to transform their rock shelters and pit houses into massive and imposing structures. At Chaco Canyon, in southwestern New Mexico, they built among the scarps bordering on a watercourse a string of magnificent buildings, extending for nine miles and housing at least 5000 people. Pueblo Bonito, the largest of them, occupied an area of three acres and contained no fewer than 800 rooms, capable of sheltering 1200 people. It was

6 *A kiva and an apartment-house in the Pueblo del Arroyo, Chaco Canyon: built in the Great Pueblo phase (A.D. 1050–1300) of the Anasazi Culture of the Southwest.*

semicircular, its rear braced against a cliff, and could be readily barricaded and defended if necessary, for its five storeys, arranged in tiers, were entered by means of ladders from the roofs. The masonry consisted of sandstone slabs, carefully squared and laid around a rubble core, and as with all Anasazi stonework its effect is precise and beautiful. However, it is possible that originally the stonework was overlaid by a smooth coat of plaster on which bright designs were painted, which would have given the entire

35

complex a singularly brilliant appearance. The inhabitants of this and the other great apartment blocks at Chaco Canyon lived in small rectangular rooms, many of them facing a sunny interior courtyard. They had no furniture and slept on grass or yucca mats, or on padded quilts. Probably the rooms were used only at night, the work of the pueblo being carried on in the sunshine of the courtyard, or on the flat roofs and terraces. Here the baskets, pottery, weapons, and agricultural implements were made. Here the women ground the corn which had been grown in the fields extending the length of the valley, irrigated by a network of ditches. The meal was placed on a block of sandstone and rolled out with a rubbing stone in the way cornmeal is still prepared throughout the Americas. However, if there was a peasant simplicity about the daily life of the Anasazi, their spiritual life was rich and profound, as is attested by the abundance of the underground *kivas*, their places of worship. There are 32 *kivas* in Pueblo Bonito alone, and scores of others are incorporated in the structure of the neighbouring buildings. From the beginning, the American Indian was a god-haunted man.

Chaco Canyon was evidently the inspirational centre of a wide area. At

7 *Family life on the roof of a prehistoric pueblo in the Southwest (about* A.D. *1000–1500).*

36

Aztec, for example, 60 miles to the north, there was a sister community whose main building, marvellously constructed of smooth green stone, was four storeys tall and contained over 350 rooms. Further to the north, a second strain of the Anasazi family had declined to step out even a few yards from the protection of the ancestral cliffs, as the Chaco Canyon people had dared to do, and made a positive art out of inhabiting cavities in the rock. In what is called the Great Pueblo period of the Anasazi culture, between A.D. 1050 and 1300, the northern Anasazi built their celebrated cliff-dwellings, at such sites as the Canyon de Chelly, Keet Seel, Betatakin, Tuzigoot, Hovenweep and Kayenta. The best known is the famous Mesa Verde, in Colorado, where high in the walls of a series of interconnecting canyons are perched hamlets and whole villages of elegant stone buildings. To see the Cliff Palace, the Balcony House, the Spruce Tree House and other miniature structures, nestling like precious stones in a setting of a smooth sweep of rock, is a delightful and breath-taking experience. Seldom in human history has a single culture created, as the Anasazi have done, two such accomplished and distinct styles of architecture as those at Mesa Verde and Chaco Canyon.

Alas, a sad fate awaited both branches of 'The Old Ones'. Between 1200 and 1350 a catastrophe occurred that drove them away from their Eden-like retreats. We do not know what it was. There is little evidence of destruction, invasion, or civil war. There may have been pestilence; or perhaps their fields became exhausted and leached out. Certainly in the year 1276 there began a fearful drought that afflicted the whole of the Southwest and which lasted for no less than 23 years, ending only in 1299. It is probable that it was the havoc caused by this visitation that forced the Anasazi to abandon their cherished settlements and undergo a cruel dispersal. Most of them seem to have moved 100–150 miles to the southeast and to have settled beside the waters of the Rio Grande, where in the so-called Regressive Pueblo period, between 1350 and 1700, they built new communities, some of which, like those at Kuaua near Albuquerque and Tyuonyi in the Bandelier National Monument, were almost as impressive as their predecessors.

The ancient Anasazi are the direct forbears of the modern Pueblo people, who live in 20 villages along the Rio Grande, from Taos in the north to Isleta in the south. In spite of the complexity of their languages, of which there are six distinct divisions, the 27,000 inhabitants of the modern pueblos possess the shy, self-reliant qualities of their ancestors which have enabled them to survive with more of their culture intact than is the case with most other American Indian peoples. It is doubtful if they possess as much confidence and zest as the Anasazi possessed a thousand years ago;

37

8 *The Cliff Palace at Mesa Verde, Colorado: a cliff dwelling of the Anasazi people (about* A.D. *750–1350)*.

and in spiritual as well as material ways they are probably more impoverished. Yet they remain resilient, highly individual, and possess an altogether outstanding artistic ability.

9 *Old Walpi, one of the pueblos of New Mexico, built by the Anasazi about A.D. 1300 and still flourishing today.*

The Eastern Forest

Even Americans who have not made the pilgrimage to Casa Grande or Mesa Verde are usually aware, through books or television, that in the distant Southwest the Indian left behind him handsome and substantial cities of stone. But they are usually unaware that across the eastern half of the United States, from the Great Lakes to the Gulf of Mexico, there once existed monuments built by Indian hands that were equally stupendous, but which have not made so deep an impression on the national memory because they were constructed of earth.

However, the structures raised by the *Adena-Hopewell* people and the *Mississippians* during the *Eastern Forest* or *Woodland* era, which was the Eastern equivalent of the Desert or Southwestern culture, were in many cases truly phenomenal. The Archaic culture had spread across the whole

39

of North America, and was remarkably homogeneous; agriculture had reached the East at about the same time as the West, although the easterners had not yet become as skilled at farming as the southwesterners, and mainly followed the old hunting way of life; in particular, they were slow to see the advantages of growing maize. But as early as 800 B.C., while the Hohokam and Anasazi were only in their own formative stages, a sizeable group of Indians were settling down in the Ohio Valley to create a striking culture. At Adena, which has given its name to the whole complex and which is near modern Chillicothe, they built with sturdy timbers some of the first truly substantial houses to be identified in America.

Even more remarkable were their burial mounds, a type of structure which, associated with various ancient cultures, would eventually cover the entire landscape of eastern America. At the centre of an Adena mound, at ground level, were one or more tomb-chambers made of carefully carpentered logs, containing up to three bodies lavishly provided with all manner of grave goods. Above these chambers hundreds of thousands of basketfuls of specially selected and graded types of earth were piled up and tamped down. Such an enterprise must have entailed an enormous output of energy, and one wonders how so much time could have been spared by so many members of the community. Nor, as the centuries went by, were the exertions of the Adena people limited to simple conical mounds. The extraordinary Serpent Mound at Locust Grove in Ohio writhes across the countryside for a quarter of a mile in the form of a 20-foot wide snake that even today, after 2000 years of erosion, is four to five feet high.

Nevertheless, if the Adena folk were preoccupied with death, for the Hopewell folk who succeeded them death was a positive obsession. It is a fair assumption that the Hopewell culture, which mushroomed into existence about 300 B.C., and which led a dramatic existence for six or seven centuries before suddenly subsiding about A.D. 400, was the child of the Adena culture. At its peak it extended from Ohio and Illinois to Nebraska and Kansas in the west and Louisiana to the south. It certainly formed an early connection with the already thriving Poverty Point villagers who, near modern Shreveport, constructed an enormous living-site that was unique in character. The wooden houses at Poverty Point were probably raised on six concentric octagonal terraces, each more than six feet high, fitted one inside the other, and covering more than half a mile. Together, the terraces added up to more than 11 linear miles. Moreover, outside the village stood ceremonial mounds of which the largest was 70 feet high and 800 by 700 feet at the base. It has been calculated that these mounds represent 20 million 50-pound basketloads of earth.

At Poverty Point, the mounds covered the cremated remains of the more important members of this hunting and fishing community. Cremation was an equally prominent practice among their Hopewell relations, who seem to have arranged their cremated or inhumed dead in neat gravecircles and then, when enough individual burials were accumulated, heaped grandiose mounds upon them. There are literally thousands of Hopewell mounds still in existence, among the most striking of which is a collection of no fewer than 23 at Mound City, near Chillicothe, and another group called Newark Earthworks, both in Ohio. The Newark people constructed enormous burial enclosures, square, octagonal or circular, enclosed by earthworks up to 14 feet in height and honeycombed with corridors and avenues. At other places, the Hopewell burial mounds are geometrical in design; while at Effigy Mounds, near Marquette in Iowa, which belonged to the so-called Effigy Mound culture which had its actual centre in Wisconsin, there was thrown up an extraordinary array of mounds, 23 in number, that are shaped like birds and bears.

The Hopewell people, who seem to have represented a confederation or

10 *A burial ceremony of the Hopewell people in the Michigan region, about* A.D. *200. Note the burial mounds in the background, the Chief Priest with the crown of antlers, and his two assistants with their faces daubed with ashes. Personal ornaments and provisions for the journey to the next world are being buried with the dead man.*

11 *Mound-builders at work in the Wisconsin area, at a time between* A.D. *600–1200. The mound in the foreground has been laid open to show a skeleton, the grave-goods, and the cremation hearth.*

loose nexus of tribes, were energetic and aggressive. They not only sent out colonizing offshoots over a huge area but persuaded many other peoples to adopt their practices. They were evidently controlled by a dominant warrior-priest class, and it may be that this class was eventually responsible for the downfall of this singular way of life. Hopewell seems to have suffered a sudden economic collapse, perhaps as a result of a surge in population, a change in the subsistence pattern, or competition for land as a result of the introduction of maize: but not before it had imbued its satellites with its own peculiar ideals. Its influence was particularly marked on the east of the Woodland region, along the whole length of the Mississippi river. Here a unified form of culture sprang up, about A.D. 800, which followed the pattern established by the Hopewell priests and chieftains. It was in many respects even more grand than its predecessor, asserting its own individuality and persisting for a full 1000 years.

The places to see the handiwork of the Mississippi people include Angel

42

Mounds in Indiana, Kolomoki Mounds in Georgia, Mounds State Park in Alabama, or the Bynum and Emerald Mounds in Mississippi itself – but there are too many for separate mention. At some of these great fortified townships as many as 100 towering mounds might be raised during the course of the centuries, most of them in the shape of flat-topped platforms of an intricate geometrical pattern. Here, with the skeletons or the pulverized bones of the dead, were interred weapons, vessels and jewelry that had been specially made for the long journey of the deceased to the Other World and for his eternal sojourn there. An intimate code of symbols associated with death was devised – skulls, spiders, warriors with wings, a weeping eye, and an eye situated in the palm of the hand. As with Hopewell, it was all very morbid and wasteful, to our way of thinking: yet it was also awesome and devout. Sometimes freshly severed heads, probably the fruit of human sacrifice, were inserted in the mounds. The Hopewell fixation with death, in fact, was perpetuated and intensified, so that in connection with the Mississippi culture the older archaeologists used to speak of a *Southern Death Cult* or *Buzzard Cult*. The burial mounds were awesome, the Emerald Mound, for instance, measuring 730 by 435 feet at the base and covering an area of nearly eight acres. Even so, the Emerald Mound is overshadowed by one of the mounds at Poverty Point and by one at Cahokia, at St Louis, Missouri, where the Monks Mound is the largest in the United States; it is 100 feet high at the summit, and almost as big as the Great Pyramid of the Pharaoh Cheops at Gizeh. Cahokia at its zenith, between A.D. 1000–1500, must have been an amazing sight. It had a population of some 30,000–40,000 people, efficient farmers who enthusiastically erected almost 150 mounds and fortified the centre of their city with a formidable log wall studded with bastions. In time the Cahokia people, perhaps feeling the pressures of overcrowding, despatched groups of citizens to set up communities elsewhere. Thus it seems likely that the compact little township at Aztalan in Wisconsin, which was enclosed by a palisade with watchtowers resembling the defences of a medieval castle, was founded by Cahokians.

An unusual feature of the Mississippi-type mounds was the manner in which they combined the functions of both burial and worship. The interments took place at ground level or on the lower levels, while a flight of wooden steps led upwards to a ceremonial hut situated on the flat platform at the summit. Egyptian pyramids had burial-chambers at their core, and were essentially gigantic tombs; Mexican pyramids, on the other hand, with a single exception, possessed no burial chambers but had shrines at the top, and were therefore not tombs but temples. The Mississippi mounds amalgamated both practices. It seems likely that they began as tombs, and added the other function as a result of direct influence from Mexico some time between A.D. 1000 and 1500.

The Mexican cultures of that era were imperialistic, and were quite capable of sending their merchants and missionaries as far afield as North America, both overland or by sea. They certainly reached the Southwest, and there is no reason why they could not penetrate the East. The Aztec *pochtecas* or merchants, for instance, were a tightly-knit warrior-guild who journeyed far beyond the boundaries of the Aztec empire. It is conceivable that the contacts between Mississippians and Mexicans became so close that the former determined to copy as well as they could, in earth and wood, the architectural triumphs of the latter; it is even feasible that groups of American Indians may have travelled in Mexico and seen those glories at first hand. Moreover the Mississippian Death Cult seems to have been swept away as abruptly as the individual cultures of ancient Mexico usually came to an end – and perhaps for much the same reason: because the tyranny of an oligarchy of priests and warrior-kings had become too burdensome to bear.

12 *The stockaded city of Aztalan, near Lake Mills, Wisconsin, as it may have looked in its heyday, between* A.D. *1100–1300. Here 500 Mississippians practised agriculture and placed their dead in burial mounds.*

When the first Europeans reached the Mississippi in the mid-1500s, most of the great mound cities were in decay and majority of the Indians of the region were leading a less demanding kind of existence.

The Plains and Prairies
Between the Eastern Woodlands and the Desert Southwest, each of them

containing peoples who enjoyed an individual and advanced way of life, there stretched the vast expanse of the Great Plains. Woodland and Desert were divided by a great band of territory, extending from Alberta, Saskatchewan and Manitoba, through the Dakotas, Nebraska, Kansas, Oklahoma, Wyoming and Western Colorado, to Texas. During the Paleo-Indian and Archaic phases, the Clovis huntsmen and their nomadic successors roamed the area, to be followed by small influxes of hunter-farmers from the woodlands to the east. About A.D. 1, Hopewellian bands reached the Missouri and flourished there for 1500 years, until the arrival of the Europeans. The typical dwelling of these Plains Village folk, as they are called, was the earth-lodge, a framework of poles and logs, often of a half-dome shape, heavily banked with earth and sods. These houses, some of large dimensions, intrigued the explorers Lewis and Clark when they traversed the territory of the Mandans in 1805. Traces of similar communities pursuing a more or less settled mode of life have been found scattered all over the lonely Plains, at such places as Mill Creek in Iowa, along the Republican river in Nebraska, and on the nearby Dismal river. They cultivated corn, beans, squash, and other crops, and hunted the deer, the antelope, and particularly the buffalo, of which animal there were estimated to exist at least three million in the Plains country before the advent of the white man and his lethal 'buffalo gun'.

Some of the Plains people went so far as to indulge in mound-building on a moderate scale; but nothing has so far been unearthed in the Plains region to rival the adobe high-rise and cliff-houses of the Southwest or the fortified townships of the Hopewellians and Mississippians; the early Plainsmen were wanderers, adrift on a vast sea of grass.

California

It is also true that nothing of eye-catching architectural merit was constructed in California and its adjoining area to the east and south, the fourth of our distinctive culture-areas. This is somewhat surprising, as California may have been occupied early – as early as 80,000–50,000 B.C., if the famous archaeologist Louis Leakey, who examined sites in the Calico Mountains near Barstow, is to be believed. At a very distant date, certainly, small groups of hunters were forsaking the broad prehistoric trackway along the eastern side of the Rockies to filter through the passes and trickle across to the shores of the Pacific. By the time such voyagers as Drake, Cook and Vancouver encountered them, their numbers had swelled to an estimated 150,000 – at least a quarter of the total Indian population of North America; yet they were apparently still living for the most part in caves and rock shelters, or in flimsy huts of rush and matting. Like their modern Californian counterparts, they enjoyed an insouciant life in the sun, basking in a benevolent climate. The seas and streams teemed with fish; the fertile forests that fringed the beaches were stocked with small game and provided pinenuts, acorns, and other food in abundance; and the warm sands themselves yielded an inexhaustible supply of shellfish. Primitive existence is always arduous, but the fishing-hunting-gathering economy of California was paradisal compared with most, though it was a different story in the barren deserts that in the course of time came into existence in nearby Nevada, northern Arizona, southern and Baja California, and northern Mexico. Here the people who chose to remain in such an adverse environment suffered appalling hardships, and never contrived to do more than scrape along in a deprived and degraded manner. They would always remain among the poorest and most primitive of Indian tribes.

The Northwest

To the north of California, on the other hand, along the Northwest Coast, which we have designated as the fifth and last of our culture-areas, an

13 *The Haida, one of the peoples of the Northwest Pacific Coast. Note the substantial buildings and 'totem poles' carved from cedarwood.*

incomparably wealthy and colourful life-style took hold. In the earliest times, when the western branch of the Wisconsin glaciers covered the land, the Northwest only offered a toehold to the Mongoloid seafarers who were the precursors of the Eskimos. With the withdrawal of the ice, Oregon, Washington, and British Columbia became positively hospitable, and soon supported a dense population of skilled and prosperous fisher-folk. From the giant cedars lining the ocean they cut long straight boards to make lofty buildings with gabled roofs. They fashioned beautiful garments from the wool of goats and husky-dogs, and were abundantly supplied with food and the necessities of a luxurious life by the whales, seals, porpoises and sea-otters that they hunted. In addition to the salmon, cod, halibut and herring that they trapped and netted, and the shellfish they scooped up, there was no lack of game and wild provender in the hinterland: and altogether they can be counted among the most enviably endowed of all American Indians.

There was never any question of the bounty of the sea, on which they principally relied, drying up; so they escaped the fate of the busy cultures of the Southwest, which were destroyed at their prime by a devastating drought. Nor, although they devised a hierarchical and authoritarian social system, did that system become so oppressive that it was beaten into the dust, as probably happened to the major cultures of the East. In fact, of all five culture-areas, the Northwestern was the only one where a clear and unequivocal transition from proto-historic to historic times can be witnessed. Whereas in the other areas the connection between ancient and modern tribes is hazy and can be only hesitantly suggested, the line of descent of the peoples of the Northwest, including the Tlingit, Haida, Chinook, Tsimshian, Klamath, Kwakiutl, Bella Bella, Nootka, and scores of others, can be positively traced.

Other early peoples disintegrated or disappeared; but the Northwesterners still harvest the seas, carve their totem poles, construct their long-houses and carry out their ceremonials, and have recently even prevailed upon a hostile white administration to lift the ban on their dramatic *potlatches* or tribal festivals. From the general wreck of the Indian way of life, terminating in our own century in almost total disruption and dispersion, the Northwest Indians remain one of the few peoples to have preserved the character they possessed before the railroads and the wagon-trains, the airlines and the interstate highways imprisoned the whole continent in chains of steel.

2

The Hunter

Our account of the ancestry of the American Indian, reaching back 30,000 years or more, should have created a measure of perspective, helping to counteract the gaudy, meretricious picture of the Indian promoted by Hollywood and the Wild West Shows. While Europe was witnessing the rise and fall of Greece and Rome, and traversing the Dark and Middle Ages, North America was displaying diverse and distinctive cultures of its own – not inferior, in their way, to those of the Saxon or the Celt.

Nonetheless, by A.D. 1500 the old high Indian cultures of the Southwest and the Woodlands were in decay, or at least in a stage of radical transformation; the grand climax of Indian history, in its original, untouched state, was over. What the astonished European would stumble upon was a great native tradition that had recently begun to decline. Of course, the colonial American later elected to view the Indian as a species of whooping savage, partly because the latter's way of life was so strange and so different from his own, and partly because he needed to denigrate the Indian in order to provide a rationale for driving him out and dispossessing him. However, in the twentieth century we no longer have such excuses. We must acknowledge that the popular image of the Indian is misleading, recognizing that he was no mere footloose nomad, but had once been a considerable artist, artisan, architect and agriculturalist in his own right. Indeed, if the European had not intervened at a moment when Indian fortunes were in a cyclical downswing, a recovery would sooner or later have taken place: and who knows to what heights the Indian might again have aspired, if an outside incursion had not occurred?

When the Europeans landed in the New World, almost 500 years ago, it would have been impossible for any group of anthropologists, even equipped with modern techniques, to have painted a simple and coherent picture of Indian existence. The canvas was already crowded and confused. For example, at the present time there are 263 distinct Indian tribes or

48

bands living in the United States, who speak between 50 and 100 languages; but as recently as 200 years ago it is estimated that there were at least 600 tribes, speaking no fewer than 300 languages.

It might be thought that a study of Indian language would provide an obvious basis for classifying the Indian peoples. Unfortunately, the study of Indian languages only leads to further confusion, since they represent only very remote inter-tribal affiliations, and are further complicated by other cultural considerations. However, it may be said that there are a number of discernible linguistic blocks in the United States and Canada, each of them introduced by bands of original settlers who, in the course of their wanderings, diffused them throughout the continent. Unfortunately, again, scholars disagree on the naming of these linguistic blocks, and many different schemes have been put forward. Since we cannot enter deeply into these intensely specialized problems, it seems best to offer a relatively straightforward six-part division, as shown in Figure 3.

It will be seen that three great language blocks predominated: The Athabascan (sometimes spelled Athapascan) in Canada, with an outlier in the Southwest; the Algonquian or Algonkian, straddling the entire continent from west to east; and the Hokan-Sioux or Siouian, occupying the Southeast and the heartland. Then there were three smaller blocks: The Eskimo-Aleut, confined to the Arctic fringe; the Penutian of the West Coast; and the Uto-Aztecan of the furthest Western desert. Even on a highly simplified map, it is apparent that much linguistic splintering and displacement eventually took place, and that even within the six blocks themselves important sub-language groups can be distinguished. Thus Muskogean was a significant complex of languages in the American Southeast; Caddoan on the southern Plains and the Dakotas; and Shoshonean in the Uto-Aztecan region. Some idea of the bewildering diversity of Indian tongues can be gathered from the fact that in the small world of the New Mexico pueblos no fewer than three separate languages are presently spoken: Tanoan, Keresan, and Zuñi. Moreover, the Tanoan language is further divided into Tiwa, Tewa, and Towa, and the Keresan language into Eastern and Western Keresan.

Not surprisingly, very few Indian tribes were able to communicate verbally with their immediate neighbours, even if those neighbours were blood relatives. When most tribes met, they were forced to use sign language, as if a Bolivian was trying to communicate with a Bulgarian, or a Norwegian with a Nigerian – though Indian sign language was often of extraordinary swiftness and complexity, greatly impressing the white travellers who saw it being used. In fact, this multiplicity of languages, while it made for cultural diversity, was one of the elements which finally

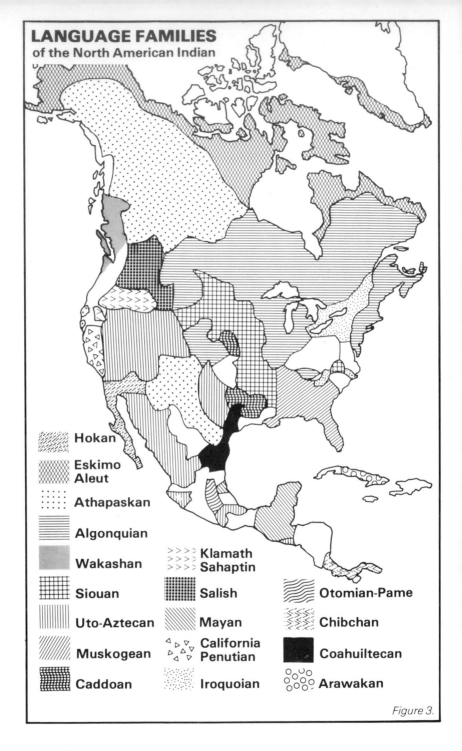

LANGUAGE FAMILIES
of the North American Indian

Hokan

Eskimo Aleut

Athapaskan

Algonquian

Wakashan

Siouan

Uto-Aztecan

Muskogean

Caddoan

Klamath Sahaptin

Salish

Mayan

California Penutian

Iroquoian

Otomian-Pame

Chibchan

Coahuiltecan

Arawakan

Figure 3.

made it impossible for the Indians to combine effectively against the white American. The handicap of the smallness of the typical tribe or band was increased by the language barrier.

Let us place the language problem, so perplexing even to experts, on one side, and refresh our memories with the divisions which we proposed for the prehistoric period. We may recall that there were five of these: the Southwest; the Eastern Forest or Woodland, consisting of the Lakes, the Northeast and the Southeast; the Plains and the Prairies; California and its Basin; and the Northwest and the Plateau. With some modification, we can use these same five categories as the framework for our picture of the Indian in modern or post-Columbian times.

Once again, this is only one of several possible schemes. For instance, the great anthropologist Clark Wissler twice devised classifications of his own, in 1914 and 1938, while such authorities as A. L. Kroeber and H. E. Driver have offered their own views. At different times, the number of culture-areas that have been proposed has varied between seven and 17. Kroeber proposed seven major areas and no fewer than 84 sub-areas – which gives some idea of the extent of Indian diversity. Our own scheme (see Figure 4) is therefore somewhat simplified, but it has the merit of being serviceable, and is easy to visualize. After each division, I have indicated some of the main tribes (many of them now extinct) that belonged to it – though naturally, with some 600 tribes extant in the period in question, only a few of the more prominent ones can be mentioned. These tribes, of course, derived from the prehistoric stocks dealt with in the previous chapter – though here, again, one encounters a maddening difficulty, in that it is usually hard and often impossible to identify an Indian tribe of the later era with its lineal ancestor. With one exception, none of the Indian languages were written down. The sole exception was Cherokee, which thanks to the exertions of a brilliant fur-trader called Sequoya, who had been educated in a mission school and crippled in an accident, was put into written form in the early 1820s. There are thus no written Indian records. To confuse matters further, a churning and shifting of the population was always in progress. Only in some of the more settled areas can some correlation be made between Indian tribes and their direct forbears. In the sedentary Southwest, for example, it seems probable that the modern Pima and Papago stem from the ancient Hohokam, and that the inhabitants of most of the modern pueblos are direct descendants of the Anasazi. However, even in the settled Southwest the links are often tenuous.

With these qualifications in mind (and omitting, while at the same time bearing in mind the importance of, the outlying areas of the Arctic and

Mexico) here are the five grand divisions in question:

1. *The Southwest:* Pima, Papago, Hopi, Pueblo Indians, Maricopa. Later arrivals: Navajo, Apache, Yaqui.

2. *The Old Forest or Woodland Area:*
   (i) East Algonquian (Abnaki, Penobscot, Mohican, Pennacook, Massachussett, Wampanoag, Narraganset, Pequot, Delaware, Powhatan).
   (ii) Iroquois Confederacy (Seneca, Cayuga, Oneida, Onondaga Mohawk. Later: Tuscarora).
   (iii) Central Algonquian (Ojibwa or Chippewa, Ottawa, Menomini, Santee Dakota, Sauk, Fox, Kickapoo, Winnebago, Potawatomi, Illinois, Miami).
   (iv) South Eastern (the 'Five Civilized Tribes': Creek, Chickasaw, Choctaw, Cherokee and Seminole; also Caddo, Natchez, Quapaw).

3. *The Plains:* Blackfoot, Piegan, Cree, Atsina or Gros Ventre, Assiniboin, Crow, Mandan, Hidatsa, Arikara, Shoshone, Ute, Gosiute, Cheyenne, Arapaho, Pawnee, Ponca, Omaha, Iowa, Kansa, Missouri, Kiowa, Osage, Comanche. The Sioux: Dakota, Eastern, or Santee Division (Mwdekanton, Wahpekute, Sisseton, Wahpeton); Teton, or Lakota Division (Oglala, Brulé, Sans Arc, Blackfoot, Minneconjou, Two Kettle, Hunkpapa); Wiciyela, or Nakota Division (Yankton and Yanktonai).

4. *California and the Great Basin:* Shuswap, Lillooet, Salish and Kutenai (Flathead), Yakima, Coeur d'Alene, Nez Perce, Bannock, Paiute, Shoshone, Ute, Chemehuevi, Walapai, Havasupai, Mohave, Yavapai, Yuma, Cocopa, Yurok, Wiyot, Wintun, Yuchi, Pomo, Yana, Maidu, Patwin, Miwok, Costanoan, Salinan, Yokut, Chumash.

5. *The Northwest:* Tlingit, Haida, Tsimshian, Haisla, Bella Coola, Heiltsuk, Nootka, Makah, Quinault, Chinook, Tillamook, Kulapuya, Klamath, Karok, Shasta.

The above tribes number just over 100 of the 600 that could once have been listed. Some were large peoples, occupying substantial tracts of territory, while others were small and occupied only a modest area. Yet the extent of a tribe's territory can be deceptive, since many tribes roamed widely but were spread very thinly, whereas others who were more populous might lay claim to only a few square miles. Thus while only slightly more than 100,000 Indians were occupying the whole of the Plains, at a density of only four or five to the mile, the same number were crammed onto a narrow strip of the Northwest coast, with a density that in places rose to 50 or 60 to the mile. This was also true of the East Algonquians of the

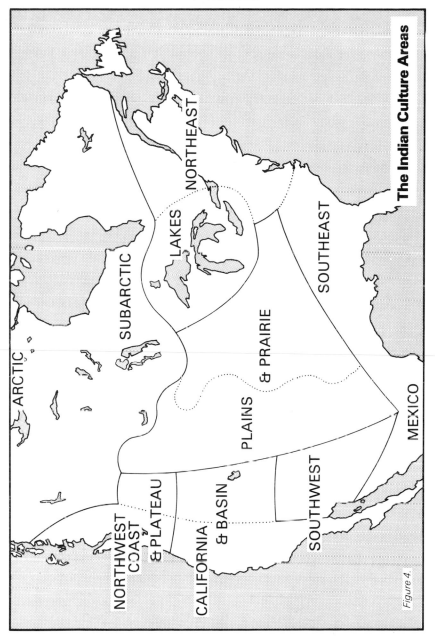

The Indian Culture Areas

ARCTIC

SUBARCTIC

NORTHEAST

LAKES

NORTHWEST COAST & PLATEAU

CALIFORNIA & BASIN

PLAINS & PRAIRIE

SOUTHEAST

SOUTHWEST

MEXICO

Figure 4.

Atlantic coast, who numbered about 100,000 and who were packed in at around 20 or 25 to the square mile.

There were perhaps no more than 750,000 to 1,000,000 Indians in the whole of pre-Columbian America, as far as can be estimated. The majority of them did not inhabit the bare windy spaces of the middle of the continent, but were crowded along its seaboards. The oceans, with the great rivers that ran into them, yielded rich bounties of fish. Even in the interior, tribes were bound to pitch their settlements close to water, the sustainer of life. The one truly populous community that existed in the interior of the country was that of the Pueblo peoples of the Southwest, clustered on the banks of the Rio Grande and its tributaries, which were wider and deeper then than now. There, the 35,000 people of that ancient and long-inhabited region achieved by far the highest population density of Indian America. There were at least 75 of them to the square mile.

Hunting

Wherever an Indian happened to live, whether he belonged to a major tribe or a minor one, he was taken up with one overriding occupation: hunting.

'Taken up' is altogether too weak a phrase. Say, rather, that he was totally absorbed by hunting. The basis of Indian existence was the food-quest, and the basis of the food-quest was the hunt. The hunting instinct had been implanted in him unnumbered ages before, while he was still a nomad on the steppes of Siberia. It was that instinct that had brought him to the Americas, where in spite of continual climate changes he had always possessed a huge territory teeming with apparently inexhaustible supplies of game.

The Indian was no vegetarian. He supplemented his food-supply with fish and vegetables, but his principal craving was for the high-protein diet that was provided by killing a wide range of animals, large, medium-sized, and small. Although, as we shall see in the following chapter, he was destined to become in many instances an accomplished farmer, he never acquired the European art of domesticating animals. Until the white man showed him the way, a mere century ago, he had no experience of owning cattle, sheep, or goats, though he is today a capable herdsman. In most cases, his whole tribal experience, even in historic times, after the collapse of the great prehistoric farming communities, was centred upon the activities of the hunt.

An Indian tribe was split into a number of hunting bands, each confining themselves to their own agreed territory, seldom coming together except in time of war or for important religious festivals. Each band had its own structure and its own leaders, and frequently its contact with other bands of

54

the same tribe was so remote that they spoke different languages or dialects. The most comfortable size of a band was usually felt to be about 100–150 persons, but it was often much smaller. When it began to swell in size, and approached the 200 mark, the problem of feeding it became serious, and the usual solution was fission. A group of families, led by a young man of exceptional character and ability, would elect to go its own way. It would thereupon hive off from the parent body. Sometimes it would do so with the blessing of its elders; sometimes it would split away as the result of a quarrel or a rivalry.

In the new band, the key people were the hunters. Wissler worked out, from historical data, that the members of a band of 100 Indians would require a minimum of four pounds of meat a day. This meant that the five to ten principal huntsmen of the tribe would need to kill an average of four deer or one elk each day, or three or four moose or two buffalo a week. A stiff task. As Wissler observes, 'The Indian male was not altogether a gentleman of leisure'. No wonder that Indian boys were given their first miniature bows and arrows and their first toy spears and knives as soon as they could walk. The hunter who possessed a steady hand, a sharp eye, a swift foot, and a strong arm, was considered a superior person.

It was the practice of hunting that above everything else bestowed on the American Indian his individual and peculiar character. There were, of course, many types of Indian. The sedentary, agricultural Indian and the wild, horse Indian differed widely in outlook and temperament. Ruth Benedict, in her famous book *Patterns of Culture*, adapted a concept from Nietzsche and Spengler and divided Indian peoples into two main psychological classes. These were the 'Apollonians', or those who were self-possessed, disciplined, detached, 'cool and Classical'; and the 'Faustians' (Spengler's term – Nietzsche called them the 'Dionysians') who were ardent, restless, aggressive, devotees of dreams and visions, 'warm and Romantic'. The 'Apollonians' were very sparing with any form of stimulant, if indeed they approved of them at all; the 'Faustians' eagerly employed drugs and stimulants of all kinds.

Yet the 'Classical' Apollonians, no less than the 'Romantic' Faustians, bore the mark of the hunter. It was the arduous, incessant responsibilities of hunting that fixed the personality of the Indian into its serious, not to say sombre mould. Hunting had its moments of excitement and abandon, but for the most part it consisted of hardship, anxiety, isolation and exhaustion. To chase wild animals on foot (and the horse, it must always be remembered, was a late arrival) not for amusement, but for survival, was a desperately demanding business. One can see the effects of it graven on the face of any pre-1890 Indian who had his photograph taken. And yet, to be sure, it was regarded as more than a humdrum, utilitarian pursuit. It was considered a manly and noble occupation. It was an art. It nurtured admirable qualities in the Indian. It gave him his endurance, his preternatural patience, above all his innate sense of being bound up with the intricate processes of nature. To be able to hunt successfully, it was necessary to understand nature in her most intimate aspects. It was the age-long, life-long devotion to the hunt that sharpened the Indian's faculties and gave him his uncanny sensitivity in moving through the landscape.

For most tribes, it was the requirements of the hunt that dictated the locations of the tribal camps and villages. Even if a tribe was one that practised extensive agriculture, it also chose a spot located in a good game area. Tribes hunted in the hinterland of their villages, and when the game began to grow scarce they knew it was time to move on. Other tribes followed the herds incessantly, in a symbiotic relationship, like that of the modern Laplander with the reindeer, while others made regular forays far from the main settlements. These expeditions were well-planned. Entire communities would leave their villages for weeks or months at a time, usually as soon as their crops had been garnered in, and would set off for the hunting-grounds. They would march by regular stages, in proper order, with scouts, outriders, advance party and rearguard. When they reached the hunting-grounds, where the game had replenished itself in the off-season, strict observances came into force. A rule of silence was imposed on the temporary camps, and anyone frightening off the game or chasing it in an irresponsible way was severely beaten by the tribal police. While the men went out to track the game, according to an organized plan, the women and children foraged for fruits, berries and roots; and when enough animals had been killed, their meat cut up, their hides and carcasses prepared, the tribe once again packed its traps and headed back to its permanent village. There the living-quarters and storage-pits had already been fumigated and set in order by the old folk, and the villagers settled down for the winter to a spell of more relaxed living.

Until the advent of the horse, all travelling was done on foot. And even when the horse arrived, it was unusual for every member of a tribe to own one, although a wealthy tribe might have a large surplus of livestock. In most tribes, the members took turns riding and walking. Nevertheless the Indian, even before he owned horses, had devised many ingenious aids to travel. From his Siberian days, in winter or Arctic conditions, he knew the use of sledges, toboggans and snowshoes, the latter carved from wood or woven with leather thongs on a frame of wood or bone. The sledges were drawn by hand, or by teams of dogs. Dogs, indeed, were the only

14 *A camp of the Chippewa, on the Canadian Great Lakes, in winter. Note the skin tipi and the dogs harnessed to haul the sled*

domesticated animal the Indians possessed. Whether in fact they actually domesticated them is doubtful, since the process may have taken place the other way around, and the wild dogs may have adopted the men. Lonely, hungry, shivering in the winter nights, the dog may have caught sight of the bright lights of the Indian encampment and slunk towards them to avail himself of warmth, food and companionship. In the Old World, dogs had been known since ancient times (the Egyptians and Assyrians bred several varieties) and are known to have existed in the New World at least as early as 5000 B.C. It is the Eskimo and the northern Athapascans who seem to have owned the larger and sturdier specimens, as evidenced by the many varieties of huskies and Arctic sledge dogs, and the breeds appear to have grown smaller as they approached the more southerly regions. The Chihuahua and the Hairless Mexican, for example, which both hail from Mexico, are diminutive. For some reason, the Hairless Mexican has an extraordinarily high body temperature, and the ancient Mexicans specially fattened it as a table delicacy. There seems little doubt that the wolf and the coyote contributed to the blood lines of the American dog, and the Indians would occasionally cross wolves with their domestic animals to improve the breed. Wolves and coyotes were often tamed as pets for Indian children.

Like the ancient Mexican (and the ancient Greek and Roman) the American Indian also ate dogs, though usually for ritual purposes. Sometimes dogs were worshipped, were solemnly sacrificed, and were given religious burial. Mostly, however, the dog was a beast of burden. He

57

was harnessed in teams to pull sledges over the ground on runners, or fitted with a harness and an ingenious arrangement of poles that enabled him to drag a pack behind him. Later this device, called by the French explorers who first saw it the *travois*, was adapted for the horse. Wheeled vehicles were unknown. The wheel was brought to the Americas by the Europeans, who employed it as a further item of that superior technology that led to rapid conquest. Some obscure genius in a corner of ancient Mexico once hit upon the principle of the wheel by accident, but its possibilities were never grasped, and it was used only on children's toys.

Until the late arrival of the horse, lifting, pulling and carrying were carried out by means of human muscle-power. Indians were familiar with the refinements of back-packing, and with such aids as placing a folded cloth or a woven pad on the head to support a water-jar. The employment of the tump-line, a cord braced round the base of the pack and supported across the forehead by a strip of webbing, was in use as early as the Basketmaker period in the Southwest, and became almost universal thereafter.

One method of travel and transportation became an Indian speciality.

15 *A Nez Perce camp in the 1870s, with a dog travois.*

This was the use of canoes, coracles, boats, and other varieties of water-craft. Wherever there was a lake, a marsh, a river, or the shore of an ocean, Indians were to be seen paddling upon it in a whole flotilla of artfully constructed vessels. There were boats that were made from reeds, like the ancient Egyptian boats of papyrus. There were boats that were sewn from skins, or hollowed out of tree trunks, or manufactured by means of a number of highly elaborate processes. No better boats have ever been constructed than the kayaks and umyaks of the Eskimo. On Lake Superior, the Ojibwa employed a 15-foot canoe that took two weeks of hard work to make, the men doing the woodwork and the women the sewing. It consisted of a birch bark outer shell; the ribs, stays, thwarts and gunwales were of white cedar; the floorboards were thin cedar strips; the seams were sewn with pine roots and their interstices coated with pine pitch. Such boats were

16 *Travelling in comfort: a Nez Perce woman and her daughter on a horse travois.*

light, and were easy to carry between rivers or across rapids. Canoes were often manhandled long distances between navigable water. On the famous 'Great Carry' in upper New York State, boats were portaged along two main routes between the Hudson, the Atlantic, and the Great Lakes. Such light boats also served other purposes. For instance, in wet weather they could be turned upside down over the smoke-hole of an earth-lodge, to keep the rain out. However, most of these craft were dwarfed by the dug-outs of the peoples of the Northwest, who ranked among the great boat-builders of the primitive world. The Haida travelled in ships up to 70 feet in length,

17 'The Howl of the Weather' by Frederic Remington. A skin boat in rough water.

carrying three tons of cargo, and manned by 60 men. They were hewn from a single huge log of red cedar, were gorgeously ornamented with painting and carving, and were steered and propelled by means of slender, highly decorated paddles. Two of these mighty vessels could be lashed together and a plank-deck laid between them to make a warship. A fleet of them in full sail was an impressive sight.

Canoes were not only important for travelling, trading, and fishing, but for bringing the hunter closer to his quarry. In regions where moose, elk and deer abounded, they often had to be pursued across watery terrain. Even the buffalo hunters of the Plains would float down the broad rivers to approach a herd.

The moose, the elk, the caribou, the reindeer, and the buffalo were the larger and more succulent prey, though moose, elk, caribou and reindeer were available only to the more northerly Indians, in the neighbourhood of the ice. These Arctic animals were formidable, sometimes standing between six and eight feet high at the shoulder. Bringing them down was difficult, despite the techniques that their pursuers had inherited from ancestors who had hunted the woolly mammoth and the mastodon, which were twice as tall. As for the buffalo, the once abundant but now extinct *Bison antiquus* was a monster that bulked almost as large as the mammoth, while even the *Bison bison* of modern times loomed higher than the average Indian and had the massive build of its relative, the ox. All these larger animals could run swiftly and tirelessly over ice, snow and tundra, and required much endurance to catch.

The catalogue of the large game was rounded out by an even more savage and redoubtable creature, the bear. All Indians held the bear in reverence. The grizzly bear of the Rocky Mountains, well named *Ursus Ferox*, was a giant which attained a height of nine feet and a weight of 800 pounds. It was capable of dragging to its lair the carcass of a 1000-pound buffalo. The polar bear of the Arctic regions was equally imposing: and although the two other varieties of bear, the brown bear and the black bear, were almost diminutive in comparison, they too possessed the same qualities of sagacity, courage, defiance, and awful strength. After despatching a bear, an Indian would often perform a little ritual such as apologizing to it, placing a pipe of tobacco between its lips, addressing it as 'grandfather' or 'grandmother', and seeking in every way to appease its spirit.

The hunters of the larger animals tended to become inseparable from, and entirely dependent upon, the great herds. There was also, however, a range of smaller and more sporadic game that was widely hunted. It included deer, antelope, and wild sheep. The so-called modern 'sportsman', with his high-velocity rifle and telescopic sight, finds them elusive targets, and it seems miraculous that the Indian could corner them on foot. There were three main species of deer that flourished in America and Canada, none of them of great size: the common or Virginia deer, the

18 *Carved boats with sails of the Kwakiutl Indians of the Northwest Pacific Coast, carrying a wedding party.*

a

b

c

d

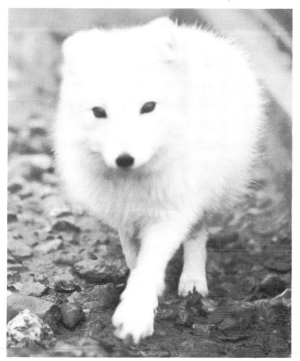

19 *Animals familiar to the American Indians: (a) American Bison (b) Brown Bear (c) Big-Horn Sheep (d) Arctic Fox (e) North American Racoon.*

e

mule deer, and the black-tailed deer. The types of antelope included the pronghorn and the wild sheep, the famous big-horn or argali of the Rockies, its horns over three feet long and forming a complete circle on each side of the skull.

In addition, the Indian ran down or trapped a long list of other creatures, most of them capable of providing sustenance. Some were coveted not for their meat, but for their fur, or for some other portion of their anatomy that could yield an article of clothing or some domestic item. Chief among these were the five varieties of the North American wolf (grey, white, pied, dusky, and black); the coyote or prairie wolf; the fox and Arctic fox; the wolverine; and the racoon. There were also a host of more humble animals almost too numerous to mention. Among them were the rabbit, weasel, ermine, mink, marten, badger, skunk, squirrel, chipmunk, gopher, prairie dog, marmot, beaver, porcupine, and the rat and mouse. These furnished many a fancy bit of Indian finery. Nor must we forget the array of mammals regularly taken by the fishermen of the Atlantic and Pacific coasts; whale, walrus, grampus, sea lion, porpoise, dolphin, and sea-otter.

Weapons

What were the weapons which the Indian relied on for success in the hunt? Considering that he remained in the Stone Age, and never used anything other than his muscles, he invented an ingenious and diversified armoury.

From the outset, he was always a highly skilled worker in stone. It provided him with his arrowheads, spearpoints, axes and clubs. In the earliest times, stone for making superior weapons was traded over enormous distances. Shiny black obsidian, which only occurs in the Southwest, was exported to the Mississippi valley; brown flint from western Tennessee was carried thousands of miles from its place of origin; and fine flint from Amarillo in the Texas Panhandle was distributed far to the east and west.

The art of flint-knapping, still in existence in many parts of the world, is mankind's oldest industry. The projectile points of the Clovis, Folsom and Scottsbluff hunters of 30,000–10,000 B.C. were as perfect in form as points being made in the nineteenth century: a continuous tradition of more than 30,000 years. Flint-working has been known in all continents at all times, deriving from independent invention or from gradual diffusion, and the American Indians practised it with rare skill. They knew how to crack the flint matrix into smaller blocks with a blow of a stone or an antler hammer. They knew how to split these smaller pieces into individual shapes, and how to refine the edges of the tools by means of delicate pressure, using softer implements of bone. Then came the final stages of polishing and sharpening, for which sand, sandstone, or some other abrasive was employed. In the Northwest, squares of sharkskin made an efficient substitute for modern sandpaper.

When completed, the points, scrapers, grooved axes, and ungrooved axes that archaeologists call celts, were inserted into slots, or bound directly with thongs of leather or sinew on to wooden shafts or handles. Sometimes the points were held in the socket by natural gum or mastic, and the bindings were coated with bituminous pitch. Every tribe had its favourite method. In the North, the tool-kit of flint and stone was supplemented by tools made from the bones of fish or seals, or from the antlers of deer, elk and caribou, rendered easier to work by soaking in water.

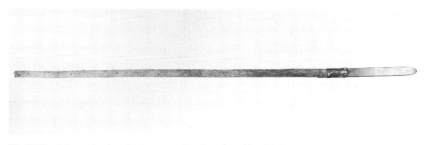

20 *White Mountain Apache lance made of sotol stalk with iron point.*

The primaeval Indian weapon was the lance or the spear. It was tipped with bone or flint, its point sharpened and hardened by charring in the camp-fire. An advance was made in manipulating this basic weapon when it was discovered that it could be turned into a javelin by throwing it, and that it could be thrown further by means of an *atlatl*. The *atlatl* (an Aztec word) was a short stick, ending in a flint or bone socket that fitted into the base of the spear. It acted as a lever, producing a longer and faster flight. It must have needed much practice to get the hang of it, but where practising with his weapons was concerned, the American Indian was as patient and persistent as the Western gunman, with his Colt and his Derringer.

No one knows the exact date when the bow and arrow made its appearance in the New World. It was being used in the Old World about 5000 B.C., but it was not until A.D. 500, at the earliest, that it seems to have reached the New World. How it got there and what tribes used it first is a mystery that is unlikely to be solved. In any event, the introduction of the bow was as great a jump in the history of weaponry as the jump from the horse to the tank. Indian fire-power, for 30,000 years confined to the spear and javelin, was immeasurably increased. Soon the American Indian, like his Old World counterpart, was choosing the toughest but most flexible

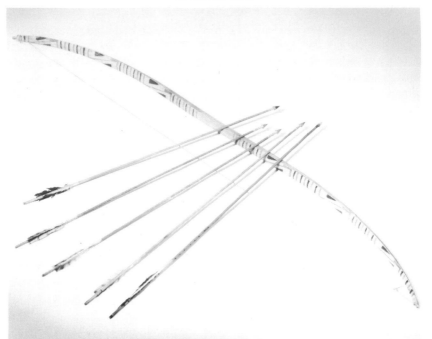

21 *Yuma bow collected pre-1900, Yuma arrows.*

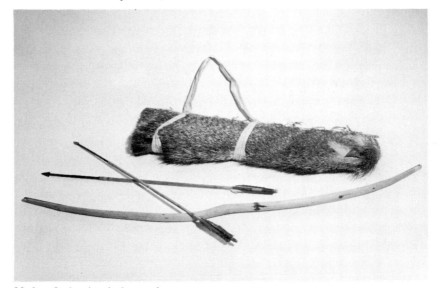

22 *San Carlos Apache bow and arrow-case.*

woods, such as the ash, yew and mulberry, and bending them or moulding them in the hot ashes of the fire to varieties of the classical form. Again, each area evolved its own distinctive style. Many bows were strengthened with a backing or an inlay of bone or sinew, and sinew or twisted fibre was used to make the bowstring and to strengthen the ends and middle of the bow. Similarly, each tribe devised its own wood or cane arrows, flighted with eagle, hawk, buzzard or turkey feathers. A competent archer could put an arrow into a moving target at 50 yards, and a white man once saw an Indian during a competition draw and fire so rapidly that he put eight arrows in the air before the first one reached the ground. The Plains Indians, galloping alongside the left flank of a buffalo, and guiding their horses with their knees, would shoot a bolt clean through the animal's heart with their handy little three-foot bows.

23 'The Buffalo Hunt' by Charles M. Russell. These Plains Indians are using the short horse-man's bow.

A few tribes invented additional means of taking game. Thus the Cherokee and Iroquois used an eight-foot-long blowgun and a delicate poisoned dart, feathered with thistledown, for hunting in forests and marshes; while the bolas, consisting of strings of pear-shaped weights, was used by the tribesmen of Louisiana to bring down duck and other birds. Some hunters were also adept at catching waterfowl by swimming beneath them, using a reed as a snorkel, or by floating among the birds with a gourd over their heads.

24 *A hunter of the arid Southwest. He has killed the jackrabbit by means of his curved throwing-club.*

On occasion, a whole community would turn out and join together in capturing game. In the Great Basin, women and children would co-operate in trapping rabbits with nets when jack-rabbits became especially plentiful. The Basketmakers of the Southwest were expert weavers of such nets. One net, discovered in the White Dog Cave on the Black Mesa, was 240 feet long, three feet wide, weighed 28 pounds, and contained nearly four miles of knotted string. No doubt it was stretched across the mouth of a canyon, and the game driven into it, with the help of the dogs whose mummified bodies were buried by their Basketmaker owners, who needed their service and companionship in the next world as well as in this one.

Indians were clever at luring animals by means of baited traps. They dug concealed pits; they constructed free-swinging snares from sappy branches. They also combined together to lure the larger herds on to ground where they could easily be slaughtered. The Stone Age technique of coaxing or scaring buffalo up a slope at the edge of a ravine persisted, and was described in the previous chapter. In fact, the Indian huntsman became as sensitive, with regard to sight, smell, knowledge of the terrain, and of animal behaviour, as the beast he was seeking. When pursuing deer, a hunter would don the skin, mask and antlers of a deer in order to slip in among the herd. Pursuing buffalo, he would make similar use of a buffalo hide, draping it over himself and over his horse, if he were mounted. Indians were also gifted at decoying birds and animals by imitating their calls, their mating signals, and the cries of their young.

As for the fishermen, they were every bit as resourceful as the huntsmen. Like the fishermen of today, Indians often fished for their private pleasure, a pleasure that uniquely lends itself to self-communing and a feeling of closeness to nature. Long before *The Compleat Angler* was written, fishermen on the Great Lakes were using rods and lines that were very similar to those used today; they were carving and painting plugs and spinners that would have done credit to any modern tackle-store. The Indian also knew the art of 'tickling' – familiar to boys everywhere – sliding a hand in a mountain stream and holding it motionless until a fish nudges against it and can be grabbed. On the Atlantic and Pacific beaches, lobsters, crabs, oysters, clams, and sea-anemones were regularly gathered as titbits.

When fishing on a large scale, the Indian was skilled at constructing dams, weirs, platforms, and elaborate pens of reeds and osiers. In these, the fish were speared, clubbed, shot with the bow, or scooped out in wicker baskets. Seine and purse-nets of plaited vines, often requiring many men to handle, were also used. The tribes of the Southeast hit upon a root, narcotic but not poisonous, which they ground up and threw in the water to stun the fish.

Fish, flesh or fowl, a part of the hunt that was as important as the chase itself was the division of the spoils. This was a serious matter, in which tradition and tribal and family relationships played a key part. Small animals could be taken back to camp and divided up at leisure, but larger ones had to be dressed out on the spot. The slayer, who recognized the beast he had killed by his personal markings on the arrow that slew it, claimed the best portions, bestowing other portions on those who had assisted him with the kill. Certain portions were set aside for specific people, or for religious purposes. After the butchering, and the removal and preliminary scraping of the hides, the meat was reduced to manageable amounts, which in turn were strapped inside rawhide containers, like skin tarpaulins, called by early French explorers *parfleches*. The *parfleches* were carried on *travois* or on the backs of the huntsmen to the temporary camp, then to the main camp. Often the women and children would make their way to the place of the kill, to help with the labour. It had to be done quickly and skilfully, otherwise the precious meat would spoil. If the meat was abundant, or there was too much of it, the tribe would hold a feast on the spot, before reducing the rest to 'jerky' or pemmican.

One factor that weighed heavily was one that is often discounted in accounts of Indian life: rain. In Hollywood films, where the cameras only turn on fine days, the weather in Cowboyland and Indianland is always idyllic. Actually, rain was a curse to cowboy and Indian alike. The cowboy,

25 *Hunters, wearing a wolf-skin disguise, approach a herd of buffalo.*

26 *Bringing firewood and fodder to a Pawnee encampment in midwinter. Note the characteristic earth-lodge, with portico and smoke-hole, and the sun-totem on a pole.*

out in all weathers, was notably bent and arthritic. He always carried his 'fish' or 'slicker' with him (and sometimes even a large umbrella) to keep off the downpour. As for the Indian, rain not only rotted his stock of new meat, but also spoiled his bowstring, made his spear slippery, stiffened his leather clothes, ruined his hides, and made his tents and belongings mouldy. When we think of the Indian, we must think of him not only in the bright sunshine, but in the misery of the wet.

The Horse

The whole business of the hunt and its aftermath – in fact, the entire existence of the Indian – was immeasurably eased with the coming of the horse.

Indian life was completely transformed. The toilsome, footsore centuries lay behind. An exciting, liberated future appeared to beckon. As Wissler says, 'The changes in Indian life brought about by this new mode of travel were even greater than those produced by the automobile in our time . . . It gave the Indian a broader outlook, new experiences, more leisure, and inhibited sedentary occupations'.

Unfortunately, though it increased the area of the food supply, and gave a fresh zest to life, it had some unpleasant side-effects. A tribe could now cover 500 miles in the course of a season, where before it could scarcely cover 50, and this new mobility stepped up the number of inter-tribal rivalries, feuds, and encroachments on neighbours' territories. It made those tribes that were already predatory and aggressive more aggressive still. It encouraged tribes which possessed a knowledge of agriculture to abandon the demanding processes of planting, tending and harvesting, and go charging off under the influence of the horse-frenzy. Worst of all, it led some of the more undisciplined and 'Faustian' tribes to embark on a rampage of killing buffalo and other animals for its own sake, a senseless slaughter that helped to deplete the food stocks.

A frenzy it was. In the 1650s, the Indians, particularly the Plains Indians, who were to surrender themselves body and soul to the new craze, possessed only a handful of horses. Twenty years later, they had acquired them in substantial numbers. Horses had been brought across the Rio Grande into the Southwest as early as 1540, when the Viceroy of New Spain permitted Vázquez de Coronado to make an armed *entrada* into the unknown territory to the north of Mexico. Coronado went in search of the fabled Seven Cities of Cíbola, whose palaces and dwellings were rumoured to be built entirely of gold, and whose wealth was said to rival that of the recently conquered Inca Empire. Coronado did not find Cíbola. He did not find it because nothing remotely resembling it existed. So after much hard fighting, and a heroic march that took him as far as Kansas, he retired to Mexico City mortally injured by a kick from a horse.

Some of Coronado's *remuda* of horses may well have escaped and run free. So probably did animals from later *entradas*, such as those of Chamuscado in 1581, Espejo in 1581–82, and Castaño de Sosa in 1590–91. But a more substantial contribution would have been made by the stock of Juan de Oñate's large-scale expedition of 1598, when the province of New Mexico was finally founded, and its capital city of Santa Fé established.

To the Indians, as to the Aztecs when they were confronted by Cortés in 1519, the first sight of men on horseback was unnerving. They thought that man and mount were welded together into a composite animal, like a centaur. Like the Aztecs before them, they fled. When they later became better acquainted with the animal, at first they showed little desire to ride them; the Indians of the period 1600–1680 appear to have eaten whatever stray horses they captured, rather than ride them. Nevertheless, they soon realized that the horse would be a boon in the hunting-field, and as a beast of burden.

Probably the turning-point came in 1680. In that year the Pueblo Indians rose unexpectedly against their now numerous and well-entrenched Spanish overlords and drove them precipitately southwards to El Paso and Chihuahua. All the belongings of the Spaniards,

27 *Three Cheyenne girls on horseback.*

28 *Cheyenne girls on the fringes of a Sun-Dance gathering.*

including their strings of horses, fell into Indian hands. By the time the Spaniards returned, in 1692, the Pueblo people and their neighbours on the Plains had mastered the art of horsemanship.

On the East coast and in the Southeast, the English and French pioneers, arriving in America later than the Spaniards, were also introducing the horse to the Indians. There, it became only a minor adjunct to the lives of the fishermen, farmers and forest-dwellers, whose wooded and watery terrain was not so ideal for raising and running stock. It was on the prairies and grasslands of the American heartland that horsemanship became a consuming passion, and it was the Spanish-bred horses of New Mexico and Texas that the Plains Indians stole or bought.

Arched around the New Mexico-Texas frontier, there was an inner ring of horsed tribes, composed of the Navajo, the Apache, the Comanche, and the Ute. In a second ring were to be found the Osage, the Kiowa, the Cheyenne, and the Arapaho. Beyond that was a third tier, composed of the Pawnee, the Crow, the Shoshone, and the tribes of the great Sioux nation, including the Dakota, Mandan and Hidatsa. And further afield still, in the distant North, were the tribes of Canada and the Canadian border, the Cree, Blackfoot, Ojibway, and those splendid horsemen, the Nez Perce, with their gorgeous Apaloosas. When once the novelty of the horse took hold, between 1650 and 1800, it spread with the same speed and enthusiasm as the spread of the motor-car and the aeroplane.

Incidentally, it is commonly supposed that all Indians rode bareback. This is not the case. Many tribes made their own rawhide saddles, on the European pattern, with decorated saddlebags to match. Nor is it true that only men were privileged to ride. Among some peoples the women and girls were as ardent and accomplished riders as the men and boys.

Firearms

Together with the introduction of the horse went the introduction of firearms. The horse and the gun were twin gifts of the white man, which together would tear huge holes in the ancient fabric of Indian life.

Firearms compounded the damage wrought among many tribes by the horse. They made aggressors more aggressive; they whipped up the tendency to indulge in the facile and irresponsible killing of game. At first, the Spaniards in New Mexico, the earliest settlers in the United States, strove to keep guns out of Indian hands. But the Indians got them in any case, either by theft, or by removing them from the dead bodies of homesteaders they had murdered. Therefore it became, strange as it sounds, official policy to supply them with what they coveted. The authorities reasoned in the way that European and American governments now reason with regard to selling arms to the Middle East or South America. Since the latter are bound to get them anyway, you might as well sell them yourself, take your profit, and bind the purchasers to you by controlling the rate of supply and the sale of spare parts. When the Spaniards, English and French sold weapons to the warrior tribes, they tried to make sure that the guns were of poor quality. Sometimes they were entirely useless, for many tribes wanted guns not to shoot but for display, as status symbols. Moreover, the Indians could not manufacture ammunition and gunpowder, and were wholly dependent on the colonists for those commodities. Nor were they able to mend their guns themselves. Lacking tools and mechanical training, they had to bring them into the settlements for repair. Tales are told of baffled Indians thwacking their guns against trees and boulders, like angry golfers smashing their clubs. In addition, unlike the white pioneers, who handled guns from the cradle, few Indians became good shots. They had no tradition or training, and even when they had reliable weapons they could seldom spare enough of their precious store of powder and shot in order to practise.

In the middle and late eighteenth century, when the Woodland Indians were increasingly enlisted as allies by the English and French, the picture gradually changed. English and French guns were generally of a higher quality than Spanish guns, and the Indians were afforded plenty of action in which to get used to handling them. By 1800, the Iroquois (without whose support of the English, America might have become a French possession) and their deadly enemies, the Algonquin, were showing disconcerting signs of becoming capable marksmen. Indeed, by the War of 1812, these two great Indian peoples were equipped with better weapons than those issued to the American and British armies. Such a situation could only enhance the bitterness of the conflict when, that war once over, the young American nation was able to turn its full attention to subduing the native inhabitants.

But let us leave, at this point, the business of warfare, to which we shall be returning later, in order to view the arts of peace which, fortunately for the vast bulk of the Indians, consumed a far more fruitful proportion of their time and energies.

3

The Home

What would we have noticed if we had been able to visit the villages and encampments of the North American Indian, at any time, say, between A.D. 1700 and 1900? Shall we take advantage of the hospitality which the Indians invariably display towards strangers, and take a short stroll together?

Whatever the type of village and the construction of its dwellings, we would first remark on the skill with which it had been sited. The Indian chose the places where he was to live with as much care as any modern town-planner. We can be sure that, even on the treeless, shadeless Plains, he would pick a spot which afforded as much shelter as possible from the full effects of sun, wind and rain. Nearby there would be water: either a natural water-hole, or else a creek or stream that contained fish, and where unwary deer and other animals would come to drink. Or the settlement would be strung out along the banks of one or other of those mighty rivers that, everywhere on the globe, nourish human culture, and which we of the modern world treat so abominably and ungratefully. In addition, close attention would have been paid to picking a site which offered a natural defence from enemy marauders and war-parties, a place that was at once inconspicuous and difficult to attack and surprise.

An Indian camp or village would normally consist of somewhere between 100 and 300 people – though we have seen that many Indian communities, particularly in the heyday of the prehistoric era, were very much larger, and could be considered townships. The camp would be divided into areas allotted to the various family groups, each numbering in the region of 30–50 men, women and children. Some camps would be completely open and devoid of any defences, whereas others would be provided with earthen walls or palisades of logs, depending on custom, circumstances, and the supply of raw materials. It was the latter that determined the shape and the construction of the individual dwellings, which differed in each of our five main cultural regions.

76

Houses

In the oldest of the settled regions, the Southwest, we have seen that at the dawn of our era the Hohokam and the Anasazi were already considerable architects. The Hohokam built the Casa Grande and other buildings of adobe, or bricks of sun-dried mud, or of caliche, which is dried stiff clay. Adobe and caliche, which the American pioneers called 'prairie marble', are not only cheap but durable, and many homes and public buildings in the Southwest are made of them to this day. As for the Anasazi, at Mesa Verde and elsewhere they translated the crude and primitive cave into a residence of fairylike quality, and in their freestanding 'blocks of flats', at Chaco Canyon or nearby Aztec, they handled stonework with an uncanny sophistication.

To the north of them, we would have seen the earth-lodges of their nomadic neighbours, the Navajo, a populous tribe of Athabascan descent who had been gradually trickling southward until they came up against the pueblos of the Rio Grande. These earth-lodges are unique in that, like the pueblos themselves, they are the only form of authentic Indian housing still in use. The Navajo reservation, largest of all Indian reservations, is thickly

29 *Modern hogan on the Navajo reservation in Northern Arizona.*

77

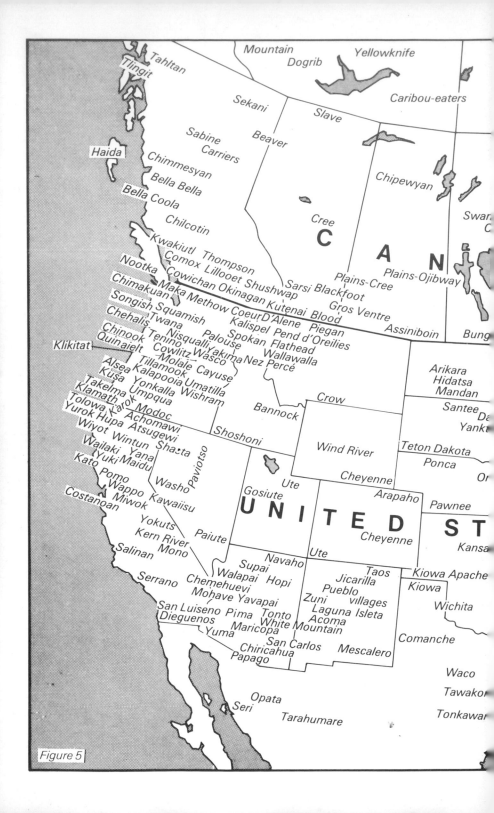

Figure 5

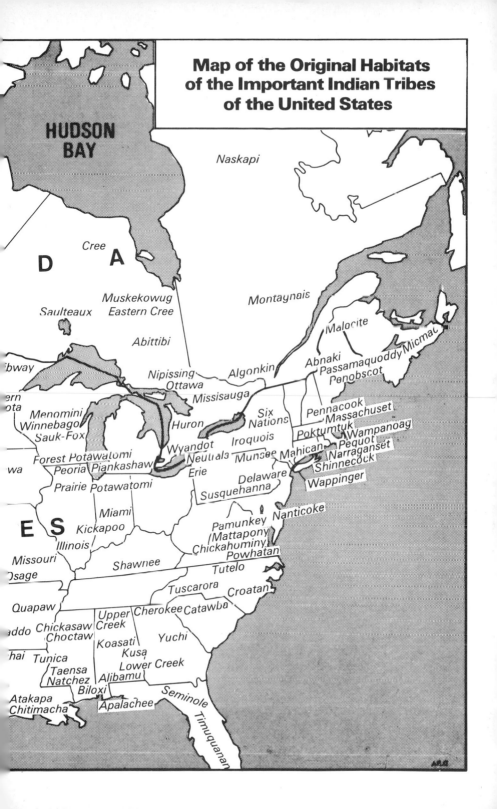

Map of the Original Habitats of the Important Indian Tribes of the United States

HUDSON BAY

Naskapi

Cree

D A

Muskekowug
Eastern Cree

Saulteaux

Montaynais

Abittibi

Malocite

bway

Nipissing
Ottawa

Algonkin

Abnaki
Passamaquoddy Micmac
Penobscot

Missisauga

ern
ota

Menomini
Winnebago
Sauk-Fox

Huron

Six
Nations

Pennacook
Massachuset

Poktumtuk Wampanoag

Forest Potawatomi
Peoria Piankashaw

Wyandot

Iroquois

Munsee Mahican Pequot
Narraganset
Shinnecock

wa

Neutrals

Prairie Potawatomi

Erie

Delaware

Wappinger

Susquehanna

Miami

Nanticoke

E S

Kickapoo

Pamunkey
(Mattapony
Chickahominy

Illinois

Missouri

Shawnee

Powhatan

Osage

Tutelo

Tuscarora

Croatan

Quapaw

Upper Cherokee Catawba
Creek

addo Chickasaw
Choctaw

Koasati
Kusa

Yuchi

hai Tunica

Lower Creek

Taensa
Natchez Alibamu

Atakapa
Chitimacha

Biloxi
Apalachee

Seminole

Timuquanan

dotted with these squat, picturesque hogans, as they are called. Their floor-plan is circular, to symbolize the sun and the universe, and their dome-shaped wooden roofs are coated with hard-packed earth. The entrance is a simple aperture covered by a blanket, facing east, again to honour the sun. Outside the main hogan, a little distance from it, would be situated the sweat lodge, a small hogan without a smoke-hole, where the family could indulge in the equivalent of a modern sauna or Turkish bath. Such sweat-baths were a common feature of Indian life throughout North America. Also near the hogan would be the *ramada*, a brush-covered frame with four poles at the corners, beneath the shade of which the older folk could snooze, the children play, and the wife sit comfortably at her loom, or preparing food for the family meal.

Earth-lodges of various types were also in use on the plains and prairies, particularly in the North, where the summers were torrid and the winters harsh. Such dwellings were cool in summer and warm in winter. The lodges of the Pawnee in Nebraska and the Mandan and Hidatsa in the Dakotas had foundations dug well down into the soil. Those of the Pawnee were round mounds, huddled close together, but those of the Mandan and Hidatsa were grandiose structures with an elaborate armature of wooden supports. Some of the Mandan lodges measured 80 or 100 feet across, sheltering several families and providing stabling for their horses, from which they could not bear to be parted. Their occupants lounged and sunned themselves on the roof. The Iroquois, too, lived packed together in long-houses, and the missionaries who occasionally sojourned among them found the heat, smoke, stink, noise, and yelping of dogs insupportable.

Across most of the central plains – which means across most of North America – the principal form of house was the *tipi*. The tipi is often mistakenly called the wigwam, a quite different structure that will be described in a moment. The tipi was the conical, painted buffalo-hide tent that is familiar from the movies. The hunting-tent was small, but the camp or ceremonial tipi might tower 20 feet high and have an internal measurement of 30 feet across, requiring up to 50 buffalo-hides in its construction. Small or large, the tipi was brilliantly adapted to its environment and to the needs of the nomads who periodically erected and dismantled it. It was easily taken down and put up, and its three or four main poles and 20 or 24 lesser poles could be arranged over the withers of horses and dogs to form a *travois* on which the folded tipi itself, as well as other goods, could be transported. At the campsite, the main poles were raised in a triangle and lashed together, the subsidiary poles were set in place, and the great leather half-moon was hoisted up and laced together with thongs of sinew. Tent pegs were driven in to hold the lower edge firm.

30 *A Mandan family with its horses and dogs inside a typical earth-lodge.*

In winter, an inner lining was tied to the poles, its bottom edge resting on the ground to keep out the draughts; but in summer the skirts of the tipi could be rolled up to admit a cool breeze. The fire was directly in the centre, so that the heat rose straight up towards the smokehole and was neatly

31 *Tipis on the open prairie.*

trapped in the narrowing cone overhead. If the prevailing wind made the smoke troublesome, then the poles could be juggled to make it blow away in another direction. Moreover, unlike earth-houses and other structures, the skin of the tipi could be decorated with beadwork, quillwork, and every sort of mythological and religious device, and with the personal badge or symbol of its occupant. The tipis of such tribes as the Cheyenne and the Blackfoot were creations of outstanding beauty and originality. Not for nothing did the Plains Indians call Heaven the 'Land of Many Tipis', a broad and sweeping landscape dotted with glistening, many-coloured tents.

32 *A Chippewa brave erects a birch-bark tipi, while his family refine maple sugar.*

The tipi was not only characteristic of the Plains, but was also in evidence elsewhere in America, though in a less gorgeous guise. Some tribes did not bother to ornament their tents, while others, especially in harsh climates, piled on mats, rugs or other insulating material higgledy-piggledy to keep in the heat. In Canada and on the Northeast coast, birch bark was used in place of skins, a material not susceptible to large-scale painting. Incidentally, the tipi is not exclusive to North America, but is known elsewhere in the world, particularly in northeastern Asia; it may in fact be

33 *A Papago woman mends a kiaha or burden basket outside her wickieup at San Xavier.*

one of the artefacts brought into Canada and America by the earliest hunters, who probably took to caves in the winter and lived in tents in the summer, though traces of something as ephemeral as wood and leather would naturally not have survived, and they are therefore only known as 'cavemen'.

The term *wigwam* is best reserved for dwellings constructed with a framework of poles, like a tipi, but with a rounded top, and covered not with skins but with woven mats or birch bark. Often the interior strengthening of the wigwam consisted of a wooden scaffolding, and they were tethered down tightly by fibre ropes, giving them the appearance of overturned boats. Where they were more flimsy and temporary, mere bundles of rushes or dried grass applied to a frame, they were called *wickieups*. Such matting or grass tents were characteristic of desert areas, like the Great Basin and the arid fringes of the Southwest, where the tribes were poverty-stricken or possessed a low level of material culture. The wickieup was the standard dwelling of the Apache, a brave but very primitive people.

Wigwams and wickieups must not be confused with the substantial thatched houses that were a feature of the southern United States. The

83

people who inhabited the parklands of the Southeast and the Mississippi Basin, where the builders of the Temple Mounds had formally raised their imposing buildings, constructed tall circular houses with stout timber colonnades. In many cases, the walls and roofs were covered with

34 *The long-house encampment of the Powhatan, from a drawing by Captain John White. The Powhatan were the leaders of the Powhatan Confederacy, a group of tribes who lived on the Atlantic seaboard of East Virginia. Pocahontas was the daughter of a Powhatan chief, Wahunsonakok.*

35 *A closer view of a Powhatan village.*

tight woven and brightly-ornamented reed mats. The circular house was also the dwelling of the neighbouring Woodlanders of the Carolinas and the Northeast coast. In these regions the long-house with its domed roof and open latticed porch and walls was also in evidence. Here, on benches stretching the whole length of the house, entire families would eat, sleep, disport themselves, and hold religious ceremonies, in the manner of the long-house societies of Southeast Asia.

It was in the distant Pacific Northwest that the long-house, like so much else, reached its maximum development. Tribes like the Haida, Tsimshian and Tlingit cut planks and beams of red and yellow cedar to build long-houses that could shelter 30 to 40 people. They were seldom less than 50 feet long and 40 feet wide, and were masterpieces of carving and carpentry. The planks were grooved, tongued, steamed into firm joints, and the roofs were shingled with bark. The exterior and interior walls, and the partitions that divided the inside of the spacious buildings into separate rooms, were carved and painted with totemic motifs. Every chief possessed his own individual set of house-boards. The ridge pole of the house was elaborately carved and painted, and outside the house stood one of the famous Northwestern totem poles, embodying the history of the clan or

85

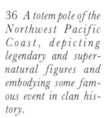

36 *A totem pole of the Northwest Pacific Coast, depicting legendary and supernatural figures and embodying some famous event in clan history.*

86

family and topped with the family emblem. Such poles, sometimes soaring to a height of 30 feet, were visible from far out to sea, and served as landmarks. They were the proud tokens of a community's power and lineage. Even today, the villages of the Northwest are bustling places, and their inhabitants are increasingly dedicated to re-establishing the crafts and folkways of their great ancestors.

Furnishing

If we had been invited, as we surely would be, to step inside an Indian dwelling, we would have found little or no furniture. The floor of beaten earth, worn flat to the consistency of glass or parquet, and scrupulously swept with a besom of grass or twigs, would either have been left bare or partially covered with furs, rugs or skins. Hangings and fetishes adorned the walls. The family would sleep around the wall of the house or tent, each member in his own appointed place, sometimes on a raised bench but more often directly on mother earth, wrapped in a warm robe. A common article of furniture was a back rest, which would support a man as he sat on the ground, rather like a modern deckchair without the seat. Certain parts of the dwelling were allotted to religious images and to the sacred medicine-bundle, and there were mysterious spots, marked with stones, which everyone avoided stepping on or passing in front of, and which were dedicated to the shades of the ancestors or had some other spiritual purpose.

The centre of the dwelling was invariably the hearth, on which a bright fire burned by day and was dampened down at night. Fire, a gift of the gods, had a sacred significance, and was sedulously cherished. It symbolized the sun, as the home around it symbolized the surrounding universe, with the door or tent-flap positioned towards the east to catch the first rays of daylight. The techniques of making fire were very ancient. In prehistoric times, the art of producing sparks by striking one flint with another, or with a piece of iron pyrites, was already known; but a commoner method was to twirl a pointed stick in a notch in another stick until sufficient heat was generated to ignite a handful of dried grass and tindery bark. Another and even more rapid way was to rotate the fire-stick by means of a bow, twisting the bowstring around the middle of the stick and working it steadily back and forth while holding the top of the stick upright in a hole in a special stone. Sometimes fire was carried from one site to another in a buffalo horn, or in an enclosed pot, or inside a mass of slow-smouldering moss. Many tribes worshipped fire; they kept an eternal flame burning in their houses and temples, and on occasion appointed a regular Keeper of the Flame to watch over it.

Clothes

The family who welcomed us into their dwelling might be dressed in a variety of clothing. The tribes of the Plains, and of the North and the East coast, would need more covering than those of the sunnier South. The latter, together with the poorer tribes such as those of the Great Basin, wore virtually no clothing, except for a loin-cloth in the case of the men and a skirt in that of the women. The southerly tribes tattooed the whole of their bodies with bizarre stripes or whorls in variegated colours, or painted themselves with white, red and brown ochres and orpiments, and some of the central and eastern tribes also practised the art of tattooing. The Plains Indians, particularly those of the warlike Caddo federation of Oklahoma, Kansas and Arkansas, tattooed themselves so heavily that the early English settlers nicknamed them the 'Pawnee Picts'.

Elsewhere, the general custom was for the women to wear a one-piece skin dress, a blouse and skirt, or a blouse and leggings. The men wore breeches and went bare-chested, and when they needed to protect themselves from rain and cold they enveloped themselves in a mantle. Shirts were only worn by men of high caste, mainly on ceremonial

37 *Women process leather in a Blackfoot encampment on the Great Plains. Note the skin tipis with their beautiful and individual decoration.*

38 *A chief of the Cheyenne, with carefully dressed hair and ceremonial decorations.*

occasions. The gorgeous costumes that are depicted in Victorian and later novels, or in the movies, were generally the creation of comparatively recent times, when the Indian adopted the silks and ribbons, sateens and velveteens of the white man, and copied the styles of the Westerners whom they encountered in the new towns, the river-boats and the Army posts. After 1860, Indian dress was everywhere transformed into a dazzling travesty of what it had originally been.

Not that the skin and fur clothing of the Indian was inferior or ill-made, before the revolution brought about by Western influence and the Wild West Shows. Indian furs were of the highest quality, stitched together into large garments with the skill of a modern furrier, while skins were treated in a wide variety of ways. Left untanned, as rawhide, with the hair and flesh removed, they were as tough as bone or plastic, and provided war-shields, bindings, and *parfleches*. The skins of buffalo, elk, moose, deer, antelope and other animals could be turned into the softest leather. The skin would be scraped, tanned by rubbing it with a mixture of brains, sour milk, elm bark and liver, and thoroughly soaked in water. After being wrung dry and stretched over a frame, it was ready for cutting and sewing into clothes, bags, pouches, shirts, leggings, footwear, arrow-cases, or the thousand and one other uses to which it could be put. Many tribes were famous for the skill with which they tanned and prepared their leather. The Crows of the Plains, for example, made their deerskin, elk skin and buffalo skin clothes and tipis so perfectly that after a rainstorm they dried out rapidly and with no sign of damage.

A leather garment or other item was seldom left plain, for the passion for decoration was innate with the Indian. It was fringed, embroidered, painted, or embellished with beadwork, shellwork, quillwork, or feathers. In addition to leatherwork, other articles of dress were fashioned by weaving, either by means of simple finger-weaving, twining, plaiting, and braiding, or employing the belt-loom or the true loom – artistic techniques that will be more fully described in a later chapter. Shirts, dresses, belts, sashes, chiefs' blankets, shoulder blankets, ponchos, and other articles were all made by Indian weavers. As for the children, they usually ran about naked until the age of five or six, when they were put into their first clothes and began to learn grown-up ways. Normally, as in modern families, great attention was paid to making sure they kept their shoes on, since there was a constant danger from rattlesnakes, ants, and other creatures. Indians possessed several pairs of moccasins, some with high tops and some with low, some with hard soles and some with soft, some for idling about in, and others for farming, working, tracking and hunting. Some were for everyday wear, some for best. An Indian going off on a hunting expedition would take

39 *A Hopi girl and her mother: different hair-styles for different tribal status.*

two or three changes of moccasins with him. In peace or war, male Indians were often tremendous swells, delighting to parade around like peacocks, endlessly preening themselves and flaunting their finery.

A distinctive feature of the Indian toilette was the style of hairdressing and headgear. Long hair was mostly the rule. It was worn simply, bound back by a thong, fillet or kerchief. Some peoples daubed their hair with mud or fat, teasing it into strange shapes to denote married or unmarried status, or to distinguish between an untried brave and a full-fledged warrior. The men of many warrior tribes shaved their heads to give themselves a more terrifying appearance. They would leave only a braided lock or stiff upstanding roach jutting up like a cock's comb. Men as well as women sported earrings, the size depending on the importance of the wearer, and both sexes draped themselves with necklaces, pendants, rings, bracelets, and anklets of every description.

The placing of feathers in the hair was not a frivolous matter. It was subject to strict usage. One warrior might be entitled to one eagle feather, another to two. The positioning of a feather or strip of fur on the head or on some other part of the body was the equivalent of displaying the insignia of rank. Only an outstanding dignitary might be allowed to wear an otter, beaver, wildcat or panther skin, and a piece of fox or racoon fur might betoken more prestige than that of a squirrel.

The most famous item of Indian headwear, the mighty war-bonnet with its multiple rows of feathers and ornate lappets falling on the shoulders, was originally devised by the tribes of the Eastern Woodlands. Thence it spread westwards to the Plains, reaching its full glory among the Sioux. Other Plains tribes adopted headdresses of a different design; the Blackfoot favoured a tall feathered crown with straight sides. The prettiest and most inventive headdresses were undoubtedly those of the tribes of California, who devised gorgeous confections incorporating the plumage of the raven and the scarlet woodpecker, and long slim reeds tipped with poppy flowers or fluffy balls of cotton. Many Indians wore purely mundane and utilitarian straw or bark hats, like panamas or sou'westers. Indian life was not a continual holiday, after all, or a permanent business of 'fuss and feathers'.

Farming

We would not have spent many hours in an Indian encampment before noticing how much of the heavy labour was carried out by the women. It was the women who performed the tedious but universal chore of rousing their children and menfolk in the morning, ejecting them from their beds, stirring up the fire, and cooking breakfast. They performed the equally tedious and necessary task of doing the housework, and the rest of their day

40 *A Crow dandy. The Crow, a tribe in Montana, were notably elegant and well-dressed. The French called them 'The Handsome Men'. Note the elaborately braided locks, artificially length-ened and often so long that they reached the ground.*

41 *A Sioux chief wears his great bonnet of eagle feathers and displays his breastplate of bone and beadwork.*

was an unceasing round of gathering wild food in season, preparing and preserving the meat and other foodstuffs that had already been gathered in, making or mending the clothes, attending to the needs of the infants, and getting ready the evening meal.

In the case of those tribes who practised agriculture – and we have seen that most Indian tribes were agricultural, to a greater or lesser degree – it was the women who tilled and tended the fields. The exception was in the pueblos of the Southwest, where from the earliest times it was the men who did the farming. Elsewhere the lot fell to the women, as it has in most other parts of the world from time immemorial. After all, it is the women, like the earth itself, who are the origin of life, in whose womb the seed is planted, who nurse it mysteriously in the dark until it issues forth into the light. In the minds of primitive peoples, there is a correspondence between the role of women and the role of the soil. And while the women were occupied in the fields, near the village, where they could keep an eye on hearth and home, their men would be ranging far afield in the performance of the equally arduous undertaking of hunting

42 *Pueblo farming. Pueblo men use their digging-sticks on a fertile patch of soil in the desert, not far from the pueblo itself, whose adobe outline can be seen in the distance. The women plant the seed in the holes made by the digging-stick. One man lies in the shade of a ramada, the timber and brushwood shelter.*

The agricultural year began in May, after the return from the early spring hunt. A solemn ground-breaking took place, and the crops were sown in the plots and patches in regular order. Corn came first, followed by beans, squash and melons. There were three major varieties of corn: flint corn, which flourished mainly in the Northeast and on the Plains; dent corn, in the Southeast; and flour corn in the Southwest. Among many minor varieties were sweet corn, pop corn, and pod corn. When Columbus reached the New World, he found cornfields that were 18 miles long, and

43 *The Potawatomi, a tribe of the Great Lakes area, set about their autumn harvesting.*

took seed corn back to Europe with him. Corn is now a more important crop than wheat, and is exceeded in world cultivation only by rice and potatoes. Many Indian tribes cultivated more than half-a-dozen types of corn, and the same number of varieties of beans, pumpkins and squashes. The Pawnees, for example, grew no fewer than ten different sorts of grain.

The corn was ready for harvesting around the end of June, on the eve of a second departure for the hunting-grounds. It was garnered in and carried in *parfleches* to the village, where it was roasted or hung up on racks in the sun, then stored in deep pits in the earth. These pits not only served as larders and granaries, but their tops could be covered with earth and scuffled over so that thieves and marauders could not find them. Getting the corn, squash, beans, pumpkins and other foodstuffs ready for storing required much dawn-to-dusk labour. In the eastern Woodlands, a different method of farming was practised. There, in the densely forested areas, the trees and brush were cut down and burnt, the layer of ash producing a rich tilth in which the seed could be sown broadcast. When one patch of forest • was exhausted, the camp would be moved, and another area burnt in turn.

It has been calculated that the North American Indian utilized 1112 different plants for food. Of these, 86 were cultivated, and of these 58 were Mexican in origin, including maize, gourds, squashes, and probably pumpkins. Among the individual products of the New World, beside corn and maize, were the potato and sweet potato, manioc (tapioca), the artichoke, every variety of bean except the broad bean, peppers, tomatoes, squashes, pineapples, guavas, pawpaws, prickly pears, chocolate and vanilla, and the peanut and cashew nut. Cotton, rubber, and sisal for making ropes were also of New World origin, while tobacco, introduced into Europe in 1558 by the Spaniards, quickly spread throughout the remainder of the world.

On the other hand, it will be seen that only one in 12 of the plants used by the Indians was cultivated. The vast majority grew wild. After many thousands of years of living off the land, there were very few roots, leaves, barks, nuts, berries, or other natural sources of sustenance, that were not

44 *Chippewa women preparing wild rice.*

45 *The Pomo tribe of Southern California attends to the acorn harvest.*

exploited in one form or another by the Indian. When they were not busy in the village, Indian women were out in the woods, meadows or deserts, their baskets on their backs and their digging-sticks or fruit-pickers in their hands. If they were detained in the village, they sent their children out on the all-important food-quest, praising or scolding them as they came back laden or empty-handed.

The number of wild foods available to the Indian are too numerous to mention. It would include sundry roots and tubers, wild rice, currants, raspberries, strawberries, wild plums, elder and sumac berries, sunflower seeds, a wide range of seed pods, the yucca, the agave, and all the multifarious forms of cactus. In California, the Great Basin and Plateau regions, there was a keen taste for lizards, snakes, crickets, cicadas, locusts, and certain juicy varieties of ant and caterpillar. Particularly sought after was wild honey, the only sweetener which primitive people knew. Climbing the trees to smoke out the bees and take the dripping combs involved much courage, and many painful stings. Maple syrup and sugar were also first introduced by the American Indian.

One other wild foodstuff was so important that it merits special mention. It has been suggested that the Indian population of the Pacific coast could only have been sustained at such a high level because the oak-trees there were so abundant in acorns, and acorn-flour was a universal staple. Bitter when gathered, the tannic acid was flushed out of the acorns by grinding them up and subjecting them to repeated washings in a stream, or by hot-water treatment in special containers. The resulting flour made tasty hot-cakes, or a nutritious mush. The Californians treated the poisonous raw fruit of the buckeye (of the horse chestnut family) in the same manner, roasting it and whipping it into a delicious mash. These gleaning activities not only yielded food, but also the raw materials for soap, shampoo, perfumes, incense, and other domestic items.

46 *Another tribe of Southern California busy with sorting acorns and other domestic matters. The woman at the right is grinding acorns into meal, and the women in the background are weaving baskets.*

The Indian, then, enjoyed a varied and balanced diet, composed of meat, fruit, and vegetables. Except in times of dearth, he did not lack for fat, protein or carbohydrate, all of which he needed to pursue his arduous existence. Nor did he have to eat his meals in a raw and unappetizing state. Indian women were excellent cooks. Travellers' accounts speak of well-served meals, consisting of several courses, soup, meat, and pudding, with assorted fruits and tit-bits to round them off.

The simplest method of cooking was in a stone-lined fire-pit, excavated in the ground, or by suspending the food over the fire. Another common method was to use large vessels of clay, wood, stone, or basketry, so tightly meshed as to be watertight, into which red-hot stones were dropped to heat the water and to cook the contents. Later on, tin buckets and frying pans were purchased from white traders for the same purpose. For table-ware, the Indian used all manner of bowls, basins and drinking-vessels, scooping up the food with pottery ladles or spoons of deer and buffalo horn. Meals were ceremonious, not slapdash affairs, though a hungry man or child could make a quick snack of any handy piece of fruit, jerked meat, or roasted corn that might be hanging inside his dwelling.

47 *Iroquois villagers on the shore of Lake Ontario. Their houses were of bark, their canoes were dugouts or of birch-bark. They grew corn and beans.*

Marriage and the Family

Just as men and women were tied to the daily round in their everyday lives, they were not free agents when it came to taking the larger steps in their individual existences. Living in a delicate relationship with nature, which might at any moment withhold its bounty, it was necessary for each member of society to bear his or her share of the ceaseless burden. There was no room for frivolity or irresponsibility. Nor was there ever a surplus sufficient for anyone to envisage escaping, or taking a vacation, or stepping back from life. Everything had to be governed by precept. Scrupulous and exact attention had to be paid to whatever had been successful in the past so that it would continue to be successful in the present. Existence was here and now: there was little provision in Indian thought for the future, and none at all for any conception of evolution or progress. It was essential to avoid rupturing those links with earlier generations that had proved effective in carrying the tribe through the perils of the past. Men had achieved a precarious condition of stasis with the universe, and with the great unseen powers that animated it, that must not be endangered.

It was understood that an undertaking like marriage, for example, could

THE HOME

scarcely be left to the unfettered choice of the individuals concerned. It was necessary to think of the survival and well-being of the tribe, whose economic and domestic arrangements would be intimately affected. Some latitude would be granted, since a feature of Indian life was a general attitude of tolerance. Couples who were obviously incompatible were not forced together. Moreover, in many tribes there was a recognition of the fact that a man might be effeminate, and unsuited for the male role. In that case, he was allowed to put on woman's clothes and do woman's work. But for most boys and girls, coming of age at 13 or 14, marriages were carefully arranged. There were matters of rank, dowry, kinship and taboo to be considered. Romantic inclinations had to be set aside, and in some tribes it was a normal custom for a very young man to marry a very much older woman, and vice versa, in order that the younger partner could take advantage of the age and experience of the other.

The normal rule in Indian society was monogamy, but a few tribes practised polygyny (polygamy). This required a society to be rich enough for some members to be able to support more than one wife, or occurred when warrior societies had quantities of female slaves. Usually, polygyny existed in conjunction with monogamy, and was practised on a voluntary basis. It might happen that a man was so contented with one of his wives he would ask her sister to join the family by marrying him; or a sister might approve so highly of her brother-in-law she would ask to wed him. In some societies, a second wife was regarded as a temporary wife, who would set up a home of her own when she found a more permanent mate. Polygyny thus enabled an unmarried woman to avoid the loneliness of spinsterhood, and the reproach of barrenness, which was felt keenly among primitive peoples. It therefore helped to ensure the continuity of the community by increased procreation. Polyandry, the system whereby a woman was the wife of more than one man, is not attested in North America, though Eskimo tribesmen were in the habit of offering their wives for the sexual pleasure of their guests, and Shoshonean women were permitted by certain tribes to have sexual intercourse with other members of the tribe while their husbands were away hunting. Other forms of marriage occasionally met with were what anthropologists term the levirate and the sororate. In the levirate, the place of a dead husband is immediately taken by his brother or cousin; in the sororate, a dead wife is replaced by her sister or her cousin. Thus a bereaved woman and her children would be provided for, and a man's motherless offspring would be looked after. Among the Eskimo, a man who killed another man had to take the dead man's dependants under his protection. Marriages were sometimes formal, a simple exchange of gifts, and sometimes solemnized with feasts and merry-making. Divorce, on the

101

other hand, was usually effected with the lack of ceremony with which it is attended in Moslem countries, where the partner is 'put away' by means of a terse declaration.

It may sound as if the Indian attitude towards marriage and similar institutions was cold and perfunctory, particularly where women were concerned. In fact, Indian societies were seldom male-oriented or male-dominated. For every society in which the male was paramount, there was another in which the emphasis was on the female – not least in many of those societies, like the Six Nations of the Iroquois, which were aggressive and warlike. Probably half of the North American tribes were matriarchal rather than patriarchal, descent being reckoned through the female and not the male line, as if we were to take our name from our mother instead of our father. As often as not, it was the wife who owned the household goods and chattels, including the house or tipi. They were hers absolutely, to be retained in widowhood or after divorce. Navajo women, for example, have never fully shared their personal wealth with their husbands, and have traditionally been more prosperous than their menfolk. They keep their profits from selling wool and weaving, and their sons remain 'mothers' boys' all their lives. Among the Iroquois, the most militaristic society of all, it was actually the women who elected the tribal leaders, deposing them when they were dissatisfied with them. And what was sauce for the goose was sauce for the gander: divorce worked both ways. A woman, too, could 'put away' her husband. He might return from the fields or from hunting and find his saddle or his entire belongings packed and placed outside the door – in which case there was nothing he could do except creep back home to his mother. Occasionally a woman would deliberately nag her husband until he beat her, thus giving her an excuse for leaving him.

In many communities, the life of the family revolved around the mother to such an extent that when a man married he had to settle down with his bride, at least for a year or two, in his mother-in-law's household, a system technically known as matrilocal residence. In short, though women might have their specific duties, their lot was not as a rule regarded as in any way inferior or demeaning, though there were admittedly many tribes which treated women as slaves or chattels. It was the Industrial Revolution, which degraded working-class women, and which rendered idle the women of the middle class, that inflicted that indignity on the women of the West. Indian women were generally spared that unpleasant experience, losing neither their dignity nor their sense of usefulness.

It was the mother rather than the father to whom the Indian child looked for guidance. Sometimes the father's role in the act of procreation was regarded as of so little account that the mother's uncles were considered more important to the child than he was. The child would call its maternal uncles 'father', and might thus enjoy the advantage of possessing more than one 'father'.

As for education, in a society organized on the basis where all must contribute, what the mother had to teach was just as important as the father. The children embarked on the acquisition of practical knowledge as soon as they were able to walk; an Indian community could not permit its children to remain unproductive until they were well into manhood or womanhood, as is the case with us. Children were treated as adults much earlier, and were judged sufficiently mature to marry at puberty. From their tenderest years, they were taught to observe and emulate the actions of their elders. Little boys fished with miniature poles and hunted with model weapons; little girls helped their mothers in the home and acted as nursemaids for their small brothers and sisters. Both boys and girls followed their mothers into the countryside to glean a handful of nuts and berries. As a consequence of the refusal to treat them as toys, or as pampered adolescents, they often possessed, and possess today, a gravity and worldy-wise demeanour that made a deep impression on white observers.

Indians were indulgent to children in the toddler stage, though illegitimate children were sometimes cruelly treated, or even strangled or smothered at birth. As early as three or four, rigorous training began. At that age, children were tattooed with bone needles, or had other marks inflicted on them, and boys would be subjected to special ordeals in order to begin the toughening process. They would be made to plunge into an icy river in winter, sting themselves with ants and centipedes, or run miles under a scorching sun with a mouthful of water that they were forbidden to swallow. Puberty rites could entail knocking out the teeth, piercing the lips and ears, and slitting the nostrils, while a girl's first menstruation required her isolation in a separate hut, sometimes without food, water, or light. Similar confinement was often prescribed for women in pregnancy and childbirth.

There is no doubt that the widespread use of the cradleboard or baby carrier must have produced a marked effect on the children who were carried about in it. Babies were tightly strapped in, and were often provided with additional constraints in the shape of a face guard and foot rest. Whether being bound hand and foot in such an apparatus is conducive to a sensation of security or insecurity is for the psychologist to decide. As for the physical effects, a doctor who worked on the Navajo reservation in New Mexico told the present writer that it produces a disproportionately large number of serious bone malformations. In some tribes, the cradleboard was

48 *A Nez Perce woman of the Northwestern Plateau with her baby in a cradleboard. (Note the baby in its cradleboard safely hitched to a tree in Plate 47.)*

fitted with a hinged flap and a cord that could be tightened in order to produce a malformation of the forehead or of the back of the head. The Chinook and the Salish of the Northwest Coast and the Flathead of the Plains-Plateau region possessed brows that were angled back until nose and forehead were in a straight line, to our eyes a grotesque phenomenon. At one time this practice was common throughout the American continent. In the prehistoric period it was practised in Ohio by the people of the Adena culture, and by the mound builders of Alabama and Florida. Moulding the head by bandaging, as in ancient Mexico, was also indulged in by southern communities. For the most part, however, the North American Indian appears to have regarded such radical disfiguration of the human form with abhorrence.

Social Systems

How, when he was dwelling in his camp or village, and was not hunting or on the warpath, did the Indian govern himself?

49 *A Flathead woman of the Northwest Plateau, painted by Paul Kane. Her forehead has been flattened in childhood by means of the type of cradleboard in which she holds her own child.*

Once again, we must remind ourselves that two centuries ago there were 600 tribes and 300 languages in North America, all with their own individual character, and that it is as impossible to give an overall description of them as it would be to generalize about the modern tribes of Africa. Even where the main culture areas were concerned, tribes living cheek-by-jowl, or even segments of the same tribe, might possess totally different social systems. Nonetheless, there are certain generalizations that hold good, and which shed light on the structure of Indian society.

For the most part, except for those authoritarian Woodland cultures described in the opening chapter, and which had largely passed from the scene in the historic era, the Indians of North America were conspicuously democratic. Their democratic inclinations were notable whether they belonged to a loosely organized society, like that of the tribes of lower California and the Great Basin, or were intricately organized like the Plains Indians. Something of a test in this respect is the nature of the office of chief. In by far the majority of cases, although the chief might enjoy great prestige, and was always immensely majestic and dignified, he seldom possessed dictatorial, let alone tyrannical powers. The rank of chieftain was seldom hereditary; chiefs were elected, or were chosen from some distinguished family. Commonly, the chief was less an outright ruler than a director, a persuader, a giver of wise counsel.

There were exceptions. Chiefs did exist who were veritable monarchs, invested with absolute authority, dispensers of life and death. The outstanding example was the Great Sun of the Natchez, heir to the builders of the Emerald Mound in Mississippi. When the French explorers first encountered him, the Great Sun conducted himself with all the brutality and arrogance of those emperors of ancient Mexico who were no doubt the inspiration of the American mound-builders. His person was so sacred that he could only be addressed from a distance, the petitioner grovelling on the ground and shouting. He and his close relatives, the Little Suns, held unchallenged sway over their 4000 subjects, who were distributed in nine prosperous villages on the northern fringes of the delta. The Great Sun dwelt in a palace elevated on a ten-foot mound, and when he went abroad, swathed with plumes and pearls, he was carried in a golden litter so that his feet would not be defiled through contact with the ground. The Creeks also had their *micos*, or village kings, whose least word was law; and far to the northeast, in the Woodlands, the Mohegan, the Miami, and one or two other Algonquian tribes, were governed by chiefs who in the course of the centuries had become autocrats.

Such cases were not typical. Chiefs, though they might sometimes prove to be high-handed and erratic, were normally 'grave and reverend signors',

106

selected for their honesty, compassion, and sagacity. Most tribes indeed had two chiefs, a civil chief, who acted as chief executive and chief justice, and a war chief. The Osage, among others, had their 'War' towns and their 'Peace' towns; the former, which supplied the military needs of the tribe, were meat-eaters, and the latter were vegetarian. Additionally, there were chiefs appropriate to various ranks and levels, such as tribal, camp, and band chiefs. The largest tribes, almost always divided into two halves, often had twin chiefs, though one of them might be the senior; while confederations of tribes might possess a paramount chieftain. An interesting institution was the Council of 50 Sachems of the Iroquois, in which the 50 leaders of the five original tribes of the Iroquois Confederacy met to deliberate matters of common policy. Similarly, the chieftains of most Indian tribes seldom dispensed advice or justice unaided: they sought the support of a committee of elders. It was the elders, acting in concert, who decided the penalties for murder, adultery, rape, assault, theft, insult, swearing, and other offences. Murder was by far the most serious crime, its punishment involving the death of the murderer or, if he had fled, the death of one of the male members of his family. Adultery was sometimes punished by death, but more frequently by cropping the ears and lips, or by cutting off the nose, or its tip. Lesser offences terminated in flogging, fines, or scratching the guilty person's flesh with thorns or sharp bones.

The unquestioned and indestructible root of the Indian community was not in fact the chieftain or the tribal council, but the family. The notion of the nuclear, biological family was fundamental. The Indians conceived of the family as an entity that was infinitely flexible and extensive. In place of our narrow conjugal family, where father and mother are supreme, the Indians often substituted the consanguine family, where important and even predominant roles were played by a wide variety of relatives. The terms 'father', 'mother', 'brother', 'sister', 'son', 'uncle', 'aunt', used by us in a specific sense, were far more widely applied. Inside the family there was also a series of highly intricate relationships characterized by what anthropologists call familiarity customs and avoidance customs. The former involved all manner of verbal and physical teasing, practical joking, and horseplay; the latter involved prohibitions of an uncomprising kind, from not using the personal names of certain relations, not eating in proximity to them, not talking to them except through a third person, and not looking them full in the face.

Even more important, in many communities, were the customs connected with the clan system. Among the poorer tribes, scraping a meagre living close to subsistence level, clans did not make a regular appearance; but among the more vigorous and populous hunting and

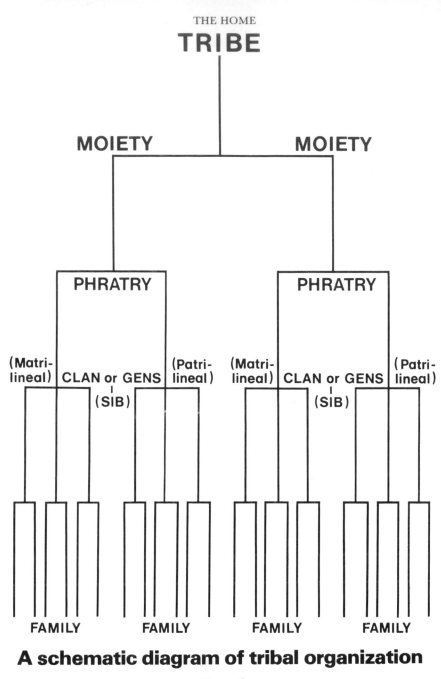

A schematic diagram of tribal organization

Figure 6

108

agricultural tribes they were universal and highly developed. An Indian, male or female, belonged to a clan by right of birth. It denoted a single blood-family, composed of all its siblings: for which reason it is often called, whether patrilineal or matrilineal, a sib (see Figure 6). An essential feature of the clan was a striking and distinctive name. The 46 clans of the Creek contained such names as Alligator, Arrow, Bear, Beaver, Bison, Cane, Corn, Deer, Fish, Panther, Salt, Spanish, Wind, and Wolf. The Osage clans included the Bear, Crayfish, Deer, Elk, and Puma. Some clans were allied, and some were hostile. Clans would link themselves with others on the basis of a shared exploit, or of some mythological or religious connection. What all of them shared was the insistence that clansmen and clanswomen must marry exogamously, outside their own clan, in order to avoid the taint of incest, and to obviate complications concerning the clan totem.

Contrary to popular belief, the clan totem (an Algonquian word meaning 'brother') was not an object of worship. Rather, it was regarded as a guardian spirit. To the Eagle clan, the eagle would be considered a guide, protector, and spiritual companion. It would be taboo to them. They would be forbidden to kill it, eat it, wear its feathers, perhaps even to touch or look at it. It would play a leading part in their mythology, and they would regard it as their earliest direct ancestor. They would meet together to sing, dance and mime its life-cycle, and to secure its magical increase.

Taboos were closely linked with totemism, but they also extended far beyond it. Almost any person, object, or activity could become the subject of a taboo. Many of them seem wildly fanciful or bizarre, although there was always a reason that was considered sound for their existence. Among human taboos might be prohibitions about touching or speaking to certain people, such as a woman who was menstruating, pregnant, or in childbirth; or there might be a ban on uttering the names of gods or dead persons. Certain stones, metals, or other materials might be shunned; and certain foods, in particular some kinds of game or flesh of animals. In most tribes there were taboos against women or unauthorized persons touching a warrior's weapons, thereby destroying their efficacy.

Frequently, a number of clans would combine together into what anthropologists term phratries. Phratries were loose associations of clans that yoked one village to another, lending cohesiveness in cases where tribes were scattered over wide areas and serving as useful working partnerships. In turn, phratries would combine to form a major tribal division, the moiety. A moiety consisted of one half of the tribe, and came into existence when a tribe, with or without a clan system, split into two parts with separate names and traditions. They occurred when a number of phratries leagued together to constitute two grand divisions within the community,

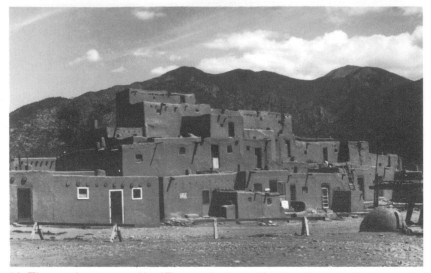

50 *The great three-storey pueblo of Taos, north of Santa Fé in New Mexico. In the foreground at the right is a typical beehive oven. The villagers are divided socially into summer and winter moieties.*

each possessing its own identity and privileges, and engaging in rivalry, albeit a friendly one. Most Indian tribes were divided into moieties. To give some random examples; among the Haida, there were the 'Ravens' and the 'Eagles'; among the Luiseño, the 'Wildcat' and the 'Coyote'; and among the Creek, the 'Whites' and the 'Chiloki' or 'Other Language'. The moieties of the Pueblo peoples of the Southwest exist intact to this day, the institution not only flourishing but functioning in a most interesting manner. One moiety supplies the government of the pueblo for the first half of the year, the other for the second. In some pueblos, they are called the 'Summer People' and the 'Winter People'. In others, they are known as the 'Squash People' and the 'Turquoise People', the word 'squash' suggesting the softness and warmth of summer, and 'turquoise' the hardness and coldness of winter.

Finally, a brief mention should be made of the question of caste and class. Caste is a rigid, exclusive phenomenon, in which certain groups of people regard themselves as inviolably set apart by virtue of birth, or of some specialized political, religious, or artistic activity. Caste was not a feature of Indian tribal life. Chiefs, sachems, shamans and religious leaders seldom maintained themselves apart from their fellows, and roles tended to be interchangeable. A sachem or wise man would also serve as a warrior or huntsman, as would a gifted artisan. There was seldom any strict line of demarcation between one calling and another. As for class, which is

51 *A Hidatsa warrior in the dress of the Dog Society. The Hidatsa were a Siouan tribe who lived on the Knife river, a branch of the Missouri in North Dakota. They were neighbours of the Mandan and Arikara.*

somewhat more easy-going than caste, since classes tend to mingle fairly freely, that too was precluded by the democratic atmosphere of Indian life. There was no hierarchy of aristocrats, middlemen, peasants, and slaves, as in other primitive societies in the Americas, Africa and Asia. Some North American tribes kept slaves, but the latter were war captives, not members of the tribe itself. At various times, certain tribes, like the Haida, Tsimshian and Tlingit of the Northwest, demonstrated something approaching a regular class system; but the only real example of a society in which one social stratum was dominated by another was among the fascinating and freakish Natchez mentioned above. The Natchez had a true nobility, consisting of the Great Sun, his mother White Woman, and their immediate descendants, who were termed Suns or Nobles. Beneath them came the Honoured Ones, and very much at the bottom of the heap came the class whose name the early white settlers translated by the expressive word 'Stinkards'. Within this Mexican-type class system, unique to North America, a certain measure of upward and downward movement was possible: but the depressing general rule was – once a Stinkard, always a Stinkard. The Natchez possessed a true class system.

The last social characteristic we shall touch on, and which should not be confused with class or caste, was the all-pervading presence of clubs or societies. There were societies of every type and description. There were clubs for men and women, for young and old, and for every kind of activity. There were singing and dancing societies, societies related to war and agriculture, and societies devoted to the age-set or age-grade of every member of the tribe. Some were completely open; others were secret, like the sinister clandestine societies of the Northwest coast. A man or woman might belong to several societies, according to their different function. On occasion, a society might overlap several tribes, like the famous Kit-Fox military society of the Plains, or the equally prestigious Grand Medicine Society of the Ojibway, Omaha and Winnebago. The latter actually preserved the rules and the minutes of their sessions written down in pictures on strips of birch bark. As for the Blackfoot, they took part with their neighbours in a society of Crazy Dogs, or Dog Soldiers, who were young and ardent warriors eager to distinguish themselves. The warrior societies of the Mandan called themselves the Black Mouth and Bull Buffalo. Among the most sociably inclined of tribes were the Oglala Sioux, who had a Head Man's society, and separate societies for war, religion, the camp police, the curing of sickness, and several more. One of the more prominent curing societies was the highly exclusive False Face society of the Iroquois, whose members sported masks depicting weird, frightening, demoniac faces.

112

But then, as we shall see in the next chapter, almost everything concerning the Iroquois, the most martial of Indian peoples, could be described as weird, frightening, and demoniac.

4

The Warrior

Next to hunting and farming, the main occupation of most Indian males was the business of warfare. Like hunting, warfare was a passion with the Indian. To kill or capture the enemy filled his dreams almost as much as to slaughter and skin the deer or the buffalo. Indeed, it was the excitement of the chase, and the skills he acquired in it, that fed his appetite for warfare. Man himself, after all, is the ultimate quarry.

The majority of Indians, when not actively engaged in fighting their neighbours, lived in a constant state of watchfulness. They were always wary, always scanning the hills or the horizon for signs of a hostile presence. Except during sandstorms, snowstorms, or drenching rain, patrols made their perpetual rounds, and sentries stood guard over the fields and dwellings. The ever-present fear of death and despoliation at the hands of marauders tended to be a chronic condition of Indian existence.

A gloomy picture. Yet there was an important mitigating circumstance. Appalling though it could be, with its own nasty catalogue of atrocities, Indian warfare was severely restricted in scope. For this there were both geographical and social reasons. In a continent the size of North America, with a native population of under a million people, except in a few relatively crowded areas, the majority of tribes were seldom forced into close or continual friction with each other. It was only in the brief final period that the possession of the horse led to frequent bruising collisions. Even then, when the horse had made many of the more aggressive tribes mobile, the scale of Indian encounters was notably circumscribed. Indian warfare never even remotely resembled European or white American military practice. The white man habitually put armies of thousands, hundreds of thousands, or millions of men into the field. The Indian had no 'armies', and a body of 300–400 Indians departing on the war-path would have been considered immense. The white man, until as recently as 1914, marched against the enemy in close order, bands playing, flags flying, bayonets

52 *'The Lookout' by W. R. Leigh. An Anasazi woman keeps anxious watch in one of the great cliff dwellings of Colorado described in Chapter One. Beside her is the drum on which she can sound the alarm.*

levelled. The little band of Indians stole through the darkness silently, a wraith, a shadow. The white man fought a stand-up slogging match, trying to overwhelm his opponent by the sheer brutal weight of numbers and fire-power. The Indian had no conception of such regular battle; he was essentially a hit-and-run artist, occasionally compelled to engage in hand-to-hand combat. The white man possessed a highly developed body of military doctrine, and was a trained, professional soldier. The Indian had no feeling for grand strategy, was a sketchy tactician, and was nothing more than a primitive warrior. The aim of the white man was to bring his enemy to battle on terms of his own choosing, to inflict tens of thousands of casualties on him, and if possible to annihilate him, accepting if necessary a heavy 'butcher's bill' of his own in the process. The Indian seldom killed more than a score or two, in a random fashion, and regarded it as a tragedy if even a single one of his own side lost his life. The white man's idea of honour and bravery was to confront his adversary eyeball-to-eyeball, refusing to yield an inch of his national territory. The Indian felt it was no disgrace to break off an engagement and run away if his leader was killed or wounded, or if things began to go badly; and as for defending the sacred soil of the homeland, he had no conception of it. He would fight to seize or to retain his traditional hunting-grounds, but he had no sense of sovereignty over the lands he lived on. Even the tribes who practised agriculture, except

115

for some of the more settled peoples, were accustomed to shifting camp to another site when their fields became leached out, feeling free to wander as they would. One must not think of the original 600 Indian tribes as resembling the petty states of pre-unification Germany or Italy, jealously guarding their frontiers. For the most part, the American Indian was peripatetic.

Why, then, were these Indian skirmishes – one would hardly dignify them by the name of proper campaigns – undertaken in the first place? Here, the characters of the white soldier and the Indian warrior run together, though the former masks his motivations under a smokescreen of altruism or patriotism, and the latter was at least frank and honest about them.

First of all, of course, there was the mouth-watering prospect of plunder. Like the white man, the Indian coveted the wealth of his neighbours. If a neighbour became weak and careless, it was an open invitation to robbery. When an Indian attack succeeded in its aim of breaking into and overwhelming an enemy camp or village, a systematic sacking took place, and the spoils were collected and carried home. In time, horses became a prize object of raiding, with the result that most Indian tribes took to tethering their mounts close to their dwellings, or actually inside them. Horse stealing was a favourite young men's sport, since it took exceptional recklessness and athletic skill to penetrate to the heart of a hostile camp.

However, while the desire for material gain was not a negligible war aim, it was mingled with other, less tangible motives. Of these, the pure element of human aggressiveness was uppermost. And we should not forget that, where the Indian was concerned, such aggressiveness was by no means exclusively male. The women thoroughly approved of the conduct of their menfolk, and if their own camp was overrun the women would snatch up weapons and fight as savagely as the men.

We have no space here to discuss the fundamental causes of human aggression. Perhaps, as Freud argued in *Civilization and its Discontents*: 'Men are not gentle, friendly creatures wishing for love, who simply defend themselves if they are attacked; a powerful measure of desire for aggression has to be reckoned as part of their instinctive endowment . . . The tendency to aggression is an innate, independent instinct in man.' In *Why War?*, Freud further observes: 'There is no likelihood of our being able to suppress humanity's aggressive tendencies', and he adds drily: 'In some happy corners of the earth, they say, where nature brings forth abundantly whatever man desires, there flourish races whose lives go gently by, ignorant of aggression or constraint. This I can hardly credit; I would like further details about these happy folk.' Certainly he would have found few

116

of those happy folk among the North American Indian, although there were a handful of tribes that were undoubtedly pacific in outlook. The Havasupai of the Southwest, for example, actually retired to the very bottom of the Grand Canyon in an attempt to secure a little peace. A drastic solution, indeed.

Anthony Storr, in his study *Human Destructiveness*, makes an interesting point:

> If we are to understand man's destructiveness, it is vital we distinguish between aggression as 'active striving', the drive towards mastering the environment, which is both desirable and necessary for survival; and aggression as 'destructive hostility', which we generally deplore, and which seems to militate *against* survival, at least of the species, if not of the individual.

We shall be noting in a moment some unpleasing examples of tribes who were consumed by a spirit of 'destructive hostility'. Where most tribes were concerned, on the other hand, Indian warfare can almost be said to have had a quality of that 'healthy' aggressiveness that Freud himself recognized as a valuable component of human activity. It was necessary to be aggressive in order to hunt: and military aggressiveness was equally useful in imparting a sense of energy, confidence, and social cohesion. For the most part, Indian warfare demonstrated only a kind of token aggressiveness. It was almost a pastime, a sport, a game that could be called off if it threatened to break the accepted rules and become too rough. Deaths were kept to a minimum, and captives were normally well treated. On the Northwest coast, some of the tribes indulged in regular tournaments, courtly affairs resembling the tourneys of medieval Europe. Most tribes had a tacit understanding that they would not inflict major damage on each other, and the long-drawn-out, implacable blood-baths and holocausts of Western warfare – like the battles of the Somme, Verdun, Rotterdam and Stalingrad – were totally unknown to the Indian and foreign to his ethos.

There were no *Millionenheeren* or conscripts in Indian war-parties. Every member was a volunteer. He was eager for booty, but much more eager for a share of the glory and prestige that were attendant on victory. These were the ultimate objects. Without the renown which he earned in war, a boy could not become a man, and a man could not matriculate from one tribal society into another, and would be condemned to lifelong mediocrity and contempt. It was essential for him to distinguish himself in war to secure a respected position in the community: there was no more striking way of

117

proving his initiative, hardihood, valour, physical and mental alertness, and dependability.

The Indian was quick to seize almost any excuse to wage war. One of the most frequent was the avenging of an insult, or of some real or imagined slight. Sometimes a tribe would be encouraged to start hostilities as the result of a dream or vision that revealed the will of the gods. Or it might be necessary to propitiate the ghost of a dead warrior. Or there might be a flare-up in a long-standing feud. Nevertheless, there were tribes who unashamedly gave a much more obvious reason: they went to war for the sheer pleasure of it – because war was fun. Ruth Underhill, in her *Red Man's America*, quotes a Cherokee warrior as saying: 'We cannot live without war. Should we make peace with our present enemy, we must at once look out for some other people with whom we can indulge in our beloved occupation'.

Even more extreme than the Cherokee in their devotion to the 'beloved occupation' were the Iroquois, whose unbridled lust for conquest led them to terrorize or subdue all their neighbours. In the seventeenth century, they went on a rampage in which they turned on their own kinsmen, the Huron, and practically wiped them out. They left not a single Indian on the banks of Lake Huron, attacked the French Canadians in Montreal, and obliterated the Neutral and Erie peoples, the Susquehannock, the Delaware, the Shawnee and the Nanticoke. By 1700, they had grown so powerful that they dreamed of heading a league of all Indians to defeat the whites. Eventually, after supporting the British in their successful struggle against the French, the Five Nations split on the question of taking the side of the British against the American revolutionaries. Those who elected to fight for the British committed such devilish atrocities that the British themselves were appalled, and George Washington, at a critical time, had to detach a sizeable army under General John Sullivan to march into the Iroquois heartland. Sullivan burned down 40 Iroquois villages, putting an end once and for all to Iroquois supremacy.

The Iroquois were unusual in that their method of waging war was deliberate. Alone among Indians, they acted according to a kind of strategic plan. After the frenzy of the fighting, they followed up their triumph with a calculated reign of terror. Such calculation was generally abhorrent to Indian taste and temperament. However, though they were wedded to warfare, even the Iroquois did not achieve the pitch of fanaticism reached by another famous people – the Comanche, the 'Cossacks of the Plains'. The Comanche, undisputed masters of Western Texas, the western part of Oklahoma, and parts of Kansas and New Mexico, were connoisseurs of war; they pursued warfare for its own sake, as a way of life, almost as a kind of art-form. After 1750, once they had become well horsed, war became the only activity they knew about or cared for. As T. R. Fehrenbach points out, in his monumental study of the Comanche, they had no material need to indulge in such unbridled warfare:

> They were rich, the *nouveaux riches* of the plains – and also the *enfants terribles*. Their war drives were not economically motivated. They bred horses, and so had all the mounts they needed to hunt buffalo. They continued raiding because Comanche society had turned into a tightening hierarchy of prestige. Men gained prestige only through war exploits, and, above all, by leading other men in battle. It was not accidental that by this time Comanche war chiefs always gave away the booty that fell to them from war raids. Most chiefs already held hundreds of fine horses – but no chief ever had enough prestige. With all the meat the bands would ever need grazing stupidly beside the camps, male life increasingly became wrapped up in a search for war. A Comanche band at peace was composed of males without a purpose, and men with no hope of gaining honour or advancement.

Comanche camp life came to be marked by fearful squabbles and scuffles between these 'touchy, arrogant, violence-orientated warriors'. More serious, the Comanche, with his *kamikaze* outlook and his motto of 'The brave die young', came to develop a truly insane horror of growing old, and even of old men, be they his own father or even his uncles. Terrified of the prospect of losing their strength and quickness, and with it their prestige, they despised the elderly man, stripping him of his honours, his goods, and even his women. In a society dominated by sneering swaggerers, it became not uncommon for older men to commit suicide – a startling departure from normal Indian practice, in which old men were venerated because age was held to be attended by wisdom.

In short, the Iroquois and Comanche outlook on warfare was abnormal, and untypical of the general attitude of the Indian.

Preparations for war

Whether their taste in warfare was obsessional or sporadic, most tribes set about making their preparations for launching an assault in much the same manner.

For the most part, war was regarded as a solemn undertaking, not to be embarked upon lightly. The decision to go to war, together with the timing and the size of the war-party, was determined by the war-council, headed by its chief, who, as we saw in the last chapter, was probably a different man from the camp or civil chief. Even the Great Sun of the Natchez was not his own war leader, but appointed his brother or maternal uncle to be the Great War Chief.

When the war leaders of the several bands had deliberated, the head war chief made the announcement. There were a number of tribes, for example the Iroquois and some of the Algonquians, who permitted any warrior who was seized with a desire to do so to organize and lead his own war-band; but as a rule such piecemeal expeditions were discouraged, since they often produced nothing but trouble and confusion.

Once war was afoot, messengers were sent to the various camps or villages, or to the specific war villages of the tribe, to bring in the braves. Sometimes, as with the Great War Chief of the Creeks, the war chief and his henchmen would personally make the rounds, singing and beating drums to attract volunteers. Most war-bands would consist of about 30 to 40 warriors, any number above that being somewhat exceptional. It must be remembered that a man could not be on the war-path and in the hunting-field at the same time, and that an overindulgence in war, unless compensated for by the seizure of much booty, could lead to painful economic dislocation. Also, if too many men absented themselves at one time from the village, then the village itself became exposed to the sudden attacks which the enemy himself might be preparing at that precise moment.

The days preceding the departure of the war-band, while the quartermasters made their practical arrangements, were marked by a mounting frenzy of rituals designed to bolster the morale of the participants. The war-bundles, the sacred arks of the war societies, were brought out and displayed; the tribal war-songs and war-dances were performed; some tribes fasted, others gorged themselves on special foods, like dog-meat; and the tribes that were 'Dionysian' or 'Faustian' by inclination took drugs, or emetics, or swallowed such potions as the 'Black Drink' which the Indians of the Southeast concocted from the leaves of the yaupon holly and the cassina holly, a practice going back to prehistoric times. Much noisy vaunting of past deeds took place, together with grandiose boasting of the deeds that were soon to be achieved. The war-pipe was ceremonially handed round, and each warrior partook of it; and many warriors, particularly on the night before leaving camp, abstained, like modern *toreros* and racing-drivers, from sexual intercourse. This was the time when magic was performed over the warrior's weapons, and when he proceeded to don his war-paint. Each tribe had its own special war-colour and war-designs, and the horse-Indian painted and arrayed his mount as well as himself. The war-horse, spared workaday service, was treated as a member of the family, sometimes as a god. Upon his intelligence and fleetness of foot his master's life depended. He was brought forth and decorated, festooned with bells, his mane and tail plaited with ribbons, his skin rubbed with aromatic herbs.

Such war-painting of man and mount was not merely intended to intimidate the enemy. It had a magical significance, rendering the wearer stronger and more formidable, placing him under the protection of the gods, making him invulnerable or even invisible. An interesting feature of this period of preparation for battle was that, if any warrior who was taking part in it had a dream or vision which suggested that he was likely to meet his death, he was entitled – indeed encouraged – to reveal it. He was then at liberty to withdraw from the war-band with no reflection on his honour

53 *'Making Medicine-Ponies' after Frederic Remington. Sioux warriors ritually prepare their horses for battle.*

and courage. It would have been folly to disregard the warnings of the gods. Even if a warrior had left camp, and was actually moving towards the enemy, he could turn back if he felt the omens were wrong. Tribes like the Comanche excepted, it was no part of the Indian's ethos to get himself killed in battle. The whole point of battle was to gain prestige: and how could you enjoy the prestige you won unless you had survived?

Weapons and armour

The Indian went into action with an eye-catching array of weapons. The native American possessed an insatiable eye for colour, and the warrior embellished his weapons with as many feathers, streamers and tassels as he wore himself.

His principal weapon was the bow, the use of which he had honed to a fine art in the everyday practice of hunting. The bow was in use everywhere in North America, either in the form of the handy, abbreviated bow used by horsemen, or the long bow of many of the California tribes, which was taller than a man.

Another universal item was the shield, emblazoned with magic formulae and fetishes. It was made sometimes of wood, as among the Algonquian and Iroquois, but more often of rawhide. The oval or circular shield of the Plains Indian, built up of layers of hide cut from the neck or chest of a bison, was stout enough to resist bullets from the white man's rifle. The painting was executed directly on to the rawhide, or on a buckskin or fabric outer covering; and it was common to keep the surface of the shield and the trophies of feathers that dangled from it swathed in some fashion until the moment of actual combat in order to prevent the power of the magical motifs from leaking away beforehand. A man's shield was such a personal possession that it was invariably buried with him.

Mounted or unmounted, all tribes made use of the spear, lance, and javelin. Other weapons of ancient origin were the many varieties of axe, club, dagger and tomahawk. Some clubs were fashioned entirely from a single hard substance, such as wood or antler; and in the Woodland area the wooden club was also a throwing-club, a missile that could be hurled with terrible force and accuracy. The wooden ball at the end of the club was usually studded with jagged flints or with the teeth of animals, and later with nails and metal spikes. The Cherokee stuck rows of garfish teeth into their clubs, making them implements to rip and tear the flesh as well as pound upon it, and the Northwest Indians braced their clubs with strips of whalebone. On the Plains and Plateau, and among the Navajo, the business-end of the club normally consisted of a polished stone, bound and glued firmly into a handle of wood or rawhide.

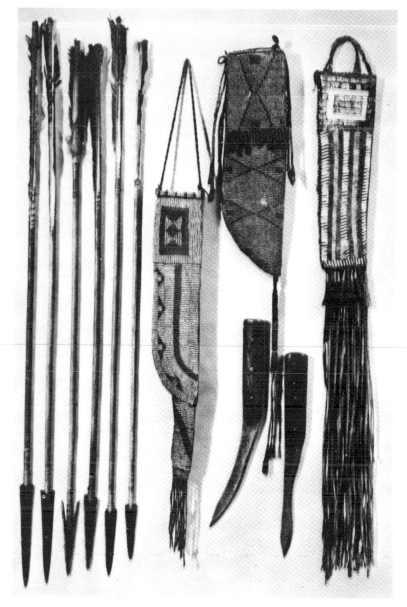

54 Weapons of the Sioux: arrows and knives and their cases. The curved knife is for skinning and scalping, the straight-bladed knife for thrusting.

55 *A Crow warrior, White Swan, with his rawhide shield and his stone club. He wears his magic necklace of bear claws.*

As for the tomahawk, the word was originally the Algonquian name for a wooden war-club, but came to be applied by the white settlers to the characteristic wedge-shaped metal weapon which was first manufactured when the Indians of the Great Lakes and the Atlantic coast began to acquire iron from the white man. Indeed, the white man soon started to manufacture the tomahawk, in New York, Montreal, London and Paris, for trading with the Indian for furs and other commodities. Based on the shape of the white man's axe, it may have been some ingenious settler who designed a tomahawk that combined an axe-blade with the bowl and stem of a pipe, an article that became immensely popular and a standard item of Indian ceremonial regalia in the Northeast. It was also the white man who introduced the taste for the large axe and the metal dagger, both of which were eagerly added to the Indian armoury. Many an English settler was stabbed and scalped with a knife stamped 'Made in Birmingham'. During the eighteenth century, the Eastern Indians, under the influence of the Europeans whom they served as allies or auxiliaries, adopted not only the guns, knives, axes and swords of the white man, but wore military coats, medals, epaulettes and gorgets of rank, with the result that the appearance of their chiefs became an odd blend of the native American and the European.

56 *San Carlos Apache war-club made of cowtail hide covering over wooden shaft and stone head.*

Since the Indian is often dismissed as a semi-naked savage, it may surprise some readers to learn that many Indian tribes had devised practical body-armour, much of it resembling the armour of the Japanese samurai. Whether such armour was invented independently in North America, or was suggested by English and Spanish plate-armour of the Colonial period, is an open question. The Civilized Tribes of the Southeast wore breastplates of cane, the Algonquians and Iroquois of reed. The Canadian tribes and the tribes of the Plateau favoured armour of wooden slats, worn over an undershirt of elkskin or hide. The Northwesterners, the supreme artists and craftsmen of Indian America, not only wore elaborate suits of armour but topped them off with helmets. The picturesque designs of these helmets were worthy of a people who also created the most astonishing series of masks in all the Americas. Some of the helmets were carved from solid pieces of whalebone, while others were elaborately carved in the shape of bird and animal heads.

The War-party

We have now brought our war-party to the moment of departure from camp.

As a rule, it would leave at night, under cover of darkness, though some parties preferred to leave by day. Everything depended on the omens, and whether traditionally the tribe had experienced better luck if it sent out its warriors at one hour rather than another.

Each man would have his rations, his corn, sweet corn, dried squash, pumpkin, beans, and slabs of dried meat, packed as economically as possible. The amount of food depended on the length of the expedition. Usually the warriors expected to be gone only a few days, but some tribes despatched war-parties that could stay in the field for weeks, even months. In that case they were expected to live off the land. Creek warriors, for example, seldom took with them more than a couple of handfuls of parched corn.

The Creeks were reputed, while on the march, to walk in single file, each man stepping in the footsteps of the man in front, to confuse the enemy scouts about the number of men in the band. The story is a tribute to the noiseless, serpent-like approach of the Creeks, and it is certainly true that the Indian war-party, like the Indian hunting-party, was subject to strict discipline. It was under the command of one of its number who had been appointed the trail-boss. The word of this veteran brave was law. He determined the route, the length of the day's march, the number of pauses for rest or refreshment, and the selection of the place to camp at night. He ensured that the party kept closed up and maintained good order.

126

In addition to the trail-boss, another warrior was deputed to carry the sacred medicine-bundle. The bundle must always be carried so that it faced towards the enemy; it must never be allowed to touch the ground; at night it must be placed on a support of forked sticks. Sometimes a war-party would take a priest or shaman along with it, and if he possessed the gift of second-sight he would be able to spy the way through woods and mountains and across deserts, and could sniff out the location of the enemy encampments.

Many war-parties moved only at night. During the day they would lie up in cover. When they reached a point close to the enemy village, they would spend at least a day, often two or three, quietly familiarizing themselves with the lie of the land. We may recall that many Indian villages were not haphazard collections of hogans or tipis, but were regular fortresses, complete with ditches, palisades, and elaborate fortifications. In that case, a war-party would obviously need to study the situation with due deliberation.

Its plan made, and each man assigned to his task, the warriors would wriggle forward, like modern commandos, as close to their objective as possible. They would try to attack at a time when their adversary was unprepared – during a religious ceremony, or when the women and children were returning at dusk from the fields, or during the evening meal. Night assaults, provided that the previous reconnaissance had been thorough, were obviously desirable, and the dawn attack, when the enemy was sleepy and sluggish, were especially favoured. For this reason, if a village feared an attack by another tribe, it posted sentinels who 'stood to' at particularly dangerous hours, like sentries in the trenches in the First World War.

There was nothing complex or subtle about the attack, when it came. The principle was that of a quick rush, followed by an equally fast retreat if the onslaught was unsuccessful. The Indian, who firmly believed in living to fight another day, considered any form of open attack stupid. The safest and cleverest tactic was speed and surprise. As the French said of the Iroquois, 'they approach like foxes, fight like lions, and disappear like birds'. It was this elusive, hit-and-run attitude to warfare that led many of the early white settlers and soldiers to stigmatize the Indian as a coward, because he would not stand up and fight in the white man's way. This was not the Indian's method. He overwhelmed the opposition at a single stroke, or he did as much damage as he could before taking himself off. If he was repulsed, or if he encountered stiff resistance, there was no point in hanging about. The villagers were usually numerically superior to his own force, and when they had got over the initial shock they would rally quickly. The retreating warriors would therefore split up into several bands, to confuse their pursuers, joining up again later at a prearranged rendezvous. One of the few Indian tribes which would 'come out and fight' were, not surprisingly, the war-besotted Comanche – which was why the French, and later the Americans, who understood this style of fighting, admired them and detested their neighbours, the Apache, who fought in the normal 'sneaky' Indian way, striking hard and vanishing. If their attack was beaten back, the war-party would shower arrows and missiles on their pursuers, try to set the huts or tents of the enemy alight with torches or fire-arrows, and melt away into the landscape.

With the coming of the horse and the gun, the Indian was to some extent seduced from his age-old, well-tried techniques of waging war. The novelty of the horse wrenched apart the lives of many Indian tribes, turning them from an habitual caution to an uncharacteristic recklessness. Open, mass attacks in the shape of ill-organized cavalry charges now became the order of the day. In any case, it was difficult for mounted braves to approach the enemy unseen, since horses are heavy, noisy animals: they stamp, they whinny, they are liable to sudden starts and frights. Even with their hoofs wrapped in soft leather and with a hand clamped over their nostrils, it is hard to disguise their presence. The horse-Indians therefore staked all on the direct, headlong assault – occasionally successful, as in the spectacular case of the battle of the Little Big Horn; but against trained, cool, steady, well-dug-in white soldiers only too often resulting in annihilation. The Indian horseman, like the Indian infantryman, was at his best when he restricted himself to raiding and to modest cutting-out operations. In the course of a mere generation or two he came, in fact, to manifest superb individual skills. White riders were constantly piqued to find themselves far outshone by their Indian counterparts. Indian horsemen seemed a part of their mounts: they could perform incredible evolutions, stop, turn, and wheel like lightning. Warriors would hang with one leg hooked over the horse's back, shooting arrows or firing a gun beneath the horse's neck; they could dangle on the horse's blind side to protect themselves when retreating; they could twist around and use their weapons on an enemy from the side-saddle position, or turn completely about and ride facing the horse's tail; they could load muskets and muzzle-loaders – powder, ball, and wadding – while charging flat out, and snatch a wounded comrade off the ground at a dead run. All of which athletic ability availed the Indian nothing when, in over-confidence, arrogance, or despair, he finally sought to fight it out with the United States cavalry and infantry on the latters' own terms.

One final aspect of Indian war-making should be mentioned. This is the

57 *A Nez Perce brave and his horse, arrayed for war. He carries his feathered coup stick.*

intriguing practice known as 'counting coup'. The word 'coup', of course, is the French word for 'a blow', and 'counting coup' was a strangely formal procedure that indicates the game-playing nature of much of Indian warfare.

When the Plains warrior – Dakota, Crow, Pawnee, Cheyenne, Arapaho or Kiowa – went out to do battle, in addition to his other accoutrements he carried with him his 'coup stick'. This was a tall pole, eight to ten feet long, with a rounded top end, and was sharpened at the bottom so that it could be stuck in the earth. It was tightly bound along the whole of its length with skin or fur, and was draped with bunches of feathers. With this stick the warrior galloped or ran at an individual enemy, and if he could touch him with the end of it he gained a certain number of 'points' which would be recognized and honoured by his war society. The principle being expressed was that it was more courageous and meritorious to encounter your opponent at close quarters then to kill him at a distance. Thus, odd as it seems, a man might gain no 'points' at all for killing a man at 50 yards with a bow and arrow, but would gain maximum 'points' for getting close enough to tap him with a stick.

Some warriors went so far as to go into action armed with nothing but a coup-stick, like an old-time British officer sauntering towards the enemy with his swagger-cane. The war societies of the Plains tribes, the Kit Foxes and the Crazy Dogs, came together, like an Olympic committee, to agree on a regular tariff of points. Thus hitting or touching an adversary with the stick earned four points, with fewer points assigned for less valiant acts. Counting coup took place in the general *mêlée*, during the cut-and-thrust combat that was the normal climax of Indian engagements: but within that combat, it signalled especially glorious conduct, like the champions of the Crusades and the Saracens in the age of chivalry.

Sports and games

We have noted that Indian warfare had what might be called its 'game-playing' aspect. The Creeks, in fact, referred to the playing of games as 'the little brother of war' – and games provided the Indian youngster with a strenuous training-ground for his martial career. The North American Indian was as devoted to sporting activities as he was to war, and before we describe the aftermath of an Indian campaign we might make a brief digression to discuss the principal sports in which the Indian indulged.

The taste for sport was inculcated early in Indian children. In fact, the little Indian enjoyed many of the same pastimes as the white child. He made cat's-cradles with string, whipped a top, bowled a hoop, bounced a ball, and pitched quoits. There were also a large number of indoor games that served to sharpen the wits, including checkers and dice cut from sticks or knucklebones. Women sometimes developed a liking for dice that alarmed their menfolk, for when the fit was on them they would neglect their homes and their work in the fields.

Some sports were of an obvious kind. There were foot-races, horse-races, canoe-races, and swimming races. It was the Indian, used to cavorting and making his daily ablutions in the great broad swift rivers of America, who introduced the crawl-stroke. (Two American Indian swimmers won medals in a free-style event in a nineteenth-century Olympics by using the crawl, and aroused the indignation of the other competitors, who thought it 'unfair'.) Indians were also fond of putting on archery displays.

Some of the more robust sports could truly have been called the 'little brothers of war'. Among these were football, indulged in with the homicidal enthusiasm of medieval England; shinny or hockey, played with a small ball and a curved stick; and lacrosse, a game that was specifically an Indian invention. Lacrosse was popular across the whole eastern half of the continent. At each end of a piece of level ground stood two tall, narrow goalposts, between which the deerskin ball had to be propelled by a hemp-strung or sinew-strung racquet. There were frequently several hundred players on each side, drawn from different tribes, moieties or

58 *Indians of the Choctaw tribe of the Mississippi-Alabama Coast, in readiness for the ball-game. Painting by George Catlin.*

59 *The Choctaw ball-game in full swing. Note the goal-posts, the scrimmages, and the knock-downs.*

clans. One side would be painted dark, the other light, and there would be many fierce *mêlées* and scrimmages, with plenty of broken heads.

The easterners also played a game called 'chunky', invented by prehistoric hunters and carried on in historic times. In this, a boulder or a round carved stone was rolled down a slope, and as it ran downhill the players would have to hurl their spears at the place where they judged it would stop. The man who came closest was the winner. The Iroquois played the same game, substituting a hollow wooden frame for the stone, the spears being aimed at the frame as it skittered along. A simple enough idea, but no doubt providing good target-practice for hunters and warriors.

It was in the Southwest that the most highly evolved of the Indian sports was played, though it had almost died out by the time the Spaniards first set foot in the area. At such places as Casa Grande, the capital of the Hohokam-Salado people, and at Wupatki, a centre of the related Sinagua people, the ancient tribes of the Southwest built spacious ball-courts. Here they played their own version of the elaborate ball-game that was a leading feature of the religion of the great civilizations far to the south, to whom they were distantly related. The clay ball-courts of Arizona cannot be compared to those of the Maya-Toltecs at Chichén-Itzá, or of the Zapotecs at Monte Albán, which were enormous, spacious structures, the size of modern stadiums. On the other hand, it seems unlikely that the pacific-minded

132

Southwesterners played the game in the lethal manner of the ancient Mexicans. In Mexico, the object of the game was to knock a rubber ball, using only the knees and thighs, through a stone ring situated high up on a wall. The players wore body-protection as heavy as that of modern American footballers, and when the game was over executions took place. Some authorities believe that the men who were slain were the losers; others believe that they were the winners, because their deaths would be a sweeter offering to the gods. It was as well for the ball-players of the Southwest that they belonged to the mildest of the North American tribes.

The treatment of prisoners and the return of the war-party

We must now return to a more sombre subject. It is a distressing one, but must be faced. It concerns the events that happened after the termination of an Indian campaign.

Most Indian warfare was, as we have said, of a restricted sort, a series of pin-pricks, seldom an all-out effort at extermination. The average Indian was satisfied with the minor skirmishing in which he could earn his personal honours and distinctions; he did not aim at pitched battles and prolonged operations. The latter demanded the large numbers, economic surplus, and heavy armaments he did not possess. Large-scale warfare was a luxury few tribes could afford. On the other hand, most tribes could certainly boast of at least one occasion on which they had soundly whipped and humiliated an important enemy. And by no means all tribes, as we have indicated, could claim to be peaceful, or to practise a policy of live-and-let-live. Some had aggressive proclivities that totally belie the notion of a Garden of Eden inhabited by Noble Savages.

Some Indian peoples behaved with fearful cruelty when they had overrun an enemy encampment and beaten its inhabitants into submission. There were no rules or conventions concerning the conqueror's behaviour: rape, robbery, and indiscriminate killing were the norm. The winning warriors ran wild. In the flames of the burning village, when they had sated their immediate desires, the victors got down to the business of taking scalps. Scalping was a widespread, almost universal procedure. An incision was scored around the victim's temples and the hair was peeled off like a bloody glove. Some of the Californian tribes took the whole head rather than the scalp alone; some Southeasterners preferred to cut off an arm or leg; the Plateau tribes simply sheared the hair; and other tribes contented themselves with an enemy's weapons and clothing. Nevertheless, all the more militant tribes collected scalps. In the Southeast, there was a vogue for women's scalps, since to take them at the height of battle meant that the warrior had reached the heart of the enemy camp. Once taken, a scalp was carefully dried and mounted on an ornamental framework. Eventually it would be hung on a special scalp pole, or in the warrior's own dwelling, or in the medicine-lodge; or else it would be used to adorn the warrior's warhorse, his person, or his war-club.

Virtually every tribe took captives. Some took only males, some only females. There were few folk like the Sanpoil, of the Plateau, who thought it degrading to enslave anyone or deprive anyone of their liberty. Fortunately, women and children, at least, were almost invariably well treated. They were absorbed without difficulty into their captor's clan or family. The Indian warrior could act pitilessly in the heat of the moment, but in a calmer mood he was tolerant; having no class or caste system, he did not regard anyone as socially inferior. Often the captives settled down so well that they refused to return to their original homes, even if an opportunity arose. This was even true of the white captives in Indian hands. We have an early account of an occasion when a tribe was forced by the Americans to yield up their white prisoners:

They delivered up their beloved captives with the utmost reluctance, and shed torrents of tears over them, recommending them to the care and protection of the commanding officer. Their regard to them continued all the time they were in camp. They visited them from day to day, and brought them what corn, skins, horses and other matters they had bestowed on them while in their families, accompanied with all the marks of a sincere affection. Nor did they stop there, but when the army marched some of the Indians solicited and obtained leave to accompany their former captives and employed themselves in hunting and bringing provisions for them on the road. Among the children who had been carried off young, and had long lived with the Indians, it is not to be expected that any marks of joy would appear on being restored to their parents or relatives. But it must not be denied that there were even some grown persons who showed an unwillingness to return. The Indians were obliged to bind several of their prisoners and force them along to the camp; and some women afterwards found means to escape and run back to the Indian towns. Some, who could not make their escape, clung to their savage acquaintance at parting, and continued many days in bitter lamentation.

It might be worth adding that the traffic in captives was not all one way. It has been estimated that at one time there were no fewer than 6000 Navajo and Apache captives in the hands of the Anglos and Mexicans, who valued them, we learn from a nineteenth-century account, 'on account of their tractable nature, intelligence, light skins, and the voluptuousness of the females'.

Beaten braves who were killed and scalped may be considered the lucky ones. The fate of male prisoners who fell alive into the hands of their adversaries was often unenviable. They were not treated gently on the way back to the conqueror's camp. The Iroquois went into battle carrying a special leather thong with which to bind their captives, and during pauses on the return march the latter were systematically thrashed. At the

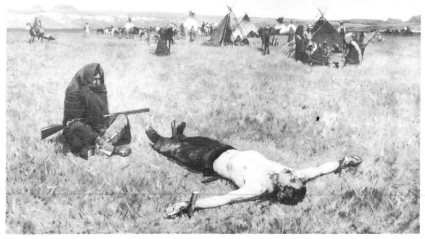

60 'The Captive' by Henry F. Farny. A Plains tribe has captured a US Soldier and pegged him out.

entrance to the Iroquois village, the inhabitants turned out with clubs and the prisoners were forced to run the gauntlet. Some were then bestowed on the families of warriors who had been killed in the campaign, and the remainder were paraded before the village women, who selected those who were to live and those who were to die. Nor was the death that was meted out either swift or merciful. The prisoners were stabbed with torches, their flesh was torn with hot irons, and slices were cut from their living bodies and eaten in front of their eyes. The chief torturers were the women, who encouraged their children to lend a hand. The torture was graduated so that it lasted for days, and when the victims flagged they were deliberately revived. Finally, the Iroquois warriors ate the dead men's hearts, and portions of the body were passed round for general consumption. The Creeks, like the Iroquois, assumed a dead man's power by eating his heart; and among them also the women were the torturers.

It is disconcerting to find even an otherwise very civilized tribe like the

Osage subjecting their prisoners to the most horrible torments; though it is not surprising to learn that their neighbours, the haughty Natchez, tied their captives to stakes and burned them, after making them dance for several days and nights in the plaza in front of the Great Sun's temple. However, until the founding of the Red Cross and the signing of the Geneva Convention, mistreatment of prisoners was taken for granted. Almost every ancient civilization, even those that are reckoned among the more enlightened, regarded their captives as less than human. Nonetheless, few peoples have inflicted pain on their defeated opponents with more hideous zest than the Apache and Comanche. The Apache – alone, be it noted, of the tribes of the Southwest – specialized in such practices as castrating the living and the dead, pegging prisoners out on antheaps, skinning them alive, crucifying them with cactus spikes, suspending them upside down and lighting a fire beneath their heads, or tying them to saguaros and shooting arrows into them. As for the Comanche, after butchering the children and raping the women, whom they later impaled or left in the desert with their heel tendons severed, they set about the business of killing their male captives methodically, inch by inch.

The return of a war-party to its village was accompanied by as much etiquette as its departure. If they had been completely successful, the returning warriors stormed jubilantly into camp; but if they had been defeated, or had suffered an unacceptable number of casualties, they would skulk in the surrounding countryside, trying to summon up enough courage to crawl home.

If the party had won a victory, though losing several men, there would be a preliminary period of mourning, lasting three or four days, before the celebrations began. But a thorough and unequivocal triumph was immediately marked by the wildest scenes, the whole village feasting, drinking and dancing until it was overcome by utter exhaustion. Then came the post-mortem on the campaign. Honours were handed out, special insignia or tattoo marks were authorized, promotions were decreed in the membership of the war grades and war societies. The plunder was divided, and the successful war-leader bestowed portions of his own share on favoured warriors and gave them items of his clothing for inclusion in their personal medicine-bundles. On the other hand, if the campaign had been lost or had gone badly, the war-leader might well be court-martialled, reprimanded, demoted, or even put to death, as was the practice among the Osage.

It might now be deemed expedient to make peace, and messengers would be despatched under safe-conduct to the enemy with an invitation to send emissaries to discuss suitable peace-terms. At the end of the conference, the treaty would be ratified by the solemn smoking of the tribal peace-pipe which, like the war-pipe, constituted a part of the personal regalia of the tribe's supreme chief. The use of the chief's own pipe was an earnest of his own and his people's good faith.

Indian warfare in the Colonial period

We know nothing of the names and achievements of any of the Indian warriors who lived before the arrival of the Europeans. There was no writing in which such things could be recorded. No annals existed. However, from the early seventeenth century onwards, until the cessation of all independent Indian activity 250 years later, the English, Spanish, French, and finally the American accounts are replete with the personalities of Indian chiefs who fought either against the colonists or for them – and it should be remembered that the latter were as numerous as the former. Many were the Indian leaders who sought to arrest the fatal tide of events by ingratiating themselves or collaborating with one or other of the colonial powers.

In the last chapter, where we shall be briefly chronicling the decline and fall of aboriginal America, we shall be noting some of the most prominent Indian personalities of that melancholy epoch. Here it is only necessary to mention that Indian warfare, in this climactic period, went through three main phases. In the first phase, the Indian warrior appears as a primitive, painted foot-soldier, punishing the sprawling hamlets of the eastern seaboard. In the second, the theatre of war has spread all across the eastern and southeastern swamps, lakes and woodlands. In this stage, the Indian, alternately the foe and the ally of the colonial powers, is influenced by the tactics and techniques of redcoat-style warfare – and the Europeans are learning reciprocal lessons from the Indian which will ultimately bring them success throughout the East. And in the third and last phase, the Indian, now horsed and provided with firearms, and with few illusions left about the intentions of the white man, stages his final, foredoomed attempts at resistance on the open plains in the heart of the continent.

To beat the Indian, the white man had to temper his own methods with those of his native enemy. If the Indian had managed to acquire the military tricks of the white man as quickly as the white man acquired the Indian's, the struggle might have been more protracted. The white man was more adaptable, and he possessed superior fire-power and discipline. The European had long been schooled in martial doctrine, and had a solid body of theory. The contest between the two sides was like the contest between the Celts under Vercingetorix or Caractacus, courageous but

137

untutored, and the highly trained and rock-steady legions of Rome. It was the amateur versus the professional. The amateur may deliver some good punches in the early rounds, but gradually he must succumb to the patience and cold expertise of the professional.

The white man, once he had established his bridge-head and made it impregnable, possessed too many advantages. He had superior weapons, and knew how to use them; he had superior knowledge of the military arts; he had superior skills in such necessary fields as transport, communication, and fortification. Gradually he came to possess superior numbers also. More important, he possessed superior morale, which military thinkers have invariably regarded as the single most decisive factor in warfare. After the short initial period when the Europeans were consolidating their position, the Indians were continually fighting on the defensive, with eventual defeat always in view; they were consistently being pushed back. Their opponents, on the other hand, possessed the interior lines; they were always working outwards from a firm base, digesting their gains before stretching out to take in more territory. By the beginning of the American era, the military experience of the young republic was growing at an increasingly swift rate. The Indian might make a fair showing against the levies of the Revolution, but after the War of 1812 and the Civil War, the U.S. Army could no longer be seriously challenged. A quick and crushing end was inevitable.

Yet the experience of the Indian Wars taught the white man many valuable lessons. It was from the Indian that the early American learned how to fight like a guerrilla, and how to shun the tight scarlet jacket for an informal costume in which he could blend with the landscape. It was the Indian who turned the American into the type of fighting man who, at New Orleans, crouched behind tree-trunks, pouring fire into the packed ranks of the advancing British, killing 2000 men for a loss of only 20. Belatedly, the British themselves picked up some tips from their setbacks in America. Sir John Moore prevailed on his superiors to allow him to form the Rifle Brigade, an infantry regiment that wore neutral green jackets, held their rifles at the trail, and carried out their manoeuvres at the trot.

Ironically, the wars of our own century are increasingly being fought in 'Red Indian' fashion. The all-out assault along a battle-front extending hundreds of miles, complete with tank armies and fleets of planes, may be in the process of becoming a thing of the past. The future pattern of warfare may come much more to resemble that of the Indian war-party – a small number of men secretly infiltrating enemy territory in order to stage a quick raid, to be followed by an equally quick withdrawal. When the Americans tried to fight the war in Vietnam, with enormous and unwieldy forces and a disproportionate supply of machinery, they were frustrated by the subtle Indian tactics of their enemies. And where combating the increasing threat of urban terror is concerned, the most effective means is the Indian one of using cadres of specially picked men, all of them fit, highly trained, eager to fight, and expert in using their weapons.

One wonders what might have occurred if the American Indian had realized the full implications of his own methods of warfare, and had known how to develop them. At the present time, it is not the Indian mode of waging war that looks old-fashioned, but that of his conqueror. Indeed, if the white man had not largely adopted the Indian's own kind of warfare, he would never have been able to subdue him.

139

5

The Medicine-Man

We must now attempt to give some account of the intricate and shadowy world of Indian religion. The Indian was not only a hunter, farmer, warrior, and family man: he was also a deeply spiritual being.

It is difficult to convey an impression of the way in which all the levels of the life of a primitive people are saturated with a sense of the spiritual world. The primitive man or woman does not regard the spiritual life as a shining ideal, as something which he thinks about mainly on Sundays; he does not keep the secular and religious sides of his nature in two fairly watertight compartments. The world of the spirit, of the unseen, of the supernatural, is all about him, at every waking and sleeping moment. Everything he sees, touches, or uses is wrapped around with a divine and other-worldly essence.

This notion of an all-embracing essence is known as *animatism*, or as *mana*. The North American Indian called it by various names. To the Sioux, it was the *wakan* or *wakonda*; to the Algonquians, the *manitou*; to the Iroquois, the *orenda*. *Mana* could attach itself to powerful personalities, such as chiefs, priests, master craftsmen, outstanding warriors. When it was personified into the shapes of gods and demons (in which case it is better called *animism*, rather than animatism), it became a property of all manner of ghosts, bogies, and monsters, as well as the creatures who sprang from and inhabited trees, rivers, mountains, and other natural features. All Indian tribes possessed an entire range of such deities. Like all primitives, the Indian was not a monotheist but a polytheist, though some god or gods might rank higher than others. Nor were there any Indian atheists, since religious feeling seems nowhere more instinctive to man than among primitive peoples, who believe that their entire welfare lies in religious observance and religious conformity.

We should draw a distinction between how we regard religion and how the Indian regarded it. For us, religion is exalted and altruistic, performed

140

61 *A Sioux medicine-man in full regalia.*

for its own sake. To the Indian, religion was active and practical: he invoked his gods by means of magical rites for a specific purpose. He wanted to secure divine intervention in order to procure a boon. True, when the Christian prays, he too is asking his deity to suspend the normal working of the universe on his behalf by means of magical intervention. But the Christian puts his case humbly, in a somewhat shamefaced way, whereas the Indian was convinced that by reciting his prayers earnestly and in the proper form he could actually compel the spirits to obey him. Furthermore, the spirits needed him as much as he needed them: he could scold, threaten, even punish them. He was not concerned with ethical problems; he did not ask the powers-that-be to make him a better or worthier man: he simply wanted something, and wanted it immediately.

The man who was qualified to treat with the other-worldly powers, and perhaps even coerce them, was the man whose name figures at the head of this chapter: the medicine-man. The medicine-man is sometimes known by the term *shaman*, which was what he was called by the Tungu Siberians, a number of whose ancestors crossed the Bering Straits to North America at the dawn of history. In many tribes, medicine-men and shamans were the sole possessors of supernatural powers and the exclusive intermediaries with the gods. In other tribes, they were a distinct class, and there was an additional corps of priests – often the tribal sachems or wise men – who carried out their own religious functions. And just as all tribes possessed both beneficient gods and malignant gods, so all tribes distinguished between 'good' magic, or white magic, and 'bad' magic, or black magic. The latter is best described as sorcery, and on occasion the medicine-man might also be endowed with the frightening capabilities of the sorcerer. However, the practitioners of black magic usually kept their unpleasant proclivities quiet. As in medieval Europe and Colonial America, witches and warlocks were not popular members of society. They practised their arts surreptitiously. Again, like wizards and witches elsewhere, the Indian sorcerer could cast his spells most effectively if he could secretly acquire something of an intimate nature belonging to his victim. A lock of hair, a drop of blood, a patch of dried spittle, the parings of the nails – these were promising materials. Not surprisingly, the Indian took scrupulous care to ensure that such personal items were burned, buried, hidden, or protected by taboos. Sometimes the sorcerer was so gifted that he could operate with such intangible objects as a man's shadow, his sleeping soul, or even his personal emanation or aura: in which case the only defence was to identify and neutralize him by killing him as quickly as possible.

62 *A Blackfoot medicine-man with bearskin robe, medicine-spear and tambourine. Painted by George Catlin.*

Religious beliefs

We have spoken of gods, goddesses, and priests. In fact, not many American tribes, by the standards of most primitive peoples, possessed a religious code that could be described as elaborately structured. Their basic beliefs tended to be simple.

While some tribes had a conception of a supreme being, others did not. The Teton Dakota believed in Wakan Tanka, the Great God. The Mojave believed in the supremacy of Matavilya, born of the union of the earth and sky. Most tribes possessed some kind of myth to account for the creation of the world. The Pomo of California attributed it to the god Madunda, and the Five Civilized Tribes of the Southeast to Breath-Holder, or the Master of Breath, who resided on high while the square world floated on the waters below. The Pueblo peoples believed that the world was created by Thought Woman, or by the Spider Grandmother, while the Eskimo and their southern relatives, the great family of the Athabascans, considered that the world owed its origin to Raven, a sly, humorous, and mischievous divinity. Raven had fashioned the world as a flat plate, poising it on four wooden pillars, so that unwary hunters might suddenly fall over the edge into the gaping void. The tribes of the Northwest thought that the world had been bent out of shape when Raven found it, and that the clever creature had wrenched it into its present form; but the Northwesterners in general were vague about the creation, and speculated that it might have been the handiwork of several other supernatural beings. The nearby tribes of the Plateau also considered that the world might be a celestial joke, for their creator-god was the equivocal Coyote, who was one of the many forms of the Trickster god who appeared throughout the entire continent. Usually, the creator god was in no way unique or even all-powerful, but merely one god among many.

Most Indian gods and goddesses took the shape of animals, birds, reptiles, in either a pleasing or a repulsive guise. They were drawn from creatures who would be familiar in the territory of the tribe in question. Almost every wild creature in America and Canada was held sacred in one locality or another. The same was true of every type of natural feature, which was either a deity in its own right or was the home of some guardian spirit. The sun, the moon, the stars, the winds, were all gods or abodes of the gods, as were mountains, woods, lakes, rivers, strangely shaped mesas and buttes, the lightning, the thunder, the storm, the rainbow.

Side by side with these personifications of nature lived gods and goddesses whose appearance was human. One of the tribes with such anthropomorphic gods was the Navajo, who worshipped a number of charming deities who can be seen in the traditional patterns of their fine

144

textiles and exquisite sand-paintings. The Navajo believed they were descended from several races of First People, who lived underground and had emerged from a badger hole situated in southern Colorado. There was an Upper World, belonging to the Holy People, and a Lower World, belonging to the Earth Surface People. The chief of the Holy People was Turquoise Woman, also known as Changing Woman. She was the sister of the moon and the wife of the sun, by whom she had given birth to the world. The moon, or White Shell Woman, was visited nightly by the sun in her home in the western ocean. In addition to these human-seeming deities, the Navajo had a host of other non-human or natural gods, such as the Wind People, the Thunder People, the Snake People, and the ubiquitous Coyote, who had playfully scattered the stars about the sky after they had been arranged there in an orderly fashion. As for snakes, the Indian was fascinated by them. They were the object of special cults among peoples as widely separated as the Zuñi of the Southwest and the Creeks of the Southeast.

Worship

How did the Indian address his petitions and his acts of propitiation towards such a diverse collection of deities?

Individually, an Indian would often go off alone into the wilderness in order to commune personally with his guardian spirit, in that spirit's own abode. Indian religion possessed an intensely private as well as a public component. Every Indian had his personal and his clan deity, in addition to the tribal deities. Alone in the wilds, he would fast, brood, prostrate himself, and will the sacred spirit to make itself manifest.

In camp, worship would be communal and formal. The gods would be summoned in the open air, by means of singing and dancing, or in the interior of a shrine. A medicine-tipi or medicine-lodge was a principal feature of most Indian villages. Invariably, the main entrance of this edifice faced eastwards, towards the rising sun, and often there were additional apertures at the west, south and north. The Sioux lodges had an eastward-facing opening in the roof, so that they could begin their ceremonies when the first rays of Father Sun touched the flames of the fire burning on the hearthstone beneath.

All medicine-lodges had their sacred fire, which was dedicated to various deities, or to the god of fire himself. If the lodge was supported by pillars, the pillars themselves were dedicated to different gods; the Arikara, for example, dedicated them to Sunrise, Thunder, Wind, and Night. Sacred stones, sacred bundles and other mysterious objects would be situated in predetermined places, and flags, emblems, streamers and drums of the medicine and warrior societies would be hung on the walls or pillars, like the stations of the Cross in a Christian church. The most sacred spot was reserved for the main altar, where a specially appointed priest or elder would keep a fire perpetually burning. When an important ceremonial took place, logs were thrown on the fire to make it blaze up. Aromatic herbs, sage, or resinous boughs were cast upon it, and drums were beaten and rattles shaken as the participants circled around it.

Close to the medicine-lodge would be situated another important religious structure: the sweat-lodge. Just as the private dwelling often had its sweat-lodge, so did the medicine-lodge. The institution was so highly esteemed that some tribes believed in the existence of a heavenly sweat-lodge, which was the palace of the high gods. The Wintun of the

63 *The Great Kiva at Aztec ruin, New Mexico, as reconstructed by its excavators. Aztec was a late Anasazi community, built between* A.D. *1100-1250 and situated 60 miles to the north of Chaco Canyon. Note the pits, baths, storage areas, niches for holy images, and the stone bench running around the whole extent of the circular subterranean edifice.*

146

Sacramento valley held that Olelbis, the Sky Father, dwelt in a gorgeous sweat-lodge made from white oaks and fragrant flowers.

The Indian sweat-lodge was the precursor of the modern sauna bath. Steam was produced by pouring cold water on heated stones. Even the modern city dweller, who takes a sauna after a game of golf or tennis, feels that he is not only opening his pores but improving his frame of mind and the state of his soul. The Indian was convinced that a good sweat put one in touch with the divine. The Delawares used the sweat-bath as a test of a man's endurance. They held that if he could bear the heat until he was on the verge of semi-consciousness, or beyond it, he would be granted an extraordinary spiritual experience. In some tribes, the sweat-bath was used for the ritual cleansing and purification of the priests and shamans, before they embarked on their ceremonials.

By far the most impressive of all Indian sacred edifices, which actually joined together the medicine-lodge and the sweat-bath, were the *kivas* of the Anasazi people of the Southwest. The Anasazi were described at some length in our opening chapter, where we mentioned the huge, beautifully constructed stone *kivas*, dating from A.D. 750–1250, which served the populous communities of Chaco Canyon, Aztec, and elsewhere. We saw that there were no fewer than 32 *kivas* at Pueblo Bonito in Chaco Canyon alone, including three Great Kivas in the spacious interior courtyard; and that the central *kiva* at nearby Casa Rinconada was built on a rocky bluff and was 64 feet in diameter. There were literally scores of *kivas* at Chaco Canyon.

The *kiva* was a vital part of the Anasazi way of life. Into these circular subterranean or semi-subterranean structures, which grew out of the humble pithouses of Basketmaker times, the Anasazi retired in order to feel themselves one with the earth, with its dark deities, as once they had retired into the depths of caves and rock shelters. The *kiva* could be said to have been both religious and domestic – except that the Indian, as we indicated at the start of the chapter, did not divide his existence into secular and sacred compartments. Every aspect of his domestic life was subtly bathed in a religious atmosphere. In addition to religious ceremonies, the *kiva* served as a place for tribal debate and deliberation. It was used as a clubhouse, a warm retreat in cold weather, a cool retreat when it was hot. It was a male preserve, into which women were invited only on special occasions. Four great postholes supported the giant timbers holding up the roof. It was furnished with stone benches, fire pits, storage areas, sweat-boxes, and niches in the walls for cult objects and images. A man could happily spend a week in one, and no doubt frequently did. The restored Great Kiva at Aztec in New Mexico has a positively luxurious air   drum-shaped, with multiple

64 *The plaza of the pueblo of San Ildefonso, New Mexico, with the steps, circular entrance and sacred poles of the kiva.*

light wells, 12 feet in height, compact, symmetrical, an underground temple reached by 14 steps. Here the ancient inhabitants of Aztec snoozed, idled, lounged, argued; here the shamans and rainmakers danced around the flickering fire in their horned headdresses, their oily bodies glistening in the ruby flames. At Coronado Monument, an abandoned pueblo on the Rio Grande, near Albuquerque, one can descend into the Painted Kiva on the main plaza by means of a ladder in the roof. On its walls can be seen birds, animals, and agricultural scenes that in their immediacy and innocence are reminiscent of one of the tombs of the nobles in the Valley of the Kings at Luxor. Like its Ancient Egyptian predecessors, it reflects an easygoing farming community, living in an unaffected harmony with nature.

It must not be supposed that the *kiva* is merely prehistoric and obsolete. On the contrary, it is still an integral part of the religion of the folk of the 20 living pueblos, descendants of the Anasazi people, scattered along the Rio Grande and its tributaries. The *kiva*, with its ladder sticking out of it, dominates the squares of the pueblos where, on the day of the festival, you can hear the drums pounding beneath the ground, playing the magic music of the gods of the underworld. Then, as you watch, a file of dancers and musicians uncoils like a multicoloured serpent from the black depths, stamping and swaying on to the dusty soil of the sun-struck plaza. The pity is that, if you are an outsider, you will never be able to peer down into the *kiva* to learn what secrets the gods whisper in the bowels of the earth.

Ceremonies

What ceremonies was the Indian accustomed to celebrate, either in the open air or in the seclusion of his holy places?

First of all, there was the regular cycle of ceremonies relating to the personal lives of the members of the tribe. These were the ceremonies for birth, puberty, marriage, and death.

The puberty or coming-of-age ceremonies tended to be particularly solemn and impressive. The modern Navajo and Apache carry out four-day rituals in which groups of boys or girls are accorded adult status. At the Navajo *kinalda*, the bodies of the pubescent girls are symbolically kneaded to make them resemble the beautiful Turquoise Woman. They grind corn and take part in races. Together, the boys and girls dance with masked figures representing the gods, finally assuming the masks themselves. The fourth night is given over to a marathon song-feast in which the whole community joins. In the Apache version of the *kinalda*, the dancers are called Gans, or Mountain Spirits. They wear black hoods, kilts, and tall headgear, and leap around the sacred fire, flourishing wooden swords and giving vent to unearthly yelps and shrieks.

65 *Pueblo Indians performing the Eagle Dance.*

149

Among the more prominent feasts were those associated with birds and animals. The impersonation of animals was important to the Indian for several reasons. If he was taking part in a dance in which he flaunted the fur or feathers of the creature which was his clan's patron, he would be drawing down its spiritual essence into himself and enhancing his own inner power. Unlike the Westerner and the white man, primitive peoples believe that they are inferior to birds and animals. The latter can run faster, see farther, hear more acutely, sense danger sooner. They can burrow as well as fly. They live in a closer harmony with each other and with nature. They can obtain the necessities of existence with less labour, and do not require the complicated apparatus of clothing, housing and weapons that are needed by naked and vulnerable mankind. Therefore, if a man wished to acquire the mysterious abilities and the keener faculties of the more clever creatures with whom he shared the earth, he had to devise rituals to do it.

The Indian felt that, although he was compelled to kill birds and animals for food and for his raw materials, he was nonetheless guilty of committing a crime against nature. To exist, he had to mar the balance and beauty of the universe by his acts of slaughter. It was an unfortunate necessity, and before he went out to hunt he performed rituals for the increase of his quarry and for success in tracking it down. Afterwards, he performed other rituals in apology and propitiation. Even though the process of hunting was exciting, and its results satisfying, he regretted that he had been forced to kill the beautiful and ingenious inhabitants of nature, his own brothers and sisters. Therefore he tended to kill as sparingly as he could, in order to disturb the natural order of things as little as possible.

In addition to animal rituals, he also carried out agricultural rituals, since nature consisted of plant life as well as bird and animal life. Like human beings, the world itself was born, bloomed, withered and died, and these phases were marked by the spring, summer, autumn, and winter feasts and dances. In some mysterious manner, just as men were the brothers and sisters of birds and animals, they were also the partners – if only junior partners – of the gods. Men were privileged to assist the gods in the task of keeping the wheel of existence turning. The co-operation of the gods was required in every phase of the agricultural process. There were ceremonies to be observed when the ground was broken, when the seed was sown, when the crops were growing, and when the harvest was reaped. There were ceremonies to bring rain, to ward off drought, to ensure crop fertility, and to minimize crop damage. Every important crop had its own festival: the Squash Festival, the Bean Festival, the Acorn Festival, the Strawberry Festival. By performing the appropriate ritual, the food supply could be assured.

By far the most important of the agricultural rituals was the Corn Dance. A Franciscan friar, writing in the seventeenth century, observed that: 'If you look closely at the Indians, you will see that everything they say and do is connected with corn. They practically make a god of it. They indulge in so much conjuring and fussing about in their corn fields that they neglect their wives, children and everything else and behave as if the only aim in life was to produce a crop of corn.'

The reverend father should have omitted the word 'practically'. Corn *was* a god. It was worshipped as such under the guise of Father Corn or Mother Corn. There were festivals for the Fresh Corn, the Green Corn, the Young Corn, the Mature Corn. The annual corn dances that take place in the pueblos of the Rio Grande, described at length by such anthropologists as Elsie Clewes Parsons, and in such books as Hartley Burr Alexander's *The World's Rim*, D. H. Lawrence's *Mornings in Mexico*, and the present writer's *A World Elsewhere*, may for the most part be attended by the public, and are lofty and moving spectacles. So too, by all accounts, were those once held in other Indian regions, such as the Green Corn ceremony of the Iroquois and of other tribes of the East and Southeast.

The form of the ceremony followed the same general pattern. The first day would feature introductory speeches, thanksgiving addresses, the smoking of tobacco, religious exercises, and prayers; the second day would be given over to a grand dance; the third day to a concert of solos and choruses; and the fourth and final day to the playing of games. At dusk each evening a feast of succotash – a stew of corn, beans, and squash – was held, and thanks and praises were raised to the Great Spirit, Lord of the Corn and of all living things. Every pueblo on the Rio Grande still celebrates its own annual Corn Dance, and although photography and tape-recording are forbidden, the outsider is allowed to witness them.

If the Corn Dance was the main observance of agricultural peoples, the Sun Dance was the main observance of the huntsmen of the high plains. Performed across the whole central portion of the continent, from Manitoba to Texas, it was a spectacular and complex ritual. In many instances it lasted not merely four days, but was prefaced by a four-day phase of preparation. In most cases, too, the Sun Dance was combined with the Buffalo Dance, since the buffalo was the chief source of food.

Celebrated by scores of tribes, the Sun Dance reached its most elaborate form among the Dakota, the Cheyenne, the Mandan, and the Arapaho. On the first three days of the principal ceremony, which took place at mid-summer, when Wakanda, the sun, was in his full heat and radiance, a Sun Pole was erected and a Sun Trail established, leading to a Sun Lodge.

151

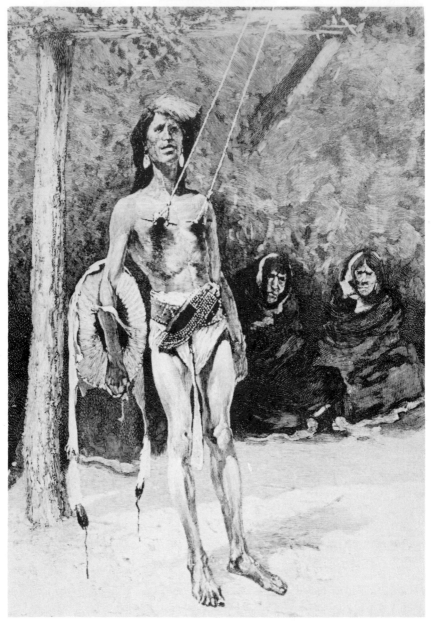

66 *A Blackfoot warrior during the Okipa, or the final stage of the Sun Dance. He dangles on strings and wooden skewers from the roofbeams of the Sun Lodge, turning continually to keep his gaze fixed on the sun. After a painting by Frederic Remington.*

152

The last day was given up to an extraordinary psychodrama, called the Okipa. This harrowing ceremony symbolized not merely steps or incidents in the career of the warrior, but also the struggle of the soul to liberate itself from the trammels of the body. It consisted of four acts, representing the warrior's capture, torture, captivity, and deliverance. It was an epic or primitive passion play, with overtones of the Crucifixion, and it struck a chill into the minds of every white man who was permitted to view it. The Indians who watched it slashed and scoured themselves, and sometimes cut off their fingers.

In the opening act, those of the Sun Dancers who had vowed to undertake the Okipa were 'captured' by members of the Buffalo Society, or some other military group. The volunteers were bound, mocked, and tortured by having wooden skewers thrust into their shoulderblades, or into the muscles of their chest and back. The skewers were inserted as roughly as possible, to increase the pain. The victim was supposed to bear the torture without a murmur, and to laugh at his tormentors as the skewers were driven home.

Leather thongs had been tied to the ends of the skewers. These were thrown over the crosstrees of the Sun Pole or Buffalo Pole, or over the roofbeams of the Sun Lodge, and the captive was hauled up into the air. There he dangled and twisted in agony, being lowered at intervals so that he could rest. In these intervals women would hurry forward to wipe away the blood. If he was suspended from the Sun or Buffalo Pole, in the open, he had to steel himself further, for he had to turn always with his face towards the full blaze of the sun, his eyes wide open.

In this third act, songs of captivity were sung by the bystanders, as the drama moved slowly towards it climax. Then, in the fourth act, the exhausted man summoned up his remaining strength to tear himself loose. By dragging at the pegs that pinioned him, by begging his friends to tug at him, by calling for his heaviest armour and weapons to lend him extra weight, he exerted all his force until his flesh parted and he was free. If he at any time faltered, or failed to stay the course, instead of being regarded as a hero he would be dishonoured and disgraced. With this final act, the Sun Dance was over, the Sun Lodge was obliterated, and the Sun Pole was stripped of its decorations and left standing naked to the elements.

The other dances of the Plains tribes were similarly fierce and energetic. In addition to the Sun Dance and Buffalo Dance, there was the Bear Dance, the Eagle Dance, the Dance of the Crazy Dogs, and the horrifying Dance of the Scalped Ones of the Pawnee. Today, at the annual gatherings at Gallup and Calgary, the dances of the Plains tribes are still flamboyant, the paint, feathers and the movements of the dancers brilliant and aggressive.

153

In contrast, the traditional dances of the Pueblo people of the Southwest are serious and restrained. Except for the secret Christian sect of the Penitentes in northern New Mexico and Colorado, who until a few decades ago mimed the suffering of Christ by actually crucifying one of their number, the dances and ceremonies of the pueblos, with their mixed Christian and Indian rituals, are pacific. They portray the same preoccupations as the dances of the Plains – mystic identification with animals and birds, the search for power over nature – but they are carried out in a less frantic manner. They have a deliberate pulse, an Apollonian rather than a Dionysian rhythm. It must also be added that even in their modern form the dances of the Pueblos are more ancient and authentic than

67 *Pueblo Indians performing a tribal dance in the 1880s.*

the present dances of the Plains Indians, which are revivals and often somewhat rootless adaptations. The beautiful, disciplined dances of the Pueblos – Pine Tree Dance, Butterfly Dance, Deer Dance, Turkey Dance, Snake Dance, and a score of others – are not undertaken frivolously, or for the benefit of tourists, but because they are believed to retain their age-old efficacy and potency.

The American government at one time banned the bloodier portions of the Sun Dance. It also stepped in to interfere with another of the prime festivals of the American Indian: the *potlatch*, or the ceremonial feast of the tribes of the Northwest. The Sun Dance was censored on grounds of brutality, the *potlatch* because, in the depressed conditions in which all Indians found themselves at the turn of the present century, it resulted in tribal ruin. For the *potlatch* was a most peculiar kind of warfare, carried on not with bows and arrows, but with wealth and property. Whenever a prominent Tlingit, Haida, Tsimshian, Kwakiutl, or an important member of a related or neighbouring tribe, built a long-house, or found it necessary to celebrate a marriage, a funeral or a similar rite, he called together his relatives and rivals for a feast at which his main aim was to dazzle them with the scale of his hospitality. *Potlatch* was originally a Chinook word, but the institution eventually spread the length of the Northwestern coast, often bringing havoc and beggary in its wake.

To demonstrate how powerful and vainglorious they were, the Northwestern chiefs and notables would bestow on their guests vast quantities of gifts which they had been amassing for that purpose for months, sometimes for years, and which often they could ill afford. They gave away the blankets that were a form of currency in that area. They gave away furs, skins, jewelry, household goods, ships, and food. They even gave away the utensils on which the food had been served. To impress the guests with his greatness, and with his contempt for riches, a chief would burn these precious objects in front of their eyes, or ostentatiously throw them into the sea. Sometimes rival chiefs would hold a joint *potlatch* at which they would take turns in destroying huge amounts of various articles, the chief who first ran out of property being the loser. Even the beautiful 'coppers', decorated shield-shaped copper plates, heirlooms which had been passed down from clan to clan and from generation to generation, were brought out in the contagious madness of a major *potlatch* and ceremonially smashed and their pieces thrown away. These Northwestern societies, arrogant, hierarchical, slave-owning, were the most prosperous societies in Indian America, and during these displays of conspicuous consumption hundreds of thousands of dollars worth of possessions might go up in smoke or be consigned to the bottom of the sea. Since the chief's family and the humbler members of his tribe contributed towards the expenses of the grander *potlatches*, the consequences of such misplaced generosity can be appreciated. On the other hand, a successful *potlatch*, marked by outstanding lavishness, was remembered and spoken about for years, and brought great honour to the clan or tribe who had organized it.

One other, very different but equally remarkable ceremony should be described: the Captive Girl Sacrifice of the Pawnee, which has received much attention from early historians and writers of fiction.

The Sacrifice was a spring rite, designed to ensure the fertility of the newly-sown crops. It was dedicated to the Morning Star, for it was the Morning Star's mating with the Evening Star that had brought light and warmth to the world. After the almost invariable four-day preparation period, a Pawnee war-party left camp as the Morning Star was rising. Its aim was to attack an enemy encampment and carry off a 13-year-old girl. The object achieved, she was brought back to camp and treated with great reverence and kindness. She was anointed with special perfumes and ointments, wore special finery, and ate special delicacies. When the time came for the four-day sacrificial ceremony, men were sent forth to procure four types of wood, elm, elder, cottonwood and willow, each symbolizing both a point of the compass and a sacred animal – bear, mountain lion, wildcat, and wolf, from which the scaffold was to be constructed.

To this scaffold the girl was conducted. It was just before daybreak. She wore a painted buffalo-hide robe. The left side of her body was painted black, for the night, and her right side was painted red, for the day and for the Morning Star. Tobacco was smoked and offered before an altar, and the whole tribe, men, women and children, sang and chanted as four priests mounted the scaffold at her side and secured her, upright and facing the east, her limbs spreadeagled, to the wooden framework. Then, as the first ray of the Morning Star appeared, a warrior stepped forward and shot an arrow through her heart. Another warrior made an incision over her heart with a sacred flint knife and daubed his face with her blood, which was allowed to drop onto an offering of buffalo meat in a pit beneath the scaffold.

Gene Weltfish, in *The Lost Universe*, his study of the Pawnee, describes the final step:

> It was full day-light, and 4 men who had been chosen by the priests to assist, untied the body and took it about a quarter of a mile to the east, placing it on the ground face down. They sang, 'The whole earth she shall turn into. The whole earth shall receive her blood.' Then they spoke of 9 things in turn: 'She will turn into a bunch of grass; the ants will find her, the moths will come and find her, the fox shall come and find her, the coyote, the wildcat, the magpie, the crow; buzzards will come and find her, and last of all will be the bald-headed eagle who will come and eat her.'

To close the proceedings, the participants in the ritual repaired to the ceremonial earth lodge to eat the consecrated buffalo meat, while the public danced, sang, and rejoiced, fought mock battles, praised Morning Star and Mother Corn, and indulged in a bout of unrestrained sexual licence (a rare event among the Indian, who was usually puritanical in that regard, even during his fertility ceremonies).

In 1816, a 20-year-old Skidi Pawnee warrior called Man Chief, son of the chieftain Knife Chief, tried single-handedly to put an end to the ceremony, which he realized was giving an excuse to the encroaching white men to express indignation. With his father's approval, he rode up at dawn to the scaffold, just as the executioner was notching his arrow, cut down the girl, sat her on a horse, and told her to gallop away to her own people. Instead of chopping him to pieces, the spectators regarded him with holy awe, since to touch the purified maiden was death, and Morning Star would take the offender in her place. He was virtually exchanging his own life for hers. However, he survived, and in 1821, when he was a member of a Pawnee delegation to Washington, he was given a handsome silver medal for his heroism. By his action, he brought the ceremony into disrepute, though it was celebrated sporadically thereafter, and an Oglala Sioux girl was sacrificed to the Morning Star as late as 1838, in an effort to avert a terrible smallpox epidemic that was laying waste whole areas of the Plains. Incidentally, the Captive Girl Sacrifice is one of the strongest instances of direct Mexican influence on the tribes of eastern and central America, as the entire bizarre ritual, complete in every detail, is represented in the sculptures and codices of pre-Hispanic Mexico.

Dreams

The Okipa and Captive Girl Sacrifices were not performed out of sadism or caprice, but for the purpose of securing blessings from the spirits who governed nature, and to enhance the spiritual resources of the tribe. They were meant to draw into men's souls the powers of the sun, the moon, the rain, the winds, the thunder and lightning, and to draw into them the mysterious essences of the beasts and the birds. The Okipa was intended not merely to test a man's endurance and capacity to suffer without whimpering, but at the height of his pain and delirium it might produce a vision that would instruct him how he was to live. In many tribes, a youngster who had not been visited by some visionary experience could not become a warrior, or even a man.

It is hard to convey the extent to which the majority of the American Indians were influenced by dreams, visions, and all such glimpses of the inner world. We in the West have learned, since Freud published *The Interpretation of Dreams* in 1900, that dreams are indeed important. They are in fact what he called 'the royal road' to the Unconscious, which even we ego-directed Westerners now recognize we must take into account. Nevertheless we are far from approaching that absolute dependence on dream and vision which is manifested by most primitive peoples, and not merely those of North America. We have doubts about the value of such manifestations that were not shared by the Indian.

The Indian, as his varied and extraordinary rituals show, possessed an

157

imagination and an inward intensity that make those of modern man seem pallid by comparison. The present author, in his book on the American Southwest referred to above, quoted the passage in C. G. Jung's *Memories, Dreams, Reflections* in which Jung describes his visit to the pueblos of New Mexico. Jung found that these people, so poor in those goods which are the index of value in the world around them, believed that they were not only brothers to each other but, in spite of having been badly used, brothers to all other men. When he was speaking to the chief of the Taos pueblo, the latter said:

> The Americans want to stamp out our religion. Why can they not let us alone? What we do, we do not only for ourselves but for the Americans also. Yes, we do it for the whole world. Everyone benefits by it.

The chief felt himself to be 'the sun of the sun'. Jung continued:

> I then realized on what the 'dignity,' the tranquil composure of the individual Indian was founded . . . His life is cosmologically meaning-ful . . . If we set against this our own self-justifications, the meaning of our own lives as it is formulated by our reason, we cannot help but see our poverty. Out of sheer envy we are obliged to smile at the Indians' naivete and to plume ourselves on our cleverness; for otherwise we would discover how impoverished and down at the heel we are. Knowledge does not enrich us; it removes us more and more from the mythic world in which we were once at home by right of birth.

The pueblo chief said a terrible and enlightening thing to Jung:

> See how cruel the whites look. Their lips are thin, their noses sharp, their faces furrowed and distorted by folds. Their eyes have a staring expression; they are always seeking something. What are they seeking? The whites always want something; they are always uneasy and restless. We do not know what they want. We do not understand them. We think that they are mad.' I asked him why he thought the whites were all mad. 'They say that they think with their heads,' he replied. 'Why, of course. What do you think with?' I asked him in surprise. 'We think here,' he said, indicating his heart.

Since they are not preoccupied with logic, or the language of the intellect, Indians are disposed to listen the more intently to the language of the heart and the instincts. In the last-named language, dreams and visions sound a predominant note. They are the voices of other-worldly powers. They reveal, with the brief and tantalizing vividness of a flash of lightning, the hidden corners of the soul. They are messages from the beyond, and from within. They unite external nature and the inner nature. They are warnings, prophecies, and revelations. They can reveal the true path and put a man's feet on it. They are enlightenment, in the sense that enlightenment means bringing light into dark places and making manifest the source of the light – which is the light of the sun, whom the Indians worshipped. They connect this world with another world which may be more real than this one; they connect waking with sleeping; they connect one plane of consciousness with another; they connect the past with the present, and the present with the future.

The Iroquois sought enlightenment and what Jung calls 'cosmological meaningfulness' by holding a Dream Festival, or a Ceremony of the Great Riddle. During it, men, women and children came forward to relate their dreams – either old dreams, which were understood and which had proved reliable guides, or new dreams, which were exciting and potentially useful, and which were not immediately comprehensible. Experts were consulted concerning the possible meaning of a dream, the whole tribe chipping in with suggestions and interpretations. The Iroquois reliance on dreaming disconcerted a seventeenth-century French Jesuit missionary, who declared:

> They have no divinity but the dream. They submit themselves to it and follow its order with the utmost exactness. Whatever they see themselves doing in dreams, they believe they are absolutely obliged to execute at the earliest possible moment. The neighbouring peoples content themselves with marking those dreams which they deem the most important: but the Iroquois would think themselves guilty of a great crime if they failed to obey a single dream. They think and talk of nothing else, and their log-cabins are given over to dreaming.

Nor were the Iroquois alone in the obsessive attention they paid to dreams. Many tribes had Dream Societies, in which dreams and visions were induced, shared, analysed. The Mojave of the Southwest were only one tribe who believed that dreams were the most important element in life, which gave success in every sort of undertaking; and in addition to ordinary nocturnal dreams, they stipulated the existence of the one ruling dream of a man's life, the Great Dream, the dream that he had dreamed in the womb, that he had forgotten during infancy and childhood, but which came back to him if he was lucky, and if he strove to recapture it, in his youth or manhood, bestowing on him insight and wisdom.

Many tribes possessed techniques which had proved beneficial in enabling individuals to have dreams and visions. Fasting, torture, swallowing emetics, dervish-like dancing, shutting up would-be dreamers

159

in dark places or isolating them in deserts or on mountaintops, were all practised. Some tribesmen, who were specially gifted and who had rigorously developed their gifts, became what modern psychologists call 'dream virtuosi', and were regarded with veneration. Shamans spent long hours in the sweat-bath to incubate and to sharpen their capacity to dream, and rival shamans would engage in dream competitions with one another. The more Dionysian or Faustian peoples took hallucinatory drugs, such as the cactus-root button, or the datura or the jimson weed, which produced short cuts to peculiarly manic and violent states of mind.

Most of the esoteric designs of Indian art – rock paintings, paintings on robes and shields, or the motifs woven into blankets – are concerned with the supernatural, as we shall see in our next chapter. These designs record memorable dreams, or are aids to dreaming, or are maps to guide the soul of their wearer along the paths of sleep and through the otherworldly universe he will traverse in dreams and visions.

Among tribes that were particularly dedicated to dreaming, one might instance the Ojibway or Chippewa of the Great Lakes area. Ojibway men and women wore charms which would stimulate dreaming, and had special 'dream songs'. They attributed all their most valued skills to dreams. David Coxhead and Susan Hiller, in their *Dreams: Visions of the Night*, write of the Ojibway:

> Wisdom and knowledge – the ability to heal, courage, creativity, and all other attributes considered valuable in human nature – were received as a form of grace in dreams or visions. Children were encouraged from early childhood to try to dream and to remember their dreams. At puberty each Chippewa boy fasted for 4 days in solitude and reverence, preparing for an experience that would determine his future. The revelation would come in a dream or vision, expressed in the form of a song he would sing only in battle when he was facing death.

Today, of course, the Ojibway, who live on their reservations in northern Minnesota, no longer go to war. Therefore they cannot release the dreams and visions that they still seek, and which are still vouchsafed to them. This is a dangerous situation, as the dreams can build up inside them and threaten to disturb their equilibrium, or even overwhelm them. The man who is subject to visions therefore erects a high pole outside his house to which he fastens a dream flag, on which he paints the subject of his dream. Everyone who sees the flag knows, as Coxhead and Hiller put it, that there lives 'Someone who was never able to sing his song, but who has the power to heal and to face death'.

Dream rituals still play a large part in the ceremonials of the North

American Indian, perhaps in none more so than in those of the Navajo, largest of the surviving Indian peoples. The Navajo Nightway Chant, or *Yebichai*, is a nine-day ritual of extraordinary colour and complexity, in which are related the dreams and visions of Bitahini, the Dreamer. The dreams of Bitahini are also the myths of the race, since dream and myth are interchangeable and inseparable. During the Chant, the participants experience a healing fusion of the mundane world with the world of dreams, the world of matter with the world of the spirit, of our small earth with the great universe beyond.

Tobacco

We have spoken of tobacco, which, though not possessing very powerful narcotic properties in itself, was nonetheless central to almost all Indian ceremonials.

The use of tobacco was one of the most widely diffused of all Indian culture traits – and not merely within North America, since with the exception of the Eskimo the native peoples of North, Central and South America all indulged in the tobacco habit. It was from the Americas that the use of tobacco spread with astonishing rapidity throughout the entire globe. Smoking in one form or another was known in many parts of the world; but it was the Spaniards who introduced it to Europe in the middle of the sixteenth century, and within another century it had been adopted wherever European voyagers or colonists were to be found.

In Europe, the newly-introduced fashion was regarded as a pleasant way to relax, an accompaniment to a sociable drink and to conversation. The American Indian also used tobacco as a form of relaxation; but from the earliest times, as with all his other activities, it also had religious connotations. Tobacco was of ancient origin, probably first seeing the light of day in North America in the southeastern region where tobacco is commercially grown today; stone pipes have been unearthed in graves and sacred sites of the Eastern Woodland culture, dating from at least 2000 B.C.

Every phase of smoking tobacco seems to have been invested with a ritual significance. There were ceremonies at the sowing and harvesting of the tobacco plant, and the embroidered pouches in which the tobacco and the pipe were kept, and the pipe itself, were surrounded by a sacred aura. It is interesting that among the Hidatsa and Mandan, to give two examples, the growing of tobacco was entrusted not to the women but to the men, and that among many Plains tribes, such as the Crow and Blackfoot, the cultivation of tobacco survived the total abandonment of agriculture that otherwise took place with the coming of the horse. The Indian, too, knew that the craving for tobacco is a hard taste to break.

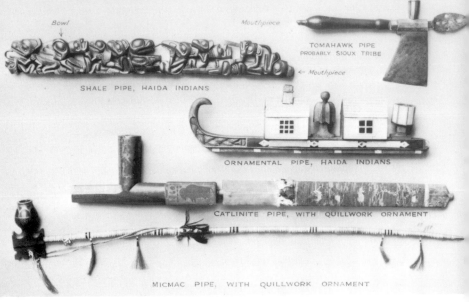

68 *Indian Pipes. The fourth from the top is carved from catlinite.*

The most commonly grown type of tobacco in the east was *Nicotiana quadrivalvus*, though as many other varieties existed as in a modern tobacconist's. The plant was seldom smoked in a pure state, but was mixed with various herbs and sweet grasses. In the east and on the Plains it was customary to combine it with the leaves of the laurel, squaw bush, or maple bush, or with the aromatic inner bark of the dogwood, cherry, red willow, poplar, birch, or arrowwood. Sometimes it was laced with buffalo dung. As for the methods of using it, these again were as plentiful and ingenious as the modern smoker could desire. Some men, taking it for their private pleasure, chewed it; others ground it up and employed it as snuff; while the peoples of the Southwest and the Great Basin rolled it in cornhusks and smoked it like a modern cigarette or cigar, sometimes inserting it in a cane cigarette-holder. Mostly, however, it was smoked in pipes, of all shapes and sizes, ranging from small and elegant smoking tubes and elbow-pipes to the capacious 'cloud-blower' of the Pima. They were made of clay, or cut from such stone as soapstone or catlinite.*⎡A dark, rich-hued orange-red stone, also known as pipestone, it only exists at a few locations in northern

*Catlinite take its name from George Catlin [1796–1872], the highly gifted painter and writer whose two-volume *Letters and Notes on the Manners, Customs and Conditions of the North American Indians* [1841] is a classic and cornerstone of Indian studies.

Minnesota, mainly in the Pipestone National Park. It has the peculiarity that, having originally been formed under water, when it is first quarried it can be carved, but hardens increasingly on exposure to the air. It was highly esteemed from the earliest times, and the eastern Sioux within whose territory it occurred made a profitable sideline from trading it not just locally but into all corners of the continent.

The tribes who lived around the Great Lakes, in Minnesota, Wisconsin, Michigan, and Ontario, made such a prominent cult of the pipe that they are sometimes called by the name of the Calumet People. The word *calumet* is an adaptation of the French word *chalumeau*, which means a reed or a reed pipe (it is the word used to describe the lowest register of the clarinet), applied to it by the early French Canadians. Indeed, it was so beaded, feathered, ribboned and sculptured that it resembled an exotic musical instrument. It was decorated in such a lavish fashion, particularly if it belonged to a priest or a chief, because it was, in fact, a sacred object.

For once, the writers of the movies were accurate when they depicted the smoking of a peace-pipe as an extremely solemn act. The smoking of the pipe sealed all contracts. The pipe itself was an earnest of peace and a token of brotherhood, and was carried around among friends, allies, and former combatants. It also served as a passport. The famous Jesuit explorer Father Marquette was given a pipe by his Indian hosts, and it provided him with perfect security as he travelled among the Great Lakes peoples. The red-garlanded war-pipe, on the other hand, was the sign of unrelenting hostility.

Another Jesuit missionary, Father de Smet, gave an interesting account of the pipe ritual among the peoples of the same region. He wrote:

> On all great occasions, in their religious and political ceremonies, and at their great feasts, the calumet presides. The savages send its first fruits, or first puffs, to the Great Wakonda, or Master of Life, to the Sun which gives them light, and to the Earth and Water by which they are nourished; then they direct a puff to each point of the compass, begging of heaven and all the elements for favourable winds.

The pipe played the part in Indian rituals which the censer played in those of Fr Marquette and Fr de Smet. It was a portable censer from which clouds of incense could be wafted at sacred objects, or towards heaven. Its soothing properties were additionally useful in inducing the requisite frame of mind in the congregation. It helped the Indian to address his prayers for assistance more effectively to the gods – for the Indian, like Sherlock Holmes, had his 'three-pipe problems'. He would accompany his requests

69 *A chief of a Great Plains tribe poses with his ceremonial pipe for George Catlin.*

70 *Portrait of Dull Knife, a chief of the Northern Cheyenne in Wyoming, with pipe.*

with a prescribed number of pipes and puffs: one puff here, a second there, and a third in another place.

Medicine

When it first reached Europe, tobacco was thought to have curative properties, and was regarded as a cure for nearly every ill. It lost its reputation as a medicine within a few decades, although smoking was considered a prophylactic against tainted and plague-ridden air until late in the eighteenth century. In North America, however, it continued to be one of the more important medical remedies, the tribal shaman blowing tobacco smoke into the ears, nostrils and mouth of the sick man to drive out the demons within.

The Indian, like all primitives, believed that sickness was unnatural, and was caused by demoniacal interference. There was no such thing as 'death from natural causes'. Illness and death occurred because of possession by malign spirits, because of sorcery, or because of a failure to perform some important ritual correctly that resulted in divine punishment. The shaman or medicine-man was sent for to diagnose the root of the trouble, and to take appropriate action. He was, after all, the specialist in demonology and supernatural affairs, and was the appropriate man to call. Few native cures were attempted without recourse to magic.

Some Indian doctors carried out their work gratis, as it were on the Tribal Health Service, while others were in private practice and charged stiff fees. A successful cure would almost always be acknowledged with some form of gift, since the 'doctor's' work was exceedingly arduous and often downright dangerous. The evil spirits could fly out of the afflicted person and attack the shaman like a swarm of bees. In many cases, the shaman had no alternative but to engage in personal combat with the evil forces, taking them at least temporarily on to himself. He was, besides, a highly trained man, who expected some recompense, in the form of a horse or a domestic animal, for exercising his skills. He usually put on a tremendous show: he sang, chanted, crooned, danced, watched for hours and days by the patient's bedside, and sometimes went into convulsions, frenzies, seizures and trances. Furthermore, if he failed to effect a cure, particularly in the case of important sufferers, he might be beaten or even put to death – a strong incentive to put forth all his powers.

It was not given to every man (or to every woman, since occasionally women also adopted the profession) to become a shaman. It was a vocation, a special election. Shamans were people set apart. Usually they gave evidence of their aptitude in youth, or even as children. Shamans were preoccupied, moody, with a taste for solitude and for lingering in lonely places. They were seldom envied, as theirs was a hard lot; indeed, in many tribes the apprenticeship and subsequent career of a shaman were so rigorous that young men had to be forced into the life. Sweat-baths, purging, fasting, gashing the body with knives and stones, perforating the tongue and penis with pine needles and cactus thorns – these were not practices to be lightly undertaken. Moreover, the shaman was often forbidden to marry, and lived alone, feared, mistrusted, isolated from his fellows. Nonetheless, his position in the tribe was important, and he was often considered second only to the chief himself.

The equipment of the medicine-man consisted primarily of his spells and formulas. These were his personal possessions, inherited from his predecessors, or bestowed on him by his guardian spirit. He had charms, ointments, prayer sticks, and magical stones. He had gourds and rattles, drums, pills and potions, medicine-spears, masks, and feather fans. He had pipes and tubes for blowing tobacco or spraying unguents on the patient, or for sucking the sickness out of him. He was often a gifted artist, and could execute the curative sand-paintings which will be described in the following chapter. Above all, he had his own special medicine-chest, in the form of his medicine-bundle. It was an heirloom, or a present from the medicine-man who had been his tutor, or from the Medicine Society from which he had graduated. Most Indians had their own medicine-bundle, which they carried around with them like a woman clutching her handbag: but the shaman's medicine-bundle was the most potent of all.

These were the contents of a Winnebago medicine-bundle: three paws of a black bear, used as bags and containing herbs; a bone tube, stuffed with small feathers wrapped in the skin of an eagle's head, which in turn was enclosed in a pouch made of otter skin; an otter skin, containing a bunch of feathers, fastened at the mouth with a piece of eagle's skin; two cane whistles; a paint bag, in the form of a tiny embroidered moccasin with legging attached, containing herbs, and closed by a bunch of buffalo hair; four snake skins; a white weasel skin, containing herbs and a cane whistle; a brown weasel skin, containing herbs; two snake vertebrae; a bone whistle; a cormorant head; a woodpecker head; a black squirrel skin; two small wooden dolls tied together; a dried eagle claw, clasping a packet of herbs and a dyed feather; an animal's eye; a horse chestnut and a tooth, enclosed in a woven sack; a diminutive wooden bowl and spoon; and eight finely woven rolled pouches, containing numerous dried herbs.

Many were the 'miracles' that the medicine-man wrought with such a bundle. A great deal of slight-of-hand and quackery took place, such as the palming of objects which were then sensationally plucked from the mouth or breast of the sufferer. However, such 'miracles' were no more insincere or

71 *An Indian of the Northwest Pacific Coast convalesces after a fight with a bear.*

cynically motivated then the cures effected by the dubious relics and weeping pictures of the Virgin in the Middle Ages. The deceit was intended to be beneficial, like the placebo prescribed by the modern doctor. Belief in the doctor is half the cure.

In the case of simple and straightforward ailments, it was not necessary to summon the medicine-man. The Indian housewife, like her modern counterpart, had her own remedies. She knew how to treat the bites of the lice, ticks, fleas, mosquitoes and other noxious insects that everywhere abounded, and which often made camp and village life miserable. For arthritis and rheumatism she prescribed sweat-baths. She could set sprains and broken limbs, and apply poultices to boils and bruises. She could mix doses for dysentery, or for the less serious forms of stomach upset and headache. Her medicine-cupboard contained such specifics as quinine, sassafras, datura, ipecac, cascara, and witch hazel, all of which later passed into the modern pharmacopeia, while Mexico and South America yielded such valuable substances as curare, ephedra (ephedrine), and a whole range of balsams and sweet gums.

In the event of the more dire sicknesses, the Indian medicine-man and the Indian housewife were as defenceless as our own doctors frequently are today. We saw in the opening chapter that pestilence might have been responsible for wiping out the population of the Anasazi cliff-dwellings, and driving the survivors down to the Rio Grande. It might have been a similar outbreak that ended the high civilization of the Mayan Empire in Yucatán and in the Petén. Europe itself lost a third of its population during the Black Death. With the arrival of the Europeans, the situation became immediately grave, as the native Americans possessed no immunity to the most ordinary European diseases, such as chicken pox, measles, scarlet fever, and the common cold, which soon carried off immense numbers of Indians. Influenza, pneumonia, tuberculosis, whooping cough, diphtheria, syphilis and other scourges also made brutal inroads.

The worst ravages were caused by two massive outbreaks of smallpox, in 1781 and in 1837. In the 1770s, although the tribes in the East had been despoiled and were about to be finally dispossessed, the tribes of the Plains were still in a stable and prosperous state. Then, in 1781, an outbreak of smallpox among the Spanish settlers at San Antonio in Texas spread rapidly northward, decimating the Comanche, crossing the Red River, and proceeding as far north as the Canadian border, where it worked havoc among the Blackfoot, Cree, and Assiniboin; the Arapaho, Shoshoni and Crow also suffered heavily. Altogether the disease may have killed as many as 130,000 Indians, halving the population of many tribes and destroying entire villages.

The outbreak of 1837 was equally terrible. It was brought the length of the Missouri river by whisky peddlers, and by the crew of a ship of the American Fur Company. The latter transmitted it to the tribesmen who had flocked to the landing-stages to sell or barter their hides and pelts. As in 1781, few Indians could grasp the fact that smallpox was contagious. They would not keep away from the boat and the germ-laden hides. Nor could they resist swooping on the infected camps of their helpless enemies, contracting the disease from the booty and the scalps that they carried off. Recourse to the sweat-bath only heightened the agony of the fever, and there are heart-breaking stories of droves of Indians drowning themselves in the river, jumping off cliffs, or cutting their throats in order to escape the pain and avoid a disgusting and long-drawn-out end. The Blackfoot, who had made a good recovery from the earlier pestilence, were this time dealt a knock-out blow. The Pawnee, Hidatsa, Dakota and Assiniboin were badly hit, and the Arikara lost 2000 of their 4000 people. The Mandan were totally destroyed. Of their population of 1600, only 31 were left alive to crawl for shelter to their kinsfolk, the Hidatsa. The Crow and Shoshoni, however, escaped more or less unscathed. Having felt the full force of the invisible horror 50 years earlier, they fled from it eastwards into the mountains, taking shelter in the crystalline and uncontaminated upper air.

Would modern American history have been any different if these two great epidemics had not occurred? Would the newly-born United States, after conquering the East, have encountered stiffer resistance on the Plains from tribes who would have been stronger in physique and morale, as well as larger in numbers? In the end, the result would doubtless have been the same, and the white juggernaut would have rolled implacably westwards. But the native Indian might have been able to give a more vigorous account of himself, which in turn would have improved his spiritual resources during the coming years of degradation and defeat. As it was, during the 1870s and 1880s, the white soldiers and settlers encountered a debilitated foe, whom they swept aside with disdainful ease.

Death and after-life

During the plague years, the Indian of the Plains and southern Canada grew accustomed to the sight of deserted villages and heaps of corpses. But what, in general, can one say of the Indian's attitude towards dying, death, and the dead?

First, despite the existence, in prehistoric times, of the fixation with death of the great Hopewell culture, and the extraordinary Southern Death Cult or Buzzard Cult of the Mississippi mound-builders, the Indian's outlook on death in the later historic epoch seems to have been notably perfunctory. Where death was concerned, he was a fatalist. As the moment of his death approached, whether it was natural or in battle, or under torture at the hands of his enemies, or on the white man's gallows, he sang his death-song. This was his own personal chant, which he had rehearsed all his life, and which was reserved for this supreme moment. It was a guttural wailing that froze the blood of the white men who heard it.

Death itself the Indian accepted with stoicism. He manifested indifference, resigning himself to it in the mood of a Moslem accepting the will of Allah. He did not make an unseemly fuss. Death in old age was nothing to be deplored. Among the Eskimo, some of the Plains Indians, and among the Apache, the elderly were sometimes left to die, when times were lean or when they were too weak to continue with the nomadic life. They did not protest their lot. More than death, the Indian feared the torture to which he might be subjected by his enemies before and after his death. Many tribes believed that scalping killed the soul, that strangling choked it, and that defacing the dead meant that the dead person took such disfigurements with him into the next world. People who were mutilated were condemned to wander forever as ghosts and werewolves.

After a man's death, his relatives would indulge in a noisy period of

170

wailing and lamentation that might last up to four days. The mourners would beat their breasts, tear their hair, and gash themselves with knives. Men too would join in the loud demonstrations of grief, to relieve themselves once and for all of all residues of sorrow. The Natchez, heirs to the death-saturated practices of ancient Mexico, had a typically bloodthirsty ritual of their own. They ritually slew the relatives, co-equals and slaves of a dead Great Sun or Great War Chief, so that the dead man might have a suitable retinue to accompany him into eternity. But this, as with almost everything associated with the Natchez, was unique, though elsewhere a man's horse or his dog might be killed and buried with him for company.

Usually the rites surrounding the cremation or interment of a dead person were simple. Either the dead man was placed in a grave, accompanied by his favourite tools and weapons, with food and water to sustain him on his journey to the next world; or he was put on a platform to be consumed by flames. Sometimes he was placed in a cave, a cleft in a rock, or under a boulder, while the Teton Dakota adopted the practice of wrapping the corpse in a cere-cloth and wedging it in the fork of a tree, where it was allowed to shrivel and decompose.

Indian graves were seldom marked in any distinctive way. Apart from the era of the fantastic burial-mounds, there were no memorials or cenotaphs. The earth was levelled, and sometimes a scrap of coloured material like a pathetic flag was tied to a twig. Soon no sign of the deceased

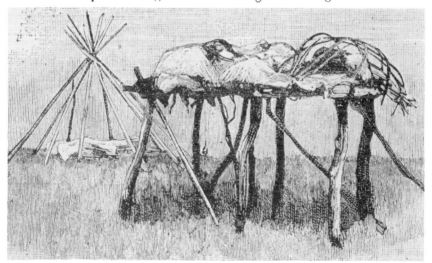

72 *A Sioux burial platform. The deceased's personal possessions, grave-goods and sacred offerings have been placed in the tipi nearby.*

73 *Plains Indians bid a comrade farewell.*

would remain above the ground. He would have merged unobtrusively into the Mother from whom he had sprung. To remove him more effectively from the land of the living, his clothes, his dwelling, and his household goods were systematically burned. Although most tribes stipulated a period of mourning that might last up to a year, strenuous exertions were usually made to ensure that all traces of the dead man's career on earth were erased. There was a general taboo on mentioning the dead man's name, and even, for a stipulated time, speaking words that might have formed part of his name. Such prohibitions were awkward, but they had to be observed. On occasion, whole genealogies and tribal histories had to be rearranged to make an 'Un-Person' of some particularly potent dead man.

The Indian, while fearless when confronted by death and dying, was terrified of ghosts. Fond as he may have been of a person when alive, when that person was dead it was essential that he should stay on the right side of the border, and not stray across it to interfere in the affairs of the living. In

74 *A burial-ground beside the Mississippi.*

any case, a person who had experienced a proper death was at peace. Only people who could not rest, who were cursed, evil, or unhappy, wandered abroad after death.

Even though he might have made a good ending, the average Indian appears to have possessed merely the vaguest notion of where his soul went after death. Many tribes did not believe in a hereafter, but the majority of Indians seem to have thought of the next world as a pleasant place, an idyllic spot where the sun shone, animals were abundant, and the rivers teemed with fish. Until the Christian missionaries arrived, the Indian had no idea of hell, of a place where one was condemned to punishment; nor did anyone go to the Happy Hunting Ground or the Land of Many Tipis as a reward of virtue. Everyone went there as of right. A warrior who died in battle expected no posthumous privileges when he got to heaven, except the pleasure of being reunited with his dead comrades. All in all, the Indian, like the majority of primitive peoples, preferred to think about this world rather than the next. Unlike Western man, who has been encouraged by religion and by the dogmas of socialism and communism to fasten his gaze on a hypothetically golden tomorrow rather than on a supposedly wretched

173

today, he was not obsessed by visions of human perfectibility. He was not a Utopian. He lived one day at a time, seeking to make the best he could of it.

Religious cults

During the past four centuries, as a result of contact with the white man, a number of Indian religious cults have sprung into existence. They ought to be noted in any survey, however short, of Indian religion.

For more than 300 centuries, Indian life and religion had existed in a condition untouched by any influence save that of other Indians. Then, with the landing of the Spaniards in the early seventeenth century, the situation was abruptly and radically altered. The brief last stage of Indian independence was inevitably marked by the material and spiritual presence of the white invader.

The Indian, whose whole existence was wrapped up in a religious aura, was bound to fall under the spell of the white man's religion. During his wars with the white man, he saw that the white man's God seemed to be more powerful and successful than his own Great Spirit. Considering that his own religion was exclusively based on obtaining favours from the gods, he was inevitably impressed by this. The white man's magic was more efficacious than his own. He therefore adopted Christian elements into his own religion, or entirely threw over his own religion and embraced the new one, or tried to combat the incoming deity by an increased strengthening of his existing religious loyalties.

The Pueblo Indians encountered the Spaniards in 1540–41, during Francisco Vázquez de Coronado's expedition along the Rio Grande (he reached Kansas, and one of his lieutenants discovered the Grand Canyon). Within a century, the Spaniards had built missions in Texas, New Mexico, and Arizona, though it was not until after Juan Bautista de Anza's great march of 1776 that they reached California. By then, they also possessed firm bases in Florida and Louisiana.

Today, in the Rio Grande pueblos, one can see the living manifestation of the fusion of the Indian and Roman Catholic faiths. The Pueblo peoples were impressed, as the Mexicans had been a century earlier, by the simple character and the vows of poverty and chastity of the Jesuit and Franciscan friars who came among them. They were also impressed by the fact that the holy fathers continued to arrive and to accept martyrdom after the Indian revolts that slaughtered them by the score and stacked up their corpses on their own altars. It must have been a powerful God who sustained them. Not that the holy fathers were as tolerant of the Indian's religion as the Indian was of theirs. The Church and the secular authorities early tried to stamp out Indian rituals – with the result, on the Rio Grande, that in 1680 the pueblos rose in revolt and swept the Spaniards from New Mexico for the space of 12 whole years. However, in the end the Christian faith, with its persuasive advocates and determined organization, made large inroads into the native religion. Pueblo religion remained substantially what it had been, with its Corn Dances, Deer Dances, Snake Dances, costumes and *kivas*: but Christian saints and Christ himself were accepted side by side into the native rituals. Today, a pueblo festival will be opened with a solemn parade of the Cross, or an image of the patron saint. In the plaza, the painted figures of the Corn God, Christ, Hernán Cortés, and the Virgin Mary will tread a solemn measure together.

At the other end of the continent, in the American Northeast, the picture was different. There, in the French and British orbit, although some Christian denominations, particularly the Quakers, made some headway among the Indian, Indians in general embarked on a fierce reassertion of their own codes. As early as the 1760s, a Delaware prophet appeared in Michigan who saw in a vision that the Indian could liberate himself by uniting with his brothers, forsaking alcohol, eschewing firearms, and concentrating Indian ceremonials on the Great Spirit alone. The prophet's doctrine spread rapidly throughout Central and Northeastern America, inspiring a great uprising of the Algonquian tribes led by the famous chief of the Ottawas, Pontiac. In 1763, Pontiac captured nine English forts, defeated a British column, and besieged Fort Detroit. But by 1765 the message of the 'Delaware Prophet' had diminished, and Pontiac had become increasingly desperate and discredited.

Forty years later, another visionary, a Shawnee called Tenskwatawa, inspired his brother, the great Tecumseh, to undertake the most determined attempt that would ever be made to weld the American Indians into a single nation. Tenskwatawa, like his Delaware predecessor, preached a complete rejection of everything white, and a return to an aboriginal Indian purity. It was Tenskwatawa who, against Tecumseh's express instructions, and after Tecumseh had been brilliantly fashioning a grand Indian coalition based on his own settlement in the Ohio valley, rashly gave the order for the Indians to attack the American army at Tippecanoe. Tenskwatawa had assured his men that the bullets of the white soldiers could not harm them. When they died, their cause died with them. The following year, Tecumseh became a British brigadier-general. He died at the Battle of the Thames in 1814.

The religious ideas of the Delaware Prophet and Tenskwatawa had taken deeper root than had been supposed. They grew in secret, eventually bursting forth as the impulse behind the sustained bout of Indian resistance, the last effort of the American Indian, that occurred between

175

1870 and 1890. They were the ideas that lay directly behind the Cult of the Dreamers, led by the extraordinary mystic Smohalla, that came into existence in Washington and Oregon in the 1860s. Smohalla was born in a village at the confluence of the Snake and Columbia rivers, and brought up as a Roman Catholic. He was kin to the Nez Perce and the Yakima. After taking part in the Yakima wars of 1855–56, he believed that he had died and had been resurrected by the Great Spirit. Because of his ability to enter deep trances, his followers gave him the name of 'The Dreamer'. He believed that the Great Spirit had first created the Indian, who was the only truly God-created stock, and that the Indian alone could claim to own the earth. He preserved the old nature rituals, but added to them the Dream Dance, intended to induce a visionary state in its participants. He meant his message to be peaceful: but when, in 1877, Chief Joseph of the Nez Perce was provoked by American cattle-rustling into his celebrated rebellion, it was Smohalla's teachings that sustained the insurgents in their gallant and prolonged but eventually unsuccessful resistance.

Smohalla was the spiritual founder, in one form or another, of the dozens of Dream Dance or Ghost Dance cults that soon came into existence. Some of them were contemplative and pacific, others preached and practised violence. From Oregon and Washington, the Dream Dance spread throughout California, branching out there to become the Earth Lodge Cult, the Warm House Cult, and the Bole Maru Cult. All these cults borrowed elements from Roman Catholicism, though twisted into the most curious shapes. Another major offshoot developed on the California-Nevada border, where in 1869 a prophet among the Paviotso Indians, named Wodziwob, began a Ghost Dance of his own. It was performed around a totem pole, and those taking part circled endlessly to the left, holding hands, and singing songs that had been imparted to Wodziwob in a dream. This very simple dance was typical of the various Dream Dances and Ghost Dances, most of which had their origin in Oregon, Washington, or California. The West Coast seems always to have had a taste for colourful and unorthodox rites.

Wodziwob was a man of commanding character, and in turn his notions were transmitted to a man of equal stature, Wovoka. Wovoka was the son of one of Wodziwob's principal disciples. He was also known as John Wilson, the name he received from the white farmer who adopted him. Wovoka, a Northern Paiute from Nevada, fell seriously ill in 1888, at a time that happened to coincide with an eclipse of the sun. Like Smohalla, he died and was brought back to life. 'When the sun died, I went up to heaven. I saw God and all the people who had died a long time ago. God told me to return and tell my people to be good and love one another, not to fight, steal and lie. He also gave me a dance to give my people'.

Wovoka's Ghost Dance spread rapidly to the Missouri river and the Rocky Mountains, and the length of the Plains. Its performance would ensure that Indian lands would be restored, that the Indian dead would arise, and that the now depleted store of big game would again become abundant. The dancers, as in Wodziwob's dance, circled slowly to the left, holding hands, wearing special shirts painted with mystic symbols that were believed to be proof against white man's bullets. They danced all night for five consecutive nights.

Wovoka's message, like Smohalla's and Wodziwob's, was intended to be peaceful. But the Plains tribes, who took up the message of the new Messiah with characteristic enthusiasm, combined it with their Sun Dance, and soon the white settlers were becoming apprehensive at the new dancing mania. The Sioux in particular became wildly excited. When the American Seventh Cavalry were despatched to keep order, the result was the clash at Wounded Knee, in South Dakota, on 29 December 1890. 200 Sioux men, women and children were massacred. Wovoka, distressed by the tragedy, increasingly modified his messianic doctrine to urge compromise with the white man. He died in Nevada as late as 1932.

Nevertheless the craze for the Ghost Dance-Sun Dance had smitten the Plains, encouraging the leaders who waged all-out war against the Americans in the 1870s and 1880s. Even when the Sioux chiefs Crazy Horse and Sitting Bull had lost their last battles, and had been assassinated by their white enemies, the Ghost Dance remained an emblem of hope and revival. Such devotees of the Ghost Dance as Albert Hopkins, Frank White, Black Buffalo, Poor Buffalo, Datekan, Paingya, and Wooden Lance carried the ritual to the Kiowa, Cheyenne, Arapaho, Wichita, and Pawnee. Thence it was taken by secondary prophets to all the important new reservation territories. The only major tribe who rejected it were the Navajo. The Navajo were reluctant to accept the Ghost Dance for the simple reason that they were scared stiff by the very thought of ghosts. The notion of an army of *chindi*, or dead people, suddenly rising from their graves and walking about was too fearful for them to entertain.

A brief glance should, finally, be taken at a southerly movement that had nothing to do with Dream Dancing or with Ghost Dancing, but which evolved on its own from the later stages of the Sun Dance. This was the movement initiated by a Comanche prophet, Isatai.

Isatai claimed to be able to raise the dead, following a visit to heaven in which he had met the Great Spirit face to face. He made the familiar promise to his followers that the white man's bullets coule not pierce them.

In 1873, he encouraged a force of Comanche, Cheyenne, and Kiowa to make an abortive attack on a band of white buffalo hunters at Adobe Walls, with the result that he lost prestige and his influence foundered. His power passed to a pragmatic young chief called Quanah Parker, who, although he surrendered to the American army in 1875, organized a confederation of Comanche, Kiowa and Apache that later proved to be highly effective.

'I can learn the white man's ways', declared Parker, who in the next 30 years would head many delegations to Washington and show himself an able negotiator. Times had changed. New methods of trying to resist the white man were called for. The episode at Wounded Knee had signalled the end of armed resistance. There was now no alternative to seeking an accommodation with the white man, which made the pursuit of religions which might, even inadvertently, spark off futile revolts pointless and counter-productive. Parker's Comanches, Apaches and Kiowas now took up, in common with others, a brand new cult, Peyotism, which advocated a more subtle and subdued, though no less obdurate, resistance to the encroachment of white culture.

The peyote plant, to which a passing reference was made earlier, is a small cactus that grows widely in Mexico and New Mexico. It contains a hallucinogen that produces highly-coloured visions that may last for 24 hours, although it is not habit-forming. It was used in ancient times in Mexico, spreading from the Rio Grande valley and taking hold on the Plains as early as the 1840s. In 1890, Peyotism made a sudden leap forward at the instigation of an Indian of mixed Delaware and French stock, John Wilson(no relation to the other John Wilson, Wovoka, who at the same time was launching his own Ghost Dance). Wilson initiated what he called the Big Moon Cult, inspired by a Ghost Dance meeting in Oklahoma that had been presided over by Sitting Bull.

Big Moon wished to guide the Indian along the 'road of peyote', in order to re-establish traditional Indian values. At first, the cult rejected all white and Christian elements; but after Wilson's premature death, his followers fell increasingly under the influence of the Latter-Day Saints, Jehovah's Witnesses, the Native American Church, and other religious splinter-groups. Under a Winnebago prophet, John Rave, it assumed a mixed pagan and Christian colouring, the eating of peyote encouraging the believer to witness the mingling of the Great Spirit with Jesus Christ. Christ was conceived as having been rejected by the white man, and thus becoming the personal Saviour of the Indian.

The peyote cult, which was also deeply concerned with healing, was avidly taken up by Indian peoples all over America and Canada. In the course of time it became wholly identified with the present-day Native

American Church, or N.A.C. Like other Indian religions, the N.A.C. has faced white persecution. The Sun Dances and Ghost Dances were officially banned in the 1880s, and could only be celebrated clandestinely, and the Code of Religious Offences was rigorously applied as late as the 1920s. Only in 1934 was the policy reversed by John Collier, the famous Commissioner of Indian Affairs, who then declared that: 'No interference with Indian religious life or ceremonial expression will hereafter be tolerated'. Today, the N.A.C. claims to have 250,000 members, and probably as many more Indians who are not members of the N.A.C. are users of peyote. Peyote is not prohibited by federal law, though its use is illegal in many states. The tribal council of the Navajo has outlawed it, in spite of which large numbers of Navajo partake regularly of the 'peyote sacrament'.

It will have been noticed that a chief aim of all the above-mentioned cults was or is the stamping out of alcoholism. In the final analysis, the white man's 'rot-gut' whisky has done as much damage to the Indian as his guns and his diseases. Spaniards, Frenchmen, Britons and Americans all used alcohol as a means of sapping the Indian's physique, will-power, and self-respect. The early colonizers and pioneer Americans realized that the Indian, with his yearning for vision and ecstasies, had a fatal propensity for the cheap shortcut offered by drink. Later, when the fabric of Indian culture began to disintegrate, alcohol had the additional appeal of deadening the sense of shame and failure. The Dream Dance, the Ghost Dance and Peyotism sought to wean the Indian from the bottle, and to substitute a more meaningful manner of achieving the state of ecstasy which, in the crisis of his culture, he increasingly needed.

We shall be discussing the problem of alcoholism, together with the other ills that afflict the modern Indian, when we deal in our final chapter with Indian life at the present time.

6

The Artist

The Indian lived intimately with nature; it was the object of his unceasing awe and reverence; he addressed constant prayer and propitiation to the spirits who were its embodiments. His bond with nature was both strong and fragile, in that it cherished him and at the same time warned him that he was pitifully frail – far worse adapted to coping with the world, he thought, than many of the wild creatures around him. In these circumstances, it was not surprising that in his art, the most personal expression of his hopes and fears, he should have given rein to these deep-seated religious feelings.

Indian art was steeped in religion. Unfortunately, with the passing of the traditional Indian way of life, and the decay of the old religion, the inner meaning of most Indian art of the high period has been lost. Today, much of it is incomprehensible not only to the white connoisseur, but even to the majority of Indians. Like the white man's art, Indian art is nowadays largely decorative, an agreeable adjunct or grace-note to life, but not an activity that derives a compelling force from a direct connection with the springs of human ecstasy and terror. In only a few places, such as the Southwest and the Northwest, and the fastnesses of the Arctic, where the framework of Indian life has to some extent persisted, can the literal magic of Indian art still be glimpsed.

Another reason why Indian art has been generally misunderstood, and therefore undervalued, is that it was executed in an unfamiliar style. Westerners would have studied it more seriously if it had been either realistic or abstract, since both these styles have established themselves in the West. American Indian art, however, is neither realistic nor abstract. It is schematic and symbolic. In this, it resembles, for example, the art of Ancient Egypt. Until recent years, Ancient Egyptian wall-painting was considered quaint and amateurish, since its conventions appeared to be so simple as to be naïve. As for Egyptian sculpture, it received critical respect only because it was supposed to be 'realistic', whereas in fact it was as heavily laden with religious and symbolic meaning as Egyptian painting. Indian art has suffered from similar critical misconceptions.

Indian art was not meant to be objective or representational. It was not meant to depict the visible surface of things, but was subjective, dealing with dreams, visions, the imagination, the interior life. Its purpose was not primarily aesthetic, though the Indian possessed a highly-developed aesthetic feeling: its purpose was magical. Indian motifs and designs, even those on everyday clothing and household utensils, were protective, curative, totemic, or supposedly productive of good luck and prosperity. Like his Ancient Egyptian counterpart, the Indian artist was not interested in painting exact portraits of people, or faithful pictures of animals. What he wanted to capture was not their physical envelope, but their soul, their ghostly essence. And how could anything as intangible as the shape of the soul be conveyed except by expressionistic and symbolic means?

With the exception of architecture, the American Indian does not seem to have created many works of art on a large scale. We have seen that the Cliff-dwellers and Moundbuilders of earlier times constructed buildings and urban complexes in a manner that rivalled the architecture of prehistoric and Dark Age Europe. On the other hand, nothing that has been found in North America – so far – can match such marvels as the wall-art of Altamira in Spain, or the equally famous cave-murals of Lascaux in France. A few modest paintings have survived in one or two of the Southwestern cliff-dwellings, most of them intrusive efforts by the Navajo, who occupied them long after they had been abandoned by the original inhabitants; and there are fragmentary murals in those *kivas* in ancient pueblos that have been opened to the public. Of course, there may be mural masterpieces on the walls of the *kivas* in the present-day pueblos, hidden from the eyes of the uninitiated, as the paintings and sculptures of Ancient Egypt once were. It would appear, however, that artistic endeavour on a larger scale was not attempted by the American Indian. His bent did not lie that way. The one noteworthy exception is the work of the master-painters and master-woodcarvers of the Pacific Northwest, creators of the splendid screens that adorned the walls of the long-houses, and of the imposing house posts, mortuary poles, memorial poles, and totem poles. (The term 'totem pole' is really a misnomer, as the poles were not strictly totemic, but emblematic or heraldic.)

Where Indian art was concerned, the only major correspondence between the art of the New World and of the Old World would appear to have been the use of pictographs or petroglyphs. Petroglyphs are the symbols that can be seen painted, pecked or incised on rocks and boulders, or in rock shelters, or on the walls of caverns. They are found all over North America. Occasionally, they feature stylized, stick-like human beings, or human feet, arms, legs and fingers. More often, they offer a repertoire of geometrical shapes (circles, ovals, squares, oblongs, triangles, trapeziums), or an amazing series of animals, birds, reptiles, and insects, or portions of such creatures. Petroglyphs are sometimes crowded into a single spot, or they can exist alone, in a remote and inaccessible place.

75 *Indian petroglyphs carved on a boulder in the Southwest.*

What was their purpose? What did they represent? In some cases, they may simply have been done by idlers, or by lovers wishing to record their feelings. Or they might have been the work of hunters, passing the time as they waited for their prey, or notching up the kills they had already made. Alternatively, they could commemorate a meeting of people of different tribes, who perhaps had come together to arrange a treaty. Many of them were certainly related to hunting magic, to increase the supply of game: but others may have had a more personal significance. When young men went out into the wilderness, to commune with themselves, and to receive the visitations of their guardian spirit, it is likely that they left a testimony to their experience in the shape of a personal symbol. The present writer has often visited a little hill, on the plain outside Carrizozo, in New Mexico. There, between 500 and 1000 years ago, the people of the Jornada branch of the Mogollon people, who were cousins of the distant Hohokam, covered the volcanic boulders of the hilltop with thousands of petroglyphs of every shape, size, and subject. It is impossible not to feel that one is treading on sacred ground. These were not, one senses, random scribbles, but the expression of something mysterious and important.

If the North American Indian evinced little interest in the more monumental forms of art, his largely nomadic way of life hardly encouraged it. Moreover, he often had a very real horror of disturbing or defacing his natural surroundings. Nature was holy. Even when he was travelling, or on the trail, it was his wish to leave behind him as little trace as possible of his passing. He sought to make no footprints, to break no branches, to disturb no leaf, to efface the ugly marks of his fires and campsites. He wanted to move through the landscape as lightly as the breeze. As we saw, even when he was buried, he tried to make his grave as unobtrusive as he could. Some Indians had such an antipathy to defiling nature that the white man could not persuade them, even when they already practised agriculture, to use the plough, because its share would cut open the living flesh of their mother, the earth.

However, if he was a stranger to what we think of as the more ambitious aspects of art (though a miniature, after all, may be just as valid and well-executed as a mural), the Indian excelled in art on the domestic scale. His weapons, his clothing, his adornments, the objects he made use of in his daily life and his religion, were shaped and decorated with unparalleled skill. On this level, the North American Indian had no rival. In addition, this artistic skill was not confined, as in our own society, to a few gifted individuals. The Indian did not consider artistic ability to be a specialized undertaking. There is good reason to suppose that the artistic instinct, which shrivels early in our society, was more widely disseminated among Indians than it is among us. Most Indians could make a pot, or a basket, or a leather jacket, or a set of harness, or paint designs on a shield or tipi. The majority of Indians appear to have been deft with their fingers. The circumstances of their lives made them practical, and their relationship with nature, with the gods, with dreams and visions, with signs and symbols, provided them with endless inspiration.

Again, one must emphasize that the bulk of the Indian art one sees today, even the Indian art one sees in museums, is not Indian art as it once existed in a pure state. Leather, wood, skins, feathers, and many other materials upon which the Indian lavished much of his craft, are perishable. The items of Indian art that have survived hard usage, the weather, or neglect, were seldom made more than a century ago – that is, well within the era when the influence of the white man had made itself felt. The number of objects that have come down to us from the earlier epochs of Indian history is unfortunately very small. As soon as they had landed, the Europeans began to trade with the Indians, for whose furs they exchanged knives, hatchets, guns, glass beads, brass bells, metal buttons, and woollen and cotton fabrics dyed in garish colours. Since the mid-eighteenth century, the Indian can be said to have been largely outfitted by the white man. His own tastes in clothing and jewelry were heightened and often coarsened by his contact with industrial civilization. The gorgeous trappings of the Indian chiefs whom we admire in nineteenth-century photographs were largely the product of the white trader or peddler.

However, the employment of mass-produced European materials did not always result in a debasing of Indian art. Sometimes, although it produced a more hectic and flamboyant surface appearance, it seemed to liberate the already vivid Indian imagination, the craving for bright and bold patterns that had been muted by natural dyes and the quieter character of primitive materials. Nor did European influence affect only the superficial aspects of Indian life. Architectural styles, styles of clothing, and the physical appearance of the Indian himself were transformed. Before coming into contact with the white man, Indian males did not wear shirts, jackets, or upper clothing, and most Indian women did not wear blouses. Later, Indian women fell under the spell of the dresses worn by the wives of the soldiers who manned the early forts and garrisons. They took to silks, satins, velvets, ribbons, to sweeping skirts and mantles. The physical appearance of the Navajo, which tourists think is 'traditional', has little in common with the way the Navajo looked 200 years ago. Even the famous Navajo jewelry is modern. The Navajo only learned to make it, under the tuition of itinerant Mexican silversmiths, in the late 1850s. There has been a total transformation of Indian life since the Spaniards crossed the Rio Grande in 1540, bringing with them horses, firearms, and other exotic marvels.

This is not to say that the Indian did not possess and continue to practise artistic talents that were predominantly his own. Contact with the Europeans started four centuries ago, but the Indian had had at least thirty times that long, and probably very much longer, to establish his own styles.

There is a considerable resemblance between Indian artefacts in all of our five principal regions, although the character of the raw materials available in each area naturally differed. In forest areas, wood was a prime material; on the plains, hides and leather; and the coastal peoples were well provided with shells and the products of sea creatures. Such materials predominated in the areas concerned. However, because of the dual operation of cultural diffusion and of trading, there are close similarities between the art and life-styles of each region, even when the regions are not actual neighbours.

Diffusion is the word used by archaeologists and anthropologists to describe the manner in which objects and ideas trickle from one people to another. In the course of history, peoples rub up against and intermingle with each other. Material objects and religious and cultural ideas can be spread peacefully, by means of intermarriage or tribal alliance; or they can be spread by means of war, when the dead are stripped of their accoutrements, or prisoners are captured from tribes with different traditions. The latter settle down with the captors and subtly influence the host culture. Another important source of diffusion is emigration. Only the presence of large groups of emigrants could account, for example, for the introduction of such major traits as Mexican ball-courts, or the temple-mounds of the American Southeast.

Even in remotest times, the hunting peoples of North America were accustomed to encountering and fraternizing with each other. The wide distribution of points, blades, scrapers and other stone tools of the Clovis, Folsom, Scottsbluff, and other early peoples is evidence of these exchanges. All tribes habitually traded. Many tribes specialized in it. The Mojave commuted between California and the Southwest, carrying commodities in both directions. The Hopi were skilled middlemen, acting as brokers for salt and skins. They distributed the fine red ochre, excellent for body-painting and religious purposes, that their shy neighbours the Havasupai dug out of the secret recesses of the Grand Canyon.

There may, for all we know, have been a heavy trade in perishable materials, including foodstuffs. Dried meats, corn meal, and various delicacies might have been exported. Occasionally we have some inkling of this. We know, for instance, that the Hohokam were exporters of salt and cotton. But most of our knowledge of trading derives, not surprisingly, from the presence of more permanent artefacts, such as types of stone and metal. More than 10,000 years ago, flint from the Alibates mine in the Texas panhandle was widely disseminated, while flint from Flint Ridge in Ohio found its way to the Atlantic coast and to Florida. Obsidian – black and glittering – was also highly prized, and was excavated from certain restricted localities in the Southwest and despatched to places thousands of miles away. We have already seen how catlinite, from Minnesota, was keenly sought after for the manufacture of peace-pipes.

When a particular people had grown wealthy, especially when it had become sedentary and built elaborate settlements, it was in a position to import all manner of luxury items. The Hopewell people, one of the most spectacular of native Indian cultures, required great masses of precious materials to satisfy the ostentatious habit of their daily life, and the even more ostentatious way in which they interred their dead beneath colossal

185

tumuli. From Alabama, they imported greenstone; from the Appalachians, sheets of mica and crystals of quartz; from Michigan and Ontario, beads of beaten copper and beaten silver. Above all, the Hopewellians were avid importers of one of the most sought-after commodities of native America: sea-shells.

Shells and beads

The Cochise people of Arizona were importing shells from the Pacific coast 5000 years ago. Their lineal descendants, the Hohokam, obtained a whole range of shells from the distant fishermen of California: cardium, conus, glycemeris, olivella, and other species. Shells have a profound appeal, because of their strange and delicate shapes and colours, and their association with the mysteries of the ocean. The Hohokam artists used large clam shells for executing designs which were the world's first essays in the technique of etching. The Hohokam were practising etching at least three centuries before its appearance in Europe. They covered the raised parts of the design with pitch or resin, then soaked away the exposed portions in acid, obtained from the fermented juice of the saguaro.

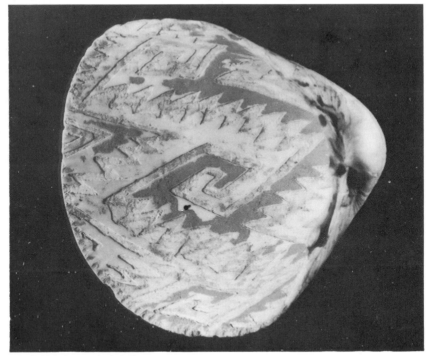

76 *A Hohokam etched shell.*

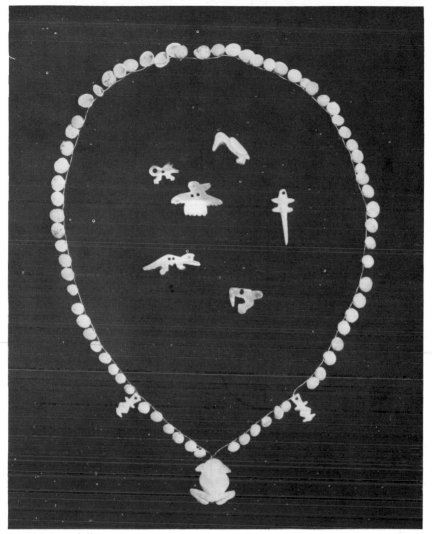

77 *Hohokam shell ornaments.*

In the cliff-dwellings and pueblos of the Southwest, the Hohokam custom of cutting rings, pendants and fetishes from shells was continued, and continues today. The pueblo jewellers, in particular the Zuñi, enhance their jewelry with pearl, coral and abalone, and trumpets made of giant conch shells brought centuries ago from the ocean are still ceremonially sounded in many pueblos. The mound-builders of the Southeast also blew conch-shell trumpets, and drank their 'Black Drink' from engraved shells.

187

From whelks they cut the elaborately engraved gorgets which priests and chiefs wore on their breasts.

The smaller shells, like the columella, cowrie, and marginella, were popular for decorating mantles, headdresses, girdles and anklets, while the dentalium became a rage across the northern plains and was used not only for adornment but as money. Dentalium shells had long been used as a regular currency by the Hupa, and other tribes of central California, who obtained them from Vancouver Island, far to the north. Each shell had a fixed value, according to its size.

The most celebrated instance of beads used for the twin purpose of decoration and currency was that of 'wampum', made by the Iroquois and the Algonquian tribes of the Northeast. Wampum consisted of discs or tubes of shell, white, pale brown, purple or lavender, which were finely shaped and ground and strung together as belts. They had ritual uses, were employed to commemorate important occasions, and were sent round with the tobacco pipe as a token of peace. The original Dutch and English settlers lost no time in manufacturing strings of wampum and putting them in circulation. Indeed, a wampum factory remained in operation in New Jersey until the First World War. Today wampum is a staple of Indian jewelry, used either alone or as spacers between beads or pieces of turquoise, coral, or other stones.

Beads of stone and shell, expertly cut, drilled, and polished, were familiar to the Indian from prehistoric times; but the making of beads by hand was a laborious business, and when the Indian became acquainted with European beads in all their profusion and variety it was a revelation to him. His whole mode of dress was swiftly revolutionized. Columbus noted in the log of his first landfall that the natives seized the necklaces of crimson glass beads he offered them and 'immediately put them around their necks'. During the sixteenth and seventeenth centuries, white traders, Spanish, French, British and Russian, sold the Indian a wide selection of large glass beads. Most were made by the glassblowers of Spain, France, England, Holland, Sweden, and Murano in Venice, and many of them were of great beauty. They bore such evocative names as the Padre Bead, the Cornaline d'Aleppo Bead, the Sun Bead, and the Chevron Bead. Today they are as greatly coveted by collectors as they were by the Indian of former days.

The large size of these beads made them chiefly useful for necklaces. It was the introduction in about 1750 of the Pony Bead (so-called because white traders carried sacks of them slung across their ponies), and a little later of the diminutive Seed Bead, that enabled the Indian to sew beads easily and thickly on leather clothing, or even to weave them on the loom. Soon beadwork had almost completely superseded the use of quills and feathers for the same purpose. In the Southwest, in recent times, an outstanding success was scored by the Hubbell Bead, a turquoise-coloured bead made in Czechoslovakia in the 1920s, and sold to the Navajo and Pueblo peoples at an Arizona trading-post. It became so popular that real pieces of turquoise were readily exchanged for it. In time, distinct regional styles of beadwork began to evolve, embodying geometrical and floral designs of an individual flavour. They were applied to clothing, hangings, or utensils in different ways: by lazy-stitching on the Plains and Plateau; by spot-stitching in the Northwest; by padding and embossing among the Iroquois; by netting and openwork in California and the southwest Basin; by plaiting on the southern prairies; and by weaving on small hand-looms by the Chippewa, Winnebago, and other tribes around the Great Lakes. Exceptionally fine beadwork is still produced on the reservations of Idaho, North Dakota, Oklahoma, New Mexico, and Arizona.

If featherwork and quill-work lost ground with the advent of the bead, they have continued in vogue among some tribes to the present time.

78 *A woman displays garments (identified as Sioux woman's dress) decorated with the typical lazy-stitch beadwork of the Central Plains and Plateau.*

Today, the hawk and eagle and other species of birds that adorned the great war bonnets and the waving headdresses are protected. Once more, the white trader has filled the gap with ostrich feathers, dyed in glaring colours; or else the humble turkey has had to be called upon. Feathered hats, masks, prayer sticks, and costumes figure prominently in the religious dances and festivals of the Rio Grande pueblos. Similarly, the wild porcupine has become a rare creature. Its quills are no longer available for the elaborate applied designs that were common on clothing and utensils across the Northeastern states and the Northern plains where it was once plentiful. The Iroquois, Huron, Ottawa, Chippewa and Winnebago, together with the Sioux, Arapaho and Cheyenne, specialized in this craft. It consisted of soaking the five-inch-long quills of the porcupine until they were supple, then wrapping, folding, or weaving them around other materials. Beadwork and quill-work were often combined, the smooth and shiny surface of the plaited quills contrasting with the areas of beadwork. In addition to quills and beads, various types of woven hair were also used for artistic effect, as well as for sewing, binding, and stringing. Human hair, as we saw in the opening chapter, was shorn from the heads of women and dead people by the Anasazi cliff-dwellers, who used it for adornment and for making nets. Horsehair and doghair were other common staples, as were moose hair and buffalo hair on the Plains.

In Chapter Three, we discussed the methods of preparing leather for clothing and for other purposes, and had earlier remarked the fact that bone, antler and horn have been basic materials ever since the first hunters slew and dismembered the mammoth and mastodon. Similarly, we touched on the types of stone tool that have been in continuous employment since the early hunters struck flakes off a flint matrix, long before 20,000 B.C.

Metalwork

Metalwork, on the other hand, reached the North American Indian as tardily as it had once reached his hunting brothers in Europe. When it did so, it arrived, as in Europe, from more sophisticated technological centres in the world beyond. The only exception in North America was the working of copper, which, as we saw, was known to the Old Copper Culture of Wisconsin, Minnesota, and Michigan in the Archaic period. At the staggeringly remote date of 5000–3000 B.C., these gifted Great Lakes people were fashioning arrowheads, spearheads, knives and axes of copper as early, or perhaps earlier, than any other people in the world. Later, the Adena, Hopewell, and Mississippian peoples, particularly those who had created the Southern Death Cult, made exquisite copper plaques, pendants and applied ornaments; while the huge 'coppers' of the Northwest coast,

79 *Zuñi women in ceremonial garb, wearing their family heirlooms of silver and turquoise, in the shape of rings, brooches, and squash-blossom necklaces. Their leggings are of deerskin.*

191

which were disdainfully destroyed during the famous *potlatches*, were carved from flattened copper sheets. Nevertheless, despite these achievements, the native Indian method of working copper remained primitive. The metal was not smelted, but extracted from the purest available veins, hammered flat in its soft state, and cut to shape. The decoration was directly incised upon it with a stone or bone graver. It was worked cold, though sometimes it was probably heated over a fire to soften it prior to flattening. The key technique of casting by means of stone or clay moulds was entirely unknown. Other metals, such as meteoric iron, lead, and silver, were hammered cold in the same way, but they were only very rarely employed.

As soon as the European had shown them easier and surer methods, a passion for making silver ornaments spread like wildfire throughout the entire Indian community. The Europeans sold the Indians sheet silver, or the Indians fashioned it themselves by trading with the white man for silver ingots and silver coins. By 1800, the Iroquois, the peoples of the Lakes and the tribesmen of the Plains were making their own brooches, buttons, earrings, pendants, combs, buckles, gorgets, bracelets, and anklets. At first, their designs were almost exclusively adopted from English, Canadian and American originals. Soon they were purchasing German silver, which is not silver but an alloy of zinc, nickel and copper. It was less expensive than sterling silver, and enabled them to expand their activities and experiment with patterns of their own.

It was the nomads of the Plains, serving as the link between the settled areas of Northeast and Southwest, who brought the taste for silver to the Southwest. Almost simultaneously, Mexican silversmiths began touring the Southwest, imparting the techniques of sand-casting by means of pumice stone and tufa moulds. The Mexicans also introduced their own Spanish and Spanish Colonial styles, which were quickly and brilliantly absorbed by the Navajo. Today, Navajo jewelry, after the lapse of little more than a century, represents one of the highest achievements of American art, closely followed by that of the neighbouring Zuñi and Hopi, to whom they passed on their skills in their turn.

The famous concho belt, and the typical Navajo bracelet are of Plains derivation, while from Spain came the shape of the Navajo beads and buttons, the silver saddles and bridles, and the squash-blossom necklace. The squash-blossom was the shape of the fastenings of the Spanish horseman's chaps or *chaparreras*, and from the bottom of the squash-blossom necklace hangs the *naja*, an upside-down crescent that was originally a good-luck device that the Spanish *conquistadores* hung on the chests of their chargers. The Spaniards themselves had adopted the *naja* from the crescentic emblem of the Moors, at the time of the Arab occupation of

192

Spain. Ordinarily, Navajo silverwork has a plain, solid character, its massiveness enhanced by the chunks of rough turquoise with which it is often studded. Zuñi jewelry, on the other hand, is miniature by comparison. Its characteristic pieces are tiny stylized birds, butterflies, insects, and mythological creatures, elegantly carried out in multicoloured mosaics of jet, coral, garnet, and small smooth chips of turquoise. The Zuñi are masters of inlay and channel work. As for the Hopi, their silver resembles that of the Zuñi in its restrained appearance, but coloured stones are seldom used, and the silver is deeply engraved with running motifs adapted from Hopi pottery. Hopi pieces are frequently executed in an overlay technique, in which two sheets of silver, the lower one blackened by the application of liver of sulphur, are sweated together. The blackened layer serves as a contrasting background for the bright designs on the upper one.

Neither Navajo, Zuñi or Hopi have ever mined silver themselves, not even at the time of the silver-boom in the Southwest. Apart from the technology that would have been involved, by the time silverwork came into fashion the white man had long since appropriated the mineral lodes. Originally, the Indian silversmith melted down Mexican silver pesos and American silver dollars. When they were banned from doing this, they purchased bar silver from dealers. Today they buy both their silver and turquoise from agents, who obtain the latter from Asia, the Middle East, and Mexico. Much so-called turquoise in modern jewelry is fake, concocted from paste and coloured glass. A little turquoise still comes from the Southwest, but it is mostly poor stuff compared with that from the 12 or 15 major sites which have now become exhausted, and which once yielded stones of a delicate difference that the trained eye could recognize at a glance. Unfortunately, most 'Navajo jewelry' on sale today is not Indian at all, but is mass-produced in Japan, in Taiwan, or by white entrepreneurs in Albuquerque or Los Angeles. The Indians themselves, who by and large have refused to capitalize on the demand for their wares by lowering their standards, have been forced to watch a gang of cheapjacks ruin the market for their products. A sad situation: but the kind of thing that the Indian has had to become used to during recent centuries.

Basketry, Pottery and Weaving

There were two artistic activities that revealed to a remarkable extent the genius of the American Indian. Together with weaving, which we shall be considering in a moment, they constitute a yardstick by which the white man can measure something of the subtlety and refinement of the Indian soul. The white man has no use for arrowheads and spearheads, and his use of feathers, sea-shells, bone and horn, buffalo hides, tipis, tomahawks and

193

80 *A Zuñi pot.*

totem-poles, is likely to be severely restricted. However, he makes daily use of baskets, pottery, and containers of all kinds, and he puts blankets on his bed. So where these basic items of everyday living are concerned, for once he is able to make a direct comparison between his own personal possessions and those of the Indian. And if he is honest, he might be compelled to admit that the Indian was accustomed to surround himself with objects that were not at all inferior to his own, and that were in many cases more satisfying to look at and to handle.

In the sphere of basketry and pottery the Indian was, and to a large extent remains, supreme. Interestingly, the making of baskets, which might be supposed to be a more complicated process than the making of pots, and therefore a derivative of the latter, occurred earlier in North America than the making of pottery. At least 10,000 years ago, in the Desert cultures of the arid West, from Oregon to Arizona, the early hunters were making coiled and twined baskets, as well as using the same techniques for making sandals and hunting-traps. Pottery, on the other hand, is not found in America until about 2000 B.C., a full 6000 years later.

Strangely, the art of pottery grew up not in the Southwest, which was so often to lead the way in cultural innovations and where agriculture had been established for 1000 years, but in the non-agricultural Woodland Southeast. In the Southwest, pottery appeared only about 500-300 B.C. In both regions, however, it seems probable that the creative impulse for making pottery came from ancient Mexico, which for most of its history was far more advanced than the lands to the north. Again, one must emphasize that there was no boundary in those days between North and Central America. There was no line on the map, no frontier on the Rio Grande, no stop for immigration. People wandered freely, bringing their chattels and their customs with them.

Eventually, the basketry of the Southwest reached a higher level than that of the Southeast or any other region. But almost all tribes of North America were superb basketmakers. They made baskets for storage, for carriage, for cookery. They made small baskets and giant baskets, round baskets and square baskets, baskets with loops and baskets with handles. They made chests, sieves, threshing baskets, corn and acorn washers, seed-beaters, back packs, fish and bird traps, hats, mats, cradles, ceremonial baskets, and baskets intended for weddings and funerals. In earlier times, it had been the practice to line storage pits in the ground with

81 *A Winnebago woman making baskets.*

195

82 *A Western Apache twined pack basket with buckskin fringes, used for gifts.*

thin twigs and strips of bark, and this in turn gave rise to the making of matting. Matting was also used to keep out the mud and drafts in caves and houses, and for wrapping around the corpses of the dead. The weave of basketry became so tight that it was employed for transporting meal, seeds, and water. Baskets were used for boiling foodstuffs, washing, dying clothes, and brewing *tiswin* or native beer and similar alcoholic beverages. An extraordinary range of materials was utilized. It included rushes, bear grass, yucca leaves, cattails, devil's claw, willow and sumac in the Southwest; cane, oak, roots and bark in the Southeast; sweet grass, hardwood, cedar and basswood in the Northeast; hazel and buffalo grass on the Plains; spruce, cedar, cherry bark and squaw grass in California and the Northwest. Almost any natural material that came to hand could be steamed, dyed, and rendered supple enough for basketry.

With the variety of materials went a variety of techniques. Coiling, plaiting and twining were combined with a truly marvellous repertoire of designs. The latter were geometrical, or human, or based on nature. Often the basket would be finished off with bells, feathers, shells, buckskin fringes, beadwork and quill-work, or with other decorative devices. The rich and riotous imagination of the Indian, his deep and inexhaustible inner life, found striking expression in his basketwork. Fine baskets are still made by the peoples of the pueblos, by the Apache and Navajo, and particularly by the Pima and Papago of Arizona. Such baskets are expensive, since they require much time and effort to make. Today they are largely made for the

83 *A large, flat basket made by the Pima, with a typical maze design. The basket is of devil's claw fibre and split cattail stems, and is stitched with willow.*

197

pleasure of artistic expression, for museums, and for the more discerning tourist. If a Pima or Papago needs a container for his own use, it is now simpler for him to buy one of metal, at the shop. The classic baskets belong to an era when mankind, including the Indian, generally paid more regard to the meaning and quality of the things it used than it does today.

In basketry, coiling and twining were the favoured methods of the West and Southwest, and plaiting of the East. In pottery, there was a similar differentiation in technique. The people of the West and Southwest made their pots by coiling successive clay sausages one on top of the other, while the people of the East and Southeast smoothed the clay on the outside or inside of a pot that served as a mould. The potter's wheel was unknown. Pottery was not as universally distributed as basketry, and there were many areas – including the whole of California and the Northwest – where pots were not made and only baskets were employed.

In the main pottery regions of the Southwest and the eastern half of the continent, the same basic shapes and designs were used. The forms of Indian pottery were somewhat more conservative than the forms of basketry. It was in decoration rather than shape that the Indian potter came into his own, although the Hopewell, Mississippi, and Death Cult peoples fashioned human and animal figurines, as do the Pueblo people today. Decoration was painted and incised with stone and bone tools, or impressed with fingers, cords, and wooden stamps and dies. The conventional shapes of the pots were redeemed by their sumptuous colours: white, brown, red, and yellow, applied with a brush, rag or scrap of fur. The colouring was put on as a liquid slip, before firing, either as a single colour or in combination. There was also a lustrous black, produced by the carbons of a closed and damped-down fire. After firing, the choicer pots were buffed with a stone or bone rubber, or wiped with a moist cloth to produce a satin finish. Sometimes specks of mica or coloured sand were mixed with the clay to impart a scintillating effect.

The best pottery made by the Indian today emanates from the Southwest. As with other Indian handicrafts, it owes its pre-eminence to the birth of an interest in Indian art which has occurred in the past half-century. Not all Southwestern pueblos make pots. Some have abandoned the craft entirely, while some have decided to concentrate on the more lucrative trade of jewelry, and others make only rough-and-ready pots for domestic use. The choicest pots are the product of the pueblos of San Ildefonso, Santa Clara, San Juan, Ácoma, and Zia. It was at San Ildefonso, in 1919, that the great potters María and Júlian Martínez introduced the famous ware in which designs in matte black paint were applied to a polished black surface. Júlian Martínez, indeed, broke

198

84 *Papago women making pots. The Papago are the neighbours of the Pima in Southern Arizona, and both are lineal descendants of the ancient Hohokam.*

radically with tradition, which had hitherto decreed that only women should make pots. Twelve years later, Rosalie Aguilar, of the same pueblo, began to fashion the equally famous carved ware. Among the other Southwestern peoples who have maintained or revived their original interest in pottery, the Hopi produce excellent pots on a restricted scale, and the Maricopa make striking bowls and high-necked jars with a brilliant blood-red finish.

In 1900, a woman of genius called Nampeyo began to make Hopi wares based on prehistoric Hopi originals; but the modern Hopi are renowned for their Kachina dolls more than for pottery or silverwork. The art of carving Kachinas, from blocks of cottonwood root ranging from three to 18 inches long, is not an ancient one. It was invented only a scant century ago, and its purpose was to assist Hopi children to memorize the appearance and characteristics of their 250 gods and goddesses. But if the dolls themselves are not ancient, the sacred spirits, who dwell on a mountain range in northern Arizona, and visit the Hopi villages every winter, most assuredly are. The village of Oraibi, indeed, on the Hopi Third Mesa, is probably the oldest continuously inhabited site in the whole United States. The

Kachinas are painted with a white kaolin undercoat, topped with gaudy poster paints, and tricked out with multicoloured feathers. Their arms, legs, heads and headdresses, weapons and implements, are carved separately and cunningly glued on, and the little figures are exquisite examples of the miniaturist's art. Since they are merely models, not cult objects, the non-Indian need not feel that there is something obliquely irreverent in buying them. They are charming portraits of the gods, or of the dancers who in the solemn festivals will represent them.

85 *Hopi Kachinas.*

200

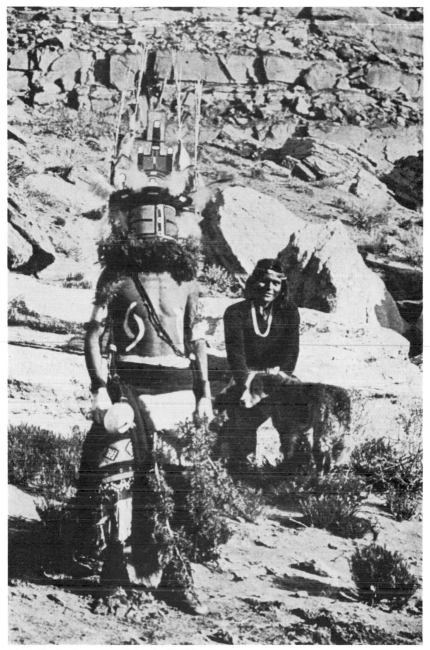

86 *A Hopi priest costumed for the Kachina Dance.*

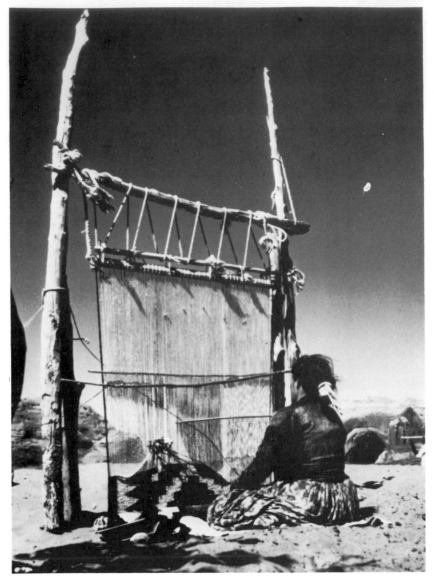

87 *A Navajo woman sits on the red earth outside her hogan and works at her large loom. (She has a small loom indoors.)*

There are fewer than 6000 Hopi, and the most remarkable Pueblo art comes from a half-dozen pueblos that contain fewer than 5000 souls between them. By far the most numerous Indian people in the Southwest today, and in Indian America, are the Navajo, who total more than 80,000. They are passable basketmakers, indifferent potters, and outstanding silversmiths; but an art which in recent centuries they have made peculiarly their own is that of weaving.

Weaving was known in North America in prehistoric times. The Adena-Hopewell people were making textiles 2000 years ago, to be followed only a little later by the Indians of California and the Plains. These textiles, however, were made by hand, not on the loom. The techniques employed were knitting, crocheting, looping, netting, plaiting, twining, and other purely manual methods. The masters of hand-weaving were undoubtedly the Indians of the Pacific Northwest, particularly the Chilkat of the extreme north, on the Canadian-Alaskan border. The Chilkat, a branch of the Tlingit, made ceremonial shirts and blankets from a mixture of shredded cedar bark and mountain goat's wool, dyed white, yellow, blue, and black. These are greatly coveted by folk-art collectors. Like the Salish of northern California, who also made notable blankets, the Chilkat eventually hit upon a rudimentary, hand-operated weaving-frame.

88 *A Navajo rug.*

89 *A Walapai woman of the California-Arizona border in her intricately decorated blanket.*

The true loom came into operation only in the Southwest. There, the Hopi became accomplished weavers, and some weaving was performed in the pueblos: but it was the Navajo who, beginning with a simple belt loom supported at one end around the weaver's waist, and at the other around a tree or house-pole, graduated to the complex vertical loom. The vertical loom may have been actually invented in the American Southwest. Originally, vegetable fibre and animal hair was employed; then came the use of cotton yarns; and from 1600 onwards the fleece of the herds of sheep brought to New Mexico by the Spanish pioneers became available. Today the Navajo, who acquired the art of weaving from the Pueblo people about 1700, have become its chief native practitioners, manufacturing blankets of daring colour and design in a score of locations on their vast tribal reservation. Chinle, Nazlini, Klagetoh, Teec Nos Pos, Lukachukai, Ganado, Wide Ruins – these are among a score of places recognized as the homes of outstanding craftsmen.

Navajo weaving is done by women. Another art in which the Navajo are pre-eminent – sand-painting – is the prerogative of the male. It falls within the province of the medicine-man, since sand-paintings possess not only a

90 *The tools and ingredients of a Navajo sand-painting.*

religious but a curative purpose. The sick person is bidden to sit upon the ground and, while chanting and prayers are offered up, the medicine-man creates the sand-painting around his patient. As the painting progresses, the sufferer's ill humours are absorbed into it, and the gods whose figures are incorporated in it exert their healing influences. Then, at the moment of sunset, the whole painstaking design is effaced, the sickness departing with it. Sand-painting – which is practised by the Navajo, the Papago, the Apache, and the people of the Pueblos – is a somewhat misleading word. Only the background of the painting is composed of sand, and instead of formal painting, with a brush, the colours are actually powdered minerals, plants, charcoal, cornmeal, and pollen that are applied by trickling them onto the sand through the fingers. The process requires precision, patience, and an exceptional memory, for it is obligatory to reproduce the complex traditional patterns entirely spontaneously, without a pattern or model.

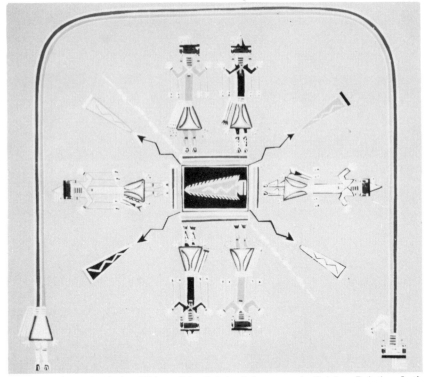

91 *A Navajo sand-painting. This traditional design is known as the Rainbow Painting. In the middle, the Messenger Fly, an invisible and all-knowing god, stands inside a hogan, around which are grouped the Rainbow People and the Talking God standing next to the cornstalks. The whole design is surrounded by a rainbow, emblem of rain and fertility.*

Painting

In painting, as in jewelry, basketry and pottery, the Southwest has led the way in the Indian Renaissance of recent years. One reason for its primacy might be that the Southwest was fortunate in escaping the obliteration that was the fate of the peoples of the East and West coasts, and the wholesale removals of the Plains and the Southeast. The Southwesterners have been exposed to humiliation and poverty, and to periods of bitter exile: but in the main they have remained on their ancestral lands, and have experienced a sense of continuity.

As a nation, the United States is abundant in artists of all kinds: yet it is so enormous, and there is so little contact between its cultural centres, that first-rate artists can flourish without their existence being suspected in distant New York or Los Angeles. The latter cities do not serve as easily accessible foci of the country's artistic activity, as do London, Paris, or Rome. For this reason, the presence of an altogether exceptional school of Indian artists in the American Southwest has, while not being completely ignored, failed to make an impact commensurate with its talents. In a smaller country, it would have gained instant and lasting recognition. For over half a century, the painters of the Southwest have been creating superlative work, of an altogether original character. In the same way that there is a deepening interest in Indian literature, so the influence of Indian art must inevitably flow, sooner or later, into the mainstream of American art, and supply a fresh tone.

Soon after the First World War, a small number of white artists, scholars and residents of Santa Fé and its environs launched what came to be known as the Santa Fé Movement. They were determined to make the world aware of the Indian's artistic potential. As a result of their enthusiasm, the Indian Art Fund came into existence in 1923, exhibitions were promoted, and gradually Santa Fé became one of the more vital centres of American artistic endeavour for white and Indian artist alike.

Amazingly, the cradle of modern Indian art was San Ildefonso – the little pueblo where María and Júlian Martínez had embarked on their career as potters at precisely this time. Even today, San Ildefonso is one of the smallest of the pueblos, with a population of only 300. More amazing still, María Martínez's brother-in-law, Crescencio Martínez, is regarded as the founding figure of the Indian movement. Crescencio, or 'Home of the Elk', was one of several young men who, at the turn of the century, had begun to experiment with the white man's water-colours. Then, about 1910, he entered on a period of intense productivity that brought him to the excited attention of the founders of the Santa Fé Movement. Unfortunately, he died young, in 1918, a victim of the Spanish influenza epidemic; but his example remained. His comrades in San Ildefonso continued working, to such effect that there were soon 20 practising painters, in addition to a host of potters, in that tiny Athens on the Rio Grande.

The ripples made by these artists spread until the other pueblos, and ultimately the neighbouring Navajo and Apache, were caught up in the fever of creativity. At San Ildefonso itself, Crescencio's nephew, Awa Tsireh (Alfonso Roybal), the son of a distinguished potter, who had Navajo blood in his veins, became an outstanding painter. Other gifted men and women who took part in the great surge of energy during the 1920s and 1930s included Chiu-Tah and Eva Mirabal at Taos, Ma-Pe-Wi at Zia, Rufina Vigil at Tesuque, To-Pove at San Juan, and Fred Kabotie among the Hopi. Simultaneously, the Navajo, with their penchant for adapting any ideas that reached them from outside sources, produced an entire company of remarkable painters, of whom Keats Begay, Sybil Yazzie, Ha-So-De, Quincy Tahoma and Ned Notah were only the most prominent. As for the Apache, one should note the important name of Allan Houser. And as if all these developments were not enough, at this same period the Kiowa, again at the prompting of white sponsors, started up a school of their own on the neighbouring Plains. Their founding father is considered to be George Keahbone, while in Oscar Howe the Sioux produced an artist whose influence would be felt on the entire Indian movement.

Today, the Indian art movement represents one of the most vigorous branches on the tree of American sculpture and painting. What are its characteristics? How may one best describe it? At first, Indian artists stayed close to the formalized, abstract, or semi-abstract motifs that were familiar to them from their work with leather, beads, quills, and pottery. With their new-found interest in their own past, they began to re-examine the magnificent geometrical designs on their ancient pottery, discovering many new points of departure. They then turned to such novelties as the realism and perspective that existed in the white man's art, seeking a way to bend them to their own purposes. Their solution was to combine realistic figures and stylized natural motifs in a spatially flattened, two-dimensional manner, not unlike, again, the art of the Ancient Egyptians. They used bright, clear, translucent colours, often the primary colours alone, retaining their own individual systems of colour symbolism. Thus, while an Indian painting presents what seems to be merely a decorative surface to the eye of the white viewer, it imparts a totally different and more profound message to the eye of the Indian.

There is nothing sombre about the Indian palette. There is no shadow or chiaroscuro. All is clean and vibrant, with an atmosphere of space, freedom, and distance. Indian art is permeated with a feeling of the great

American landscape, and when one studies it one comes to realize how dark and claustrophobic much European art seems in comparison. It might perhaps be compared, if only in mood, to the joyous *plein air* canvases of the Impressionists. Moreover, the Indian artist has sacrificed nothing of the spiritual quality of his work. Its apparent naivete is misleading: the old religious values are still there.

In recent decades, Indian artists have successfully experimented with the abstract mode, fusing it with the abstract motifs present in their basketry and pottery, and with the abstract shapes of their religious symbols. They have also taken to sculpture, and have manifested an ability to paint extended and integrated murals that demonstrates that there is no medium or genre to which they will not aspire in the future, and to which they will not bring their own unique vision.

It would seem, therefore, that although the traditional handicrafts have tended, with some very important exceptions, to go into a decline, the artistic abilities of the North American Indian have suffered no diminution, but have begun to manifest new ambitions and new outlets. As the Indian peoples advance with fresh hope and vigour into the twenty-first century, one can expect to find that not only individual artists, but the spirit and outlook of Indian life as a whole, will demand increasing attention. In turn, it will inject into the art and culture of the white man something of its own special character.

7

The Reservation

The earliest significant contacts between Indian and European took place in the first half of the sixteenth century. In 1534, Jacques Cartier sailed down the St Lawrence; in 1539, Hernán de Soto claimed Florida for Spain; in 1540, Francisco Vázquez de Coronado entered the Southwest. Thereafter the pace of European intrusion steadily quickened. The first – unsuccessful – English colony was established at Roanoke in 1585; Juan de Oñate settled in New Mexico in 1598; the Jamestown colony was planted in 1607; Quebec was established in 1608; the Plymouth Pilgrims landed in 1620; and in 1626 the Dutch governor of the New Netherlands bought Manhattan island for $24.

Because of the size of the continent, and the small number of the European colonists, the Indian did not feel threatened by the white man or begin to resent his presence for another century. Until the mid-1700s, most Indians did not know the European existed, or had only heard rumours about him. Relations were generally friendly, and although there was friction, this was mitigated by the fact that there appeared to be plenty of elbow-room for everybody.

Until the time of the American Revolution it seemed to the Indian that, if the necessity arose, the white man could be contained, in spite of his horses and muskets. There were times when it actually appeared that he had fixed a limit to his territorial demands. In 1763, King George III decreed that his subjects were under no circumstances to encroach upon the lands beyond the Appalachians; and although Indian fears had been aroused by the extent of European penetration in the East, by 1776 the white man had advanced no further than the Ohio River. At that natural boundary-line he could surely be held.

In the Southeast, on the eve of the Revolution, European influence was restricted to the coastline of Florida, Louisiana, and to a few small blockhouses inland. In the Southwest, the Spanish colonists on the Rio

Grande had at one time been driven back into Mexico by the Pueblo Revolt of 1680, and their colony in Arizona had foundered because of Indian hostility; while on the Pacific coast the Europeans were represented by nothing more than a few mild and peaceful religious missions. Throughout most of the eighteenth century, the Indian was not confronted by the European as an enemy, but courted as an ally. Some tribes fought with the English against the French, others with the French against the English. They were richly rewarded. They were encouraged to take booty, their chiefs were given the rank of colonel or brigadier-general in the white man's armies and were awarded medals, decorations, and pensions. Indian leaders were taken to London and Paris to be fêted and flattered, and were presented to the kings of England and France. When the Europeans were so fond of making war on each other, and when their divisions could be so profitably exploited, where was the danger to the Indian?

With the birth of the American Republic, the picture changed. The white man was no longer a colonist; he was a citizen of a vigorous, confident, aggressive young nation. He was united, he was single-minded, he had closed his ranks. He would endure vicissitudes and set-backs, such as the War of 1812 and the Civil War: but his strength, numbers, and resources had now swelled to an extent that the Indian could not challenge him. And with the growth of his numbers, he needed Indian land. The Indian might try to resist him, and might even score some sporadic successes: but the end of the issue was now never seriously in doubt.

For the Indian, the past two centuries have been a period of unparalleled turmoil. They have been an epoch of torment from which he has hardly yet begun to emerge, and of which he will always bear the scars. His pride and his power were broken. He was herded off his immemorial ranges and penned up in alien territories. From being the lord and the master of all he looked upon, he sank to a condition more pitiable than that of the meanest slave. When the black man was being granted his freedom, the enslavement of the red man was just beginning.

The story of the Indian's decline is involved and hard to disentangle. Largely it was the result, as all human affairs are in the final melancholy analysis, of battle and bloodshed. Treachery and massacre played their roles, as did famine and pestilence. Yet active warfare was only a part, if the largest part, of the sequence of events. The Indian tragedy was also shot through with attempts at passive resistance, legal manoeuvring, diplomatic forays, and frustrated alliances. Peace was tried, as well as war. Between 1778, when the Delaware signed a treaty with the United States that dangled before them the prospect of statehood, until 1868, when the United States sealed a pact with the Nez Perce, the Indians ratified no fewer than

370 separate agreements with the United States, all of them dishonoured and discarded. The Indian today refers to his 'Trail of Broken Treaties'.

By chicanery, sickness, and warfare the Indian's hold on his continent was eroded. He was no match for his opponent in negotiation or in military skill. Yet, as always, the fault did not lie exclusively on one side. The Indian too could ignore treaties, murder women and children, and torture prisoners. Many Indians collaborated with the white man. Some did so sincerely, trusting the white man's word, believing that the white man's civilization was superior to his own, or reckoning that the Indian's only chance of survival lay in submission. Other Indians were quislings. They collaborated for money, sold off their tribal lands for personal gain, and sought the white man's support in internal power-struggles. It was not the white man alone who could behave dishonourably: and it should be recorded that, at every stage of the dismal saga, there were white statesmen, soldiers, writers and churchmen, even some white settlers, who struggled against the ghastly train of events. They were not many, not as many as there ought to have been, and certainly not enough to resist the tide of greed and hysteria; but they raised up their voices and they should not be forgotten.

From the outset, it was the settler who did most of the damage. Always the key factor was the pressure the people on the frontier could bring to bear on the central authorities. They had newspapers, they had their own rascally and fanatical politicians, and above all they had votes. (The Indian did not become a United States citizen until 1924, and was not finally enfranchised until 1948.) The government, while it usually professed humane sentiments, and on a few occasions acted on them, was too weak and cowardly to withstand the clamour of such a vocal group. And, to be fair, the members of the government, unlike the settlers, were engaged with more problems than the Indian problem alone.

Until the advent of Andrew Jackson, a certain decency in government was usually in evidence. George Washington, who as a young man had taken part in Indian wars, and had been a friend of the Seneca chiefs, acted in his habitually straightforward and sensible way. Jefferson, on the other hand, was a disappointment. With regard to Indian affairs there was a distinct gap between his liberal professions and his behaviour in office, between what he put down on paper and what he did in practice. He was the originator of the removal programme, and in the words of the author of *The Removal of the Choctaw Indians*, he invited those dealing officially with the Indians 'to practise fraud and intimidation, and his ideas implied a human cattle drive'.

So strongly had Jefferson implanted the notion of removal that, in the

212

fiercely nationalistic aftermath of the War of 1812, it was impossible to eliminate or soften it. It is greatly to the credit of John C. Calhoun, President Monroe's young Secretary of War, that he strove for eight years, between 1817 and 1825, to resist the frontiersmen and their demagogic representatives. While realizing that drastic measures would be forced on him, he sought to delay them, and when delay proved impossible, to implement them in a humane manner. It was Calhoun who, in 1824, established the Bureau of Indian Affairs and placed at its head Superintendent Thomas B. McKenney. Between 1824 and 1830, the Board attempted to implement Calhoun's enlightened policies: but all efforts at fair dealing were brought to an end by Jackson's accession to the presidency in 1830. Jackson, belligerent by nature, had already behaved with notable cruelty towards the Indian during his years as a general. In office, where he became the begetter of cronyism and the spoils system, it was inevitable that he would deliver the Indian over to land-sharks, bullies, and exploiters. In 1830, he enacted the Indian Removal Act, which decreed the instant removal of the Indian to the Trans-Mississippi West. From that date until 1890, with a brief remission during the Civil War, the worst elements in politics and in the army brought the destruction of the Indian to a rapid and remorseless conclusion.

The European Conquest

The simplest way to present the near-elimination of the Indian is in terms of the culture areas with which we have already become familiar. The Indian was extinguished successively in one of these areas after another, as the white man set up his rule. First the Northeast and its Atlantic seaboard were the cockpit of the Indian-European confrontation; then the Great Lakes and the North; then the Southeast and Florida; then California, the Northwest coast, and the Great Basin; and finally the Plains. These were the steps by which the white man conquered each region, consolidated his grip, and either exterminated its inhabitants or relegated them to strips of inhospitable terrain.

As we saw, it was in the Northeast that the European planted his first colonies. To begin with, the colonists were vulnerable, starved for resources, and intimidated by the scale of the country. It was the Indian who provided them with stores of food, clothing and materials. Squanto, one of the chiefs of the Wampanoag, helped the Pilgrim Fathers to weather their first harsh winter. Pocahontas, daughter of Powhatan, paramount chief of 34 Algonquin tribes, twice rescued the rambunctious freebooter Captain John Smith from execution. She married the Virginia planter John

213

C. Smith taketh the King of Pamavnkee prifoner. - 16 o 8.

92 Captain John Smith personally takes prisoner, in 1608, a chief of the Pamunkey, a tribe of the Powhatan Confederacy.

93 *Indians attack an early colonial settlement.*

Rolfe, became a Christian, and died of smallpox at Gravesend in England, in 1617, at the age of 22.

Pocahontas, like La Malinche, the Mexican consort of Hernán Cortés, acted as an intermediary between her own people and the Europeans. And like La Malinche, she was unable to avert the inevitable clash between the Indian and the interloper. With the death of Powhatan, in 1618, his brother Opechancanough, a fierce old man who secretly hated the colonists, organized the first of the Indian wars. In March, 1622, the Indians suddenly massacred 300 of the settlers, who later retaliated by murdering the Indian chiefs they invited to a peace conference. Then, for 22 years, there was an uneasy peace, until Opechancanough, now nearly 100, incited a second rising in which 500 whites were slaughtered. They struck back, annihilating the Indians in their turn.

Further to the north, during the Pequot War of 1637, the colonists had begun the tactic of inciting one Indian people to attack another. With the help of the Mohegan and the Narragansett, the colonists put the greater part of the Pequot to the sword, the rest being sent to Bermuda as slaves. They were the first of more than 400 tribes who were to disappear in the next 250 years.

For 30 years, hostilities in the Northeast were sporadic, until the outbreak, in January 1675, of the so-called 'King Philip's War'. In this conflict, Metacomet, chief of the Wampanoag, whom the New Englanders called 'King Philip', sought to drive the colonists into the sea. The Narragansetts sided with the Wampanoag, and were defeated with them at the battle of Kingston in Rhode Island the next year. King Philip was captured and beheaded. The Mohegan again sided with the colonists, though their disloyalty to their own kind would eventually do them no good. New England had been effectively cleared of Indians, and today only a small cluster of the original inhabitants still exist.

From the Northeast, the battleground shifted northward, to the region of the Great Lakes and the Ohio and Illinois valleys. Here lived the most populous and most warlike concentration of Indians in North America. It was here, between 1750 and 1830, that the cardinal clashes between Red Man and White Man would occur, and where the issue was effectually decided.

Unfortunately for the Indian, his position in this area had already been weakened by an ugly prelude to the struggle that lay ahead. Between 1630 and 1675, the Iroquois Confederacy, or the Five Nations (Mohawk, Seneca, Oneida, Cayuga, Onondaga, and later the Tuscarora), had carved out a place for themselves on the Hudson River by savagely subduing their Algonquian neighbours. In doing so, they had undermined what might later have been the nucleus of a more united and spirited resistance to the French, English, and Americans. Worse still, when the Indians picked sides with one or other of the European nations, seeking to ingratiate themselves with the power they judged most likely to become dominant, some of the tribes were bound to make the wrong choice. Thus while the Iroquois, Seneca and Mohawk declared for England, the Ottawa, Ojibway,

94 *Pontiac, the Great Chief of the Ottawa. Portrait attributed to John Mix Stanley, a one-time resident of Detroit.*

217

Delaware, Shawnee, Miami, Sac, Chippewa, Huron, Potawatomie and other tribes opted for the French. The French lost, and their Indian allies suffered the consequences. Then, after Wolfe had beaten Montcalm at Quebec, and the French had signed the Treaty of Paris, it seemed logical for many tribes to shift their allegiance to the victorious English, in the coming clash with the rebellious Americans. Even the eloquent and intrepid Ottawa chief, Pontiac, who had sensed the true pattern of things to come, and who had sought for two years to unite the Indians against the European incursion while there was still time, was finally compelled, after capturing nine English forts, to ally himself with England, before dying by an assassin's hand.

In Joseph Brant, the Mohawk war-chief, whose Indian name was Thayendanegea, the English gained the services of a soldier and leader of the first order. Intelligent, English educated and trained, he proved a steadfast and resolute partisan. He mobilized and held together for England the ranks of the Five Nations, the Oneida alone abstaining. Twice he visited England to meet George III, to have his portrait painted by Romney, and to consult with the English authorities. While still in his mid-thirties, he headed an army partly composed of English regulars. He won a string of battles; and when the end came, after the battle of Johnstown, he took his people to Canada, vowing to play his part if the English ever undertook an invasion of the infant Republic. He died in Ontario, in 1807 at the age of 65, on land deeded to him by the English crown.

When the War of Independence ended, the fathers of the young Republic, who had been compelled to detach troops from the main battle at critical moments to combat the threat from the Indian, were in no mood to be benevolent. Their tempers were even more sorely tried when, in 1793, the Miami of Ohio, under chief Michikimkiva or Little Turtle, ambushed an American column and killed 900 men. It took an army of 3000 soldiers, under General 'Mad Anthony' Wayne, to catch up with them and defeat them two years later, at the battle of the Fallen Timber.

Even then, the Republic's troubles in the Ohio valley were not over. In their extremity, the Indians of that area had thrown up a commanding personality who outshone even Pontiac and Joseph Brant, and who made his influence felt far beyond his homeland. The Shawnee chief Tecumseh, or Shooting Star, almost single-handedly, by sheer force of character, nearly achieved the Indian dream of halting the white man's progress by forming a united front. Tecumseh envisaged the creation of a single Indian nation, concentrated in an independent buffer area between Canada in the north and the United States in the south, recognized and guaranteed by

218

both powers. He negotiated with the Canadians and Americans, and between 1808 and 1811 he made a series of protracted journeys that carried him among the Ottawa, Delaware, Wyandot, Ojibway, Kickapoo, and other northern tribes, and among the Creek, Choctaw, and Chickasaw, far to the southeast. If the English had had more foresight, and the Americans had acted in good faith, or if Tecumseh's Indian coalition had shown better cohesion, Tecumseh might just possibly have created a third independent

95 *Tecumseh, the warrior-statesman of the Shawnee, in the uniform of a British Officer, and wearing a British decoration. His red cap is ornamented with porcupine quills and a black eagle feather.*

nation on the soil of North America. In the circumstances, the likelihood was never more than remote: but that does not detract from the towering quality of his conception, or from the honourable nature of his failure. Tricked by the Americans, he was defeated at the battle of Tippecanoe in 1811. He died in the War of 1812, fighting as an English brigadier-general at the battle of the Thames, in Ontario. He was 45.

Tecumseh's dream died with him. One of his lieutenants, Black Hawk,

96 *A painted and tattooed chief of the Seminole of Florida, one of the Five Civilized Tribes. He carries the characteristic tall bow of the region.*

leader of the Sauk and the Fox, tried to keep what remained of Tecumsch's confederacy alive in Illinois and Wisconsin. At the battle of Wisconsin Heights, in 1832, he was eventually trounced, captured, and delivered up in chains by Lieutenant Jefferson Davis to General Winfield Scott. Many members of the Middle Western tribes, such as the Delaware, Potawatomie, and Kaskaskia, had long since seen the storm approaching, and had already given up their lands and moved across the Mississippi, in an attempt to get away from the white man.

Increasingly secure on its northern and northwestern frontiers, the United States could now bestow its attention on the next of the major areas – the South and the Southeast. It had little to fear from the two principal tribes of that area, the Cherokee of Tennessee and the Choctaw of Mississippi and Alabama. These powerful peoples had generally striven to maintain peaceful relations with their white neighbours. The initial United States target was therefore two warlike tribes in the distant South, the Creek of Louisiana, and the Seminole of Florida.

For most of the eighteenth century, the Creek and Seminole had got along excellently with the Spanish, and particularly with the French, who more than any other of the colonial powers had known how to ride the Indian on a light rein. The Creeks, though agricultural, were a restless people. Their blood was mingled with that of the European traders and adventurers who had been present in the area for 300 years. Three of their principal chiefs, Alexander McGillivray, William Weatherford, and William McIntosh, had Scottish fathers and Indian mothers. McGillivray was a colourful character who became successively an English colonel, a Spanish administrator, and a United States brigadier-general. McIntosh had also sided with the Americans. Weatherford, however, was irreconcilable. In August 1813, he precipitated the Creek War by slaying 500 settlers in a fortified plantation on the Alabama river. Down came Andrew Jackson to avenge this cowardly atrocity; but it was twelve months before he managed to bring Weatherford to bay at the battle of Horseshoe Bend with a force of more than 5000 men. He then confiscated and handed over to American settlers, including many of his own friends, more than half the territory of the Creeks – 23 million acres.

Although Florida was officially annexed by the United States in 1821, warfare between the Seminole and the Americans did not break out until 1832. The precipitating factor was the Treaty of Payne's Landing, whereby the Seminole agreed to be removed to Oklahoma, together with the Creek, in return for a lump sum of $15,000 – of which $7000 was immediately to be paid to the white settlers for 'damages'. The bulk of the Seminole refused to

97 *Osceola, the gallant young Creek who led the Seminole Resistance in Florida. Painted by George Catlin during his captivity in Fort Moultrie, South Carolina, shortly before his death.*

222

accept the treaty and took to the warpath, under the leadership of an energetic and gifted young warrior, Osceola. Osceola, who had both Creek and European blood, was only 30, and was not a chief; but for two years, between 1835 and 1838, he led his adversaries a dance in the swamps and bayous of his homeland. On Christmas Eve 1835, his braves wiped out a white column, killing an American general and four of his officers. Osceola, a handsome, romantic figure, was eventually captured by General Jessup, whom he had previously defeated, when he came in to parley under a flag of truce. Jessup clapped him and his companions in irons.

Osceola died in prison three months later, but Seminole resistance was undiminished. General Zachary Taylor suffered heavy casualties in securing a precarious victory, and his opponents were only dragged out of the marshes and into captivity in the fall of 1841. Most of them were immediately despatched to Oklahoma.

Ironically, the Choctaw chief Pushmataha and 700 Choctaw warriors had fought under the command of General Claiborne against the Creek. They then enlisted under General Jackson and distinguished themselves against the English at the battle of New Orleans. The Cherokee, their northern neighbours, had also waged war against the Creek, and had fought with Jackson at the battle of Horeshoe Bend.

Excellent fighters, the Choctaw and Cherokee, unlike the lawless and marauding Creek, had become men of peace. They wanted to prove to the white man that, given the opportunity, and if left to themselves, they could make a productive contribution to North American society. They were, after all, 'Civilized Tribes'. Agricultural by tradition, they had taken advantage of the white man's example, and had become expert farmers and husbandmen. They owned immense herds of cattle and horses. They had long given up living in tipis, and dwelt in solid frame houses. They built roads, schools, and churches. As a result of Sequoya's invention of the alphabet, most of the Cherokee were literate; they had their own newspaper, *The Phoenix*. In 1819, the Cherokee elected as the President of their National Council the great John Ross, a blue-eyed young man whose father had been a Scots immigrant, and who had been brought up by the Indians under the name of Tsan-Usdi, Little John. In 1826, he inspired the formation of a duly constituted Cherokee Nation, with a capital at New Echota, Georgia. In 1828, he was invested with the title of Principal Chief.

The Choctaw and Cherokee were intelligent, adaptable, and advanced. Their destruction was perhaps the worst crime to be laid at the door of the white frontiersman. Their fate had long been determined. As early as the first decade of the nineteenth century, their removal westward had been

98 *John Ross, the Principal Chief of the Cherokee Nation, and a survivor of the 'Trail of Tears'. A photograph taken in 1858 when he was on an official visit to Washington DC as the leader of the United Cherokees.*

urged. Under the implacable Jackson, whom John Quincy Adams used to refer to as 'the barbarian', the policy was implemented. Between 1831 and 1834, two-thirds of the Choctaw nation, together with their neighbours, the Chickasaw, were carted and shipped westwards to 'Indian Territory'. Their individual compensation was a blanket and 13 dollars.

In 1838, General Winfield Scott and 7000 soldiers descended on the Cherokee and drove them into stockades, preparatory to escorting them west. They were only released when John Ross, realizing that his legal struggle with the American government was hopeless, begged to be allowed to lead them himself. In the winter of 1838, 15,000 Cherokee prepared to follow the Choctaw to 'Indian Territory'. 4000 of the emigrants died on the six-month trek, among them John Ross's wife. To this day, the episode is known to the Cherokee as *Nuna-da-ut-sun'y*, 'The Trail Where They Cried', or 'The Trail of Tears'. Such was their leader's character, that even a succession of such terrible events failed to break them. In Oklahoma, Ross gathered the remnants of his people around him, re-founding the Cherokee

Nation with a fresh constitution, and with a new capital at Tahlequah. He died in 1866, in Washington, during the course of one of his many attempts to persuade an obdurate government, now more than ever resolved to eliminate the Indian, to behave with some degree of justice and generosity.

While the Indians of the eastern United States had been locked for 300 years in an unremitting contest with the European, those of the West had so far remained relatively untouched. During the Spanish occupation of the Southwest and California, which lasted until 1819, the number of European settlers, priests and soldiers had been diminutive, and the actual area they farmed, occupied or administered around the Spanish towns and missions was similarly restricted. Between 1819 and 1848, when the same area was under Mexican rule, the same conditions applied. The Mexican was spread so thinly as to be virtually insignificant; and although the Mission Indian, as he was called, was the victim of epidemics, and a certain amount of sporadic brutality, most Western Indians, living far from the white occupied territories, were hardly troubled at all. The majority were probably unaware that the intruder existed, and many tribes regarded the white man's presence as positively beneficial, both spiritually and materially.

Estimates of the original Indian population of the East coast vary widely. There seem to have been at least 250 tribes, grouped into a score of small nations. They spoke more than 100 distinct dialects. It seems unbelievable, but within 20 years of the arrival of the white American, practically all of them had disappeared: hanged, shot, poisoned, tracked down by professional hunters with dogs, deliberately starved, or decimated by deportation.

This chapter of mass murder began in 1848. In that year, following the Treaty of Guadalupe Hidalgo, the United States, 43,000 of whose troops were occupying Mexico City, acquired all of Mexico lying north of the Rio Grande. For this slice of territory, larger than the whole of Europe, the United States paid Mexico the sum of 15 million dollars.

Only a year later, the Gold Rush began. Such was the rush of speculators, criminals, opportunists, desperadoes, and people who had been pitiful failures in the East into the new territories, that within three years the white man far outnumbered the Indian. In a single year alone, 100,000 immigrants descended on California, to make a hell out of what until then had been something of a Garden of Eden. Of the villainous acts of those early settlers and miners it is best not to speak. Readers whose stomachs are strong enough to pursue the course of West coast history between 1850 and 1875 may consult the work of Sherburne F. Cook or Robert G. Cowen, as well as the classic little book of Theodora Kroeber referred to in the opening chapter.

White penetration of the Southwest was slower to materialize, but eventually the area received its own swarm of rapacious land-grabbers and gold and silver miners. Their effect was only a shade less lamentable. The Indian population was halved, or reduced by two-thirds, during the years 1850–1900. The larger Southwestern tribes, such as the Pima, Papago, Navajo, and the Pueblo peoples, kept themselves alive by dogged tenacity, or were otherwise so small and defenceless and lived in such arid areas that eventually the white man ceased persecuting them and mercifully forgot them. It was the warrior tribes of the Plains, mostly horsed, who challenged the white man militarily, and were broken in pieces for their pains.

The last stand of the American Indian, ending a way of life that had existed for 30,000 years, took place during the 1870s. The first of the four memorable Indian wars that broke out or reached their climax in that critical decade took place in the Southwest. Cochise, the venerable leader of the Chiricahua band of the Apache, had been holding out in the mountains for nine years. The other five groups of the Western Apache, including the bellicose Mescalero Apache, had already been suppressed and penned into makeshift reservations. At that time, the Apache did not possess, or deserve, an especially savoury reputation. But it is impossible not to admire the fight, against staggering odds, which they sustained for so long. Their resistance was the more amazing when one reflects that the Western Apache never numbered more than 5000 to 6000 men, women and children.

Cochise, a dignified and impressive chieftain, took to the warpath in 1861, after escaping with three bullets in his body from a parley with the Seventh Cavalry that was supposed to have been protected by a flag of truce. At first he acted in league with the legendary Mangas Coloradas, or Red Shirt, and together the two warriors almost won the battle of Apache Pass against 3000 American soldiers who had been sent from California to suppress them. Five months later, in January 1863, Mangas Coloradas was killed. He was enticed into negotiations, again under a flag of truce, arrested, tortured with red-hot bayonets, and shot 'while attempting to escape'.

It was not until more than eight years later, in September 1871, that a humane and just American general, George Crook, whom the Apache respected, and whom they called Grey Wolf, persuaded Cochise and his 200 warriors to make peace and enter the reservation. Even then, Apache resistance intermittently flared up. Between 1871 and 1886, successive Apache chiefs or warriors persuaded other members of their band to jump

99 *Chato, a leader of the Chiricahua Apache, one of the six tribes that made up the Apache nation. In March 1883, Chato led 26 Apache warriors through the American Southwest and Mexico, dodging 500 American and 4000 Mexican troops and travelling 120–160 kilometres (75–100 miles) a day. They killed twice their own number and lost only two men. His exploit was equalled and surpassed by other Apache leaders.*

227

100 *Quanah Parker, Comanche chieftain and leader of the Comanche, Apache and Kiowa in peace and war. A photograph taken in 1895.*

the reservation and go on the rampage. Some parties consisted of as many as 100 warriors, others of only a dozen. Large or small, they wrought fearful havoc. Victorio, Nana, Chato, Loco, and Ulzana, among others, performed feats without parallel in the annals of guerrilla warfare. The last Apache war-leader was Geronimo, who was not in fact a chief but a garrulous, vicious, half-mad tribal trouble-maker. The American army had to call back General Crook to deal with him and talk him into surrender. Crook was then promptly withdrawn, and the 500 remaining Chiricahua Apache were shipped off, the innocent with the guilty, in a sealed train to prison-camps in Florida and Alabama. There, in the course of the next 20 years, most of them died of homesickness and despair. Only in 1913 were 200 of them permitted to crawl back to their native mountains.

Even so, the Apache fared better than the Comanche, who spearheaded the second insurrection of the 1870s. Today the Comanche survive as only an insignificant remnant of a once spectacular tribe. In 1874, 30-year-old Quanah Parker, the fiery young chief of the Kwahadi Comanche, the son of a Comanche father and a white mother, led 700 Comanche, Kiowa and Cheyenne against a band of 30 white buffalo hunters holed up at a post called Adobe Walls, on the Staked Plains. The battle raged for three days, but the Indians were unable to storm the post in the face of the buffalo hunters' big-bore guns, and could kill only three of them. On the surface, the incident would seem to bear some resemblance to the kind of spontaneous, maverick Indian raid which was satirized in the first paragraph of this book. In fact, Parker's purpose was serious, although it proved abortive. In 1867, under the terms of the Medicine Lodge Treaty, the principal tribes of the southern Plains had been granted reservations which were supposed to be inviolate, and where they could hunt the buffalo, on which their existence depended, undisturbed. Instead, the white buffalo hunter, who was a callous ruffian of the same stripe as the California gold-seeker, poured onto the Plains, into territory guaranteed to the Indian, and totally destroyed the animal which for centuries the Indian had revered and worshipped. The white hunter eliminated the Plains buffalo in four years, between 1870 and 1874, the brief period when the eastern market for hides and tallow opened and as suddenly collapsed. In 1860 there were an estimated 100 million buffalo on the western Plains; in 1900 there were 1000. A single member of the riffraff who hunted them thought nothing of slaughtering 200 of them between sunup and sundown with his monstrous 'buffalo gun'.

After his unsuccessful action, Parker stayed on the Staked Plains until the following year, when he was rounded up by General Miles, George Crook's superior. Like the Apache, the Comanche were despatched by that brutal

101 *Red Cloud, the chief of the Oglala Sioux, who won his war against the United States. A photograph taken on the Pine Ridge Reservation in South Dakota, where he lived in a house built for him by the US Government. He carries his pipe, symbol of his authority.*

102 *Fort Laramie, on the Platte River, Nebraska, where Red Cloud signed his successful treaty which created the Great Sioux Reservation.*

103 *Tatanka Iyotake, Sitting Bull, chief of the Hunkpapa, a branch of the Teton or Western Sioux. The Sioux of the Sioux.*

officer to virtual extinction in Florida. The fate of the American Indian would increasingly resemble that of the American buffalo.

It was also in defence of their vital hunting-grounds that the Sioux and Cheyenne took up arms against the Americans on the northern Plains.

In 1865, Chief Red Cloud, of the Oglala Sioux, forcibly detained an army detachment sent to reconnoitre the Bozman Trail through Montana. When the army ignored the warning, and entered the Powder River country of Wyoming, the result was 'Red Cloud's War'. In 1866, a detachment of 80 soldiers was slaughtered outside Fort Kearney, and two years later, by the terms of the Treaty of Fort Laramie, the military authorities conceded the contest and agreed to remove their garrisons and dismantle their forts and posts. Red Cloud became the only Indian to win a war against the United States.

Nevertheless, his decision to make peace and retire to the newly-established Great Sioux Reservation in Nebraska infuriated many of his younger warriors. They refused to follow him on to the reservation. Under the spirited leadership of Crazy Horse, then aged no more than 19, they remained on their old hunting-grounds. In 1876, old General Crook was sent to coax them on to the reservation. They not only refused but, additionally infuriated by the depredations of miners in the Black Hills of Dakota, they cut off his supplies and attacked him at the Rosebud river. Crook, after a day's battering, retreated, and Crazy Horse took his 1200 Oglala Sioux and Cheyenne through to the valley of the Little Big Horn. There he joined forces with the main force of 3000 warriors, under the command of Sitting Bull, chief of the Hunkpapa Sioux.

Sitting Bull, who was in his middle forties, was an extraordinary personage. He was not only a chief and a warrior, but also a visionary and a medicine-man. A few days earlier, he had performed the Sun Dance, in order to obtain divine guidance, and his back and chest still bore the open wounds. He was too weak to take part in the coming battle, and had to remain in his lodge: but he was the strategist and the master-mind, leaving its actual conduct in the capable hands of Crazy Horse. The Sioux were fortunate in that their opponent was the glory-hunting General Custer, a mendacious and incompetent officer who had been suspended from duty for cruelty and misconduct. Notwithstanding, he had been reinstated by his patron, General Sheridan, now in charge of the War Department. Sheridan's own stated policy towards the Indian was that he should be exterminated. Before the battle of the Little Big Horn, on 25 June 1876, his protégé not only disregarded the instructions of his superiors, but in his contempt for his enemy made the elementary mistake of dividing his forces.

233

104 *Julius Meyer, a US Government agent, poses with a group of famous warriors of the Teton Dakota. Standing next to Meyer: Red Cloud (Oglala). Sitting, left to right: Sitting Bull (Hunkpapa); Swift Bear (Brulé); Spotted Tail (Brulé). A photograph taken by Frank Currier in 1875.*

234

105 'The Duel' by Charles Schreyvogel. Indians and the US Cavalry in action.

Within an hour, Custer and 224 men of the Seventh Cavalry were dead

It was a great victory, but it would have been better for the Indian if he had never won it. The news of the disaster roused the white American to a pitch of frenzy. The cry went up for vengeance. That winter, General Miles with a strong force pursued Crazy Horse across the plains, until the latter was compelled to seek surrender and sanctuary with the more compassionate General Crook. A few months later, the young chief was killed. He had learned of plans to seize him and send him in chains to the Dry Tortugas, and in trying to escape he was bayonetted in the back. Sitting Bull, after a sojourn in Canada, was shot in a skirmish on the Standing Rock Reservation in 1890, when a white agent thought he too was seeking to escape. His 17-year-old son was murdered with him.

The last scene in the drama was quickly played out. Appropriately, it took place in the remotest corner of the United States, as if to symbolize the manner in which the Indian had been driven back until finally he had no room left.

Since 1855, the Nez Perce had been occupying lands in Oregon and Idaho that had been awarded to them by treaty. A numerous and gifted

106 *Himmaton-Yalatkit, 'Thunder Coming Up Over the Land from the Water'. Chief Joseph, heroic leader of the Nez Perce.*

tribe, they had been given their name by French trappers, either because they inserted shells in their nostrils or because, like many tribes, they slit the nostrils of their Apaloosa horses to draw more air into the lungs and give them greater speed. When gold was discovered on their reservation, the white commissioners tried to reduce its size by more than three-quarters. The dispute came to centre on the fertile Wallowa valley, which young Chief Joseph, after protracted legal resistance, was compelled to give up or face removal by the army. While he was preparing to move, violence broke out, several whites were killed, and the troops sent to keep order were beaten at the battle of White Bird Canyon. In the 18 skirmishes that followed, Chief Joseph's war-leaders, Five Wounds, Looking Glass, and Toohoolhoolzote, continued to make rings around their adversaries.

After a clash with General Howard and 600 men in a two-day battle at Kamiah, in Idaho, Joseph, who even at the outset had never had that number of warriors at his disposal, realized that he had to choose between surrender and flight. He decided to try and take his remaining 200 warriors and 600 women and children to asylum in Canada. The Nez Perce then conducted an orderly retreat, closely pursued by Howard, that rivalled and perhaps even outdid the masterly retreats of the Apache. The remnants of the tribe moved east through the Lolo Pass of the Bitterroot Mountains; crossed four states; twice traversed the Rockies; drew Howard, whose force now numbered 2000 men, through the Yellowstone; and forded the Missouri. When Howard cornered him and his little worn out company in the Bear Paw Mountains, Joseph had traversed 2000 miles and was only 30 miles from the Canadian border. Even then, his braves fought furiously for five days, inflicting heavy losses, and Howard had to employ his cannon.

On 7 October 1877, after Howard had received further reinforcements, Joseph surrendered. The message addressed to his conqueror is famous:

I am weary of fighting. Our chiefs are killed. Looking Glass is dead. Toohoolhoolzote is dead. The old men are all dead. It is now the young men who say 'yea' or 'nay,' and he who used to lead them, my brother Olicut, is dead. It is cold. We have no blankets. The children are freezing. Some of my people have taken to the hills, and have no covering and no food. No one knows where they are. Perhaps they too are freezing. I want to look for them and try to find them. Perhaps they are dead.

Hear me, my chiefs. I am tired. My heart is sick and sad. From where the sun now stands, I will fight no more forever.

Chief Joseph's lament was only one of a number of such declarations that convey to a later generation something of what his utter and crushing defeat meant to the Indian.

237

The neighbours of the Nez Perce were the Flatheads. Their chief, Charlot, refused to vacate the Bitterroot valley in Montana for white settlers, and after a 30-year resistance was compelled as a very old man to take his people across the border into Canada. Here are a few sentences from a speech which he made in 1876. It was printed in translation in one of the more enlightened Montana newspapers:

Since our forefathers once beheld the white man, more than seven times ten winters have snowed and melted. He has filled graves with our bones. His course is destruction. He spoils what the Spirit of this country made beautiful and clean . . . What is he? Who sent him here? We were happy when he first came. We thought he came from the light. But now he comes like the dusk of the evening, not like the dawn of the morning. He comes like a day that has passed, and night enters our future with him. 'To take and to lie' should be burnt on his forehead, in the way he burns his name on the sides of the horses he steals from us. Had the Great Spirit signed him with a warning mark, we could have rejected him. But we did not reject him. In his weakness and poverty we fed him and cherished him. We befriended him and showed him the fords and passes across our lands. And he invited us to put our names on his papers, making us promises that he swore by the Sun and in the name of his own Chief. He promised to give us things that he never gave us, and which he knew he would never give us. And after the promises he threatened us, with his soldiers, his jails, his iron chains . . . My people, we are poor. We are fatherless. The white man has inflicted his doom on us, on the few of us who may survive a few days longer . . . As you know, he his cold, he is merciless, he is haughty and overbearing. You look at him, and he looks at you back – and what do you see? His fishy eyes slide over you. Cunning and envy fit him as closely as his hands and feet . . . Did his laws ever give us a single blade of grass, a tree, a duck, a grouse, a trout? He sneaks up on you like the wolverine that filches your goods. He comes more and more often. He seizes more and more. And he dirties what he does not take.

Such was the mood of the Indian in the 1870s. It was a mood that was to last for another half-century. Only now, and by no means everywhere, is it beginning to lighten a little.

We have seen that the policy of removing Indians by force or fraud from their tribal lands, which led inevitably to bloodshed, had been initiated in a spasmodic way in the seventeenth and eighteenth centuries, becoming systematized in the early nineteenth. Jefferson formulated large-scale plans to clear him from the Mississippi in 1802, extending the scheme to Indiana in 1803, Louisiana in 1804, and Arkansas in 1808. In such men as William

Henry Harrison, governor of Indiana Territory between 1800 and 1812, he found willing tools. Harrison quashed Indian titles to land in Indiana, Illinois, Ohio, Michigan and Wisconsin, compulsorily purchasing it at one cent an acre. By the last of his 15 compacts with the Indian, the Treaty of Fort Wayne in 1809, he seized 2½ million acres and drove Tecumseh to take up arms against the United States. Against such determined men, the Indian was helpless. In the five years between 1853 and 1857, the United States acquired 157 million acres of land, through 52 different treaties, none of which were subsequently honoured.

By 1860, the removal concept was clear and the process well advanced. It was only marginally interrupted during the Civil War, when the Confederate government introduced an imaginative new approach to the Indian question that was unfortunately terminated by the Northern victory. By 1880, 25 tribes of the shrinking number that still survived had been re-located in what is now Oklahoma, and most of the others had been transferred a greater or lesser distance from their homeland. There was some discussion of the possibility of constituting an Indian Territory, a separate State to be wholly occupied by Indians; but the idea lapsed when it was realized that it would mean ceding too large an area, and one which might later prove to contain choice mining or farming locations. It was the need to repossess such locations on the reservations that had been duly established that would involve many unfortunate tribes in successive removals. The Mescalero Apache, for example, were removed eight times before they were allowed to settle in a spot for which the white man had no use. In actual fact, the wretched business of removal could itself be made to turn a profit. Shady white operators would pay bribes of as much as $20,000 to secure contracts to provide the Indian with weevil-infested biscuits and army surplus blankets. The famous Sioux chief Spotted Tail asked the government: 'Why does not the Great Father put his red children on wheels, so he can move them about more easily?'

In the early 1880s, the extent of Indian land holdings was 138 million acres. Fifty years later, in the early 1930s, as a result of the cheating made possible by the Dawes Severalty Act of 1887, and its continuation, the Burke Act of 1907, Indian holdings had been reduced by almost two-thirds, to 52 million acres. The Dawes Act had itself allotted 30 million acres to individual Indians; by 1934, 29 of those 30 million acres had found their way into the hands of the white man. At a rate of 1½ million acres a year, or 4500 acres a day, the Indian was losing even the vestigial territory that had nominally been granted to him. Even when the Indian had been given land by allotment, he was usually unable to live on the best parts of it because they had been 'leased' to the white man.

There was, of course, as indicated at the beginning of this chapter, a body of white notables who attempted to protest at this hideous procession of events. We noted that the Bureau of Indian Affairs, established in 1834, had struggled to ameliorate the situation: but in 1849 it was merged with the Department of the Interior, losing what little independence it had ever enjoyed. Even then, as early as 1854, its Commissioner, George Moneypenny, had not abandoned the effort to halt the removal policy, or at least to mitigate its more abominable features. In 1869, a new Board of Commissioners to administer Indian affairs was created by President Grant. At its head he actually placed an Indian, Ely Parker, a member of the Seneca people who had been one of his staff officers in the Civil War. Unfortunately, the members of the Board too often proved to be time-servers, or else corrupt. Parker himself had to be removed at an early stage for incompetence. Nevertheless, in addition to such courageous individuals as Helen Hunt Jackson, organizations like the National Indian Association, the Indian Rights Association, and the National Indian Defence Association, though small, performed vigorous and useful service.

As early as 1793, Congress had voted the sum of $20,000 annually to provide the Indian with domestic animals and farming equipment. George Washington believed that the salvation of the Indian lay in the adoption of the white man's ways. In 1819, Congress established a further fund to 'civilize' the Indian; but by mid-century the programme had been abandoned, and politicians of all persuasions were openly declaring that the Indian was dirty, backward, unteachable, irrelevant, an obstacle to progress, and should be positively encouraged to die.

By the mid-1920s he was, in fact, moribund. The tiny medical unit set up inside the Indian Service in 1910 was powerless to stem the diseases that were devouring him. The Indian's birth-rate fell below his death-rate. A whole people, who once bestrode a continent, were perishing.

Yet it was now, when the Indian's fortunes appeared to have reached their lowest point, and his end seemed inevitable, that a gradual reversal began to occur.

Revival

The factor that started to tip the scale in the other direction was the Teapot Dome scandal. President Harding had appointed as Secretary of the Interior in his none-too-sweet-smelling administration a lawyer called Albert B. Fall. Fall had made his name in the Southwest, where he had been a judge and the associate and defender of cattle-barons, land-sharks, gamblers, gunmen, and murderers. One of his first actions as Secretary of the Interior was to introduce an Indian Omnibus Bill that would have stripped the Indian of whatever possessions were still left to him. When oil was discovered at Teapot Dome, on the Navajo reservation of Arizona, Fall decreed by executive order that the oil belonged to the government, not to the Navajo. He and his friends were already accepting bribes in respect of this and other oil properties, and in the upshot they were indicted and sent to jail. At the same time, Senator Robert M. LaFollette contrived to kill the Indian Omnibus Bill.

At last, the American public began to feel some stirrings of conscience at such cynical antics. Sentiment began to veer in favour of the Indian. Fifty years had passed since the battle of the Little Big Horn, and the Indian had long ceased to be a major threat, or even a minor irritation. There had been some other straws in the wind. The public had been impressed by Theodore Roosevelt's characteristic enthusiasm, as a dedicated outdoors-man, for all things Indian. It also remembered the fighting record of Indian soldiers in the First World War. The shift in feeling was reinforced by the appearance in 1928 of a monumental report, called the Meriam Report, issued by the Brookings Institution. The document denounced in plain terms the misdeeds of the Federal Government, the Indian Bureau, and the Senate Committee on Indian Affairs. President Hoover continued to encourage the impluse towards reform, which culminated in 1933 in the appointment by President Roosevelt of an altogether outstanding man to the post of Commissioner of Indian Affairs.

John Collier, who had been trained as a social scientist, was vigorous and determined. In his term of office, which almost exactly spanned that of Roosevelt's presidencies, he secured a 'New Deal' for the American Indian. In 1934, he brought about the termination of the policy of severalty, by means of an Indian Reorganization Bill, and in the years that followed, with immense pertinacity, he engineered a revolution in the way the white man regarded the Indian and in the way the Indian had been taught to regard himself. It was Collier who, by such measures as lifting the existing bans on Indian ceremonials, on Indian folkways, and on the wearing of Indian dress, began to reawaken in the Indian a sense of dignity and self-respect.

There have been setbacks in the progress of the Indian since Collier's retirement in 1946. Indeed, it might be more accurate to say that there has been less actual progress than a stabilization of the Indian condition, an arrest of the miseries of his long decline. The Bureau of Indian Affairs has not maintained the momentum imparted by Collier, and today is generally resented or actively detested by the Indians themselves. Indians do not occupy high positions in its hierarchy, and scarcely participate in its decisions. Jamake Highwater, the editor of Fodor's *Guide to Indian America* (1975), declares in the section devoted to the Bureau that:

A familiar Indian joke is that the first two swear words learned on a reservation are S.O.B. and B.I.A. Many of the long-term white staffers are leaving the service, and unfortunately those people most inclined to leave are the most sympathetic and best educated, while the old-timers, mostly retired military personnel attracted to the political jobs, linger on. The trend of B.I.A. bureaucracy is more to perpetuate itself than to achieve social goals.

In conclusion, what, the reader may ask, is by contrast the situation in Canada? What prompted Chief Joseph and Chief Charlot, and such earlier leaders as Pontiac and Joseph Brant, to guide their peoples out of the United States into the shelter of the other great country of North America? Why did the soil of Canada seem so inviting? One cannot do better than to quote the opinion of John Collier, in his *Indians of the America*. He wrote:

Canada's policy was, from the first, based on the English policy of respecting the Indian landholdings and keeping faith with the tribes. It was also concerned with conserving natural resources. The Hudson's Bay Company, formed by Charles II of England in 1670, was itself a conserver of Indian life and society. As such, and through the medium of the Indians, it became the earliest institution in the modern white world to apply itself to the conservation of natural resources. The resources were the fur-bearing animals; but these existed within the web which included the forest and the man. In the United States the web was reft asunder; in the Hudson's Bay area, after a good deal of early destruction, the web was permitted to regenerate itself, and is nearly intact today.

Canada made Indian treaties thriftily and never broke them; neither did Canada drive the tribes at one another's throats nor fight them. She formulated out of practice, a brief, flexible body of Canadian Indian law which is eminent for fairness of spirit and for common sense. She did not force land allotment on her Indians; she did not appropriate their communal funds or divert them into her costs of administration; she did not tolerate corruption in her Indian Service. She provided an orderly, dignified transition for Indians out of the tribal and into the general life, but she did not force the process by way of the many kinds of bludgeoning and confiscation employed in the United States. And this is still true in the present day . . .

Genius, vision, adventurousness are not greatly present in Canada's Indian record. But it means much that there is one Commonwealth in the Western world – there is only one – which from beginning to end has shown moral integrity in dealing with Indians and has kept the faith.

Today, the Indian in the USA lives on 200 reservations, in 26 states. The reservations vary from a few acres with a score of Indians to hundreds of thousands of acres with a corresponding number of occupants. The Indian population is variously estimated at between 550,000 and 800,000. It is difficult to obtain an exact figure, since much of the Indian population is constantly in movement between the reservations and the white urban centres where lucrative employment – or sometimes simply employment – is to be found. In any case, the Indian, like the Chicano, the black, and the Puerto Rican, tends to become suspicious and unco-operative where such a manifestation of officialdom as census-taking is concerned.

It is probable that at any one time about half the Indian population is on the reservation and half off it. Indian men and youths increasingly leave the reservation for cities that are close at hand, such as Phoenix, Albuquerque, Oklahoma City, Tulsa, Denver, Rapid City, Portland and Seattle. Some of them travel further afield to San Francisco, Los Angeles, Chicago or Minneapolis. The desire of the Indian, the peasant, and the poor in general to abandon the land, and to add to the overcrowding of the cities, is a world wide problem.

In the case of the American Indian, several important factors are at work. First, many reservations are too infertile to provide their inhabitants with a decent living, and many of the Indian tribes, particularly the hunting tribes, have never taken to the settled ways which the white man has sought to impose on them. Secondly, in the back of the mind of the older generation of Indians is the memory of the order, issued by General Sheridan in 1871, that an Indian must not leave the reservation assigned to him without the written permission of his white agent. Not so long ago, Indians were prisoners in the hands of white jailers, and to escape from the reservation was thus the equivalent of an escape from prison. Thirdly, the Indian population of America is now very young – and young men are energetic and ambitious. Now that some prospect of recovery is in the air, the Indian birth-rate is rapidly rising. In the 1860s, the Navajo were rounded up by Kit Carson and conducted on their own 300-mile 'Trail of Tears' to the Bosque Redondo, at Fort Sumner. Their number declined to fewer than 900. Extinction seemed unavoidable. Somehow they found the will to endure, and in recent years their number has risen to more than 125,000, of whom 60 per cent are today under the age of 19, and a further 25 per cent under 40. Clearly there is no room for so many dynamic young people on the reservation, even though the Navajo reservation is 16 million acres in extent. It is the largest reservation in the United States, and its size seems generous – until one realizes that, before the 1860s, the Navajo roamed over an area twice as large, and that at one time their reservation was so drastically reduced by the white authorities that some of its bleaker parts

243

had to be restored to prevent the tribe from literally starving to death.

Like many American reservations, the Navajo reservation is beautiful but inhospitable. It consists largely of desert or semi-desert that the white settler did not consider worth seizing even under the provisions of the Dawes Act. There is no choice for a bright and active young man except to forsake his poverty-stricken mesas and head for the city.

Unfortunately, the young Indian, whose abilities are needed more on his reservation than in the town, is fatally handicapped in his new environment, and can seldom make a success of his fresh start. Fifty per cent of the Indians who seek a new life in the city eventually creep back home again, bitter, perplexed, and defeated. His main handicap is his lack of education. Many Indians receive no schooling at all, and others average only five years of schooling compared to the white boy's 11. Few enter high school, and fewer still proceed to college. In addition, the Indian is bewildered by the tempo of life in the city. He suffers from homesickness, loneliness, and unfamiliarity with the English language. He feels cut off from his family and friends, and from the supportive structure of the tribe.

On the reservation, the Indian possesses individuality, status, and a sense of belonging. In other respects, his situation there is not enviable. Some tribes, with better land than others, have become excellent farmers and stockmen. They successfully operate such businesses as hotels, ski resorts, and lumber-yards. Other tribes have remained unskilled, apathetic and hostile to white culture. In general, as the Bureau of Indian Affairs itself has pointed out, 'the land on reservations is not sufficiently productive to provide a livelihood for the population'. In 1976, when the average income of an American family was $6400, only ten per cent of Indian families earned more than $4000 a year. 75 per cent earned less than $2000 a year, 50 per cent less than $1000. The Indian earns an average wage of $30 a week, against $130 a week for the white and black man. And between 40 and 60 per cent of the Indian population is, in any case, permanently unemployed.

On the reservations, 75 per cent of the inhabitants occupy shacks, shelters, huts, or abandoned cars and buses. The same proportion haul their water from pools, tanks, or rivers, which are often polluted. Not surprisingly, as a result of insanitary conditions, inadequate housing, poor diet, alcoholism, and a lack of medical services, the Indian's expectation of life is substantially lower than the white man's – 45 years compared to 72 years – and he suffers to an excessive degree from syphilis, tuberculosis, pneumonia, dysentery, trachoma, and diseases of the bone and the inner ear. The Indian is the low man on the American totem pole.

He also suffers from ills of his own making. Many of the leaders he elects to govern him are often found guilty of corruption and embezzlement, or at the best of poor fiscal judgment and a lack of responsibility and accountability. Many reservations are riven by the feuds and factions endemic to all human communities, but which can be disastrous in communities situated as precariously as those of the modern Indian. Moreover, the problems of sickness, unemployment, and tribal in-fighting are immensely compounded by the main Indian social problem: drunkenness. Its causes lie in recent Indian history. They can be readily understood, and arouse sympathy. Nevertheless, on a single Western reservation, in one year, 44 per cent of all males and 21 per cent of all females were arrested for drunkenness. In Gallup, where many Navajo go to drink, there are 54 bars to serve 50,000 people, and arrests for drunkenness reach 10,000 a year. The roads around many reservations are death-traps. Drunken drivers cause more fatalities in a year than occurred in many of the Indian wars. The incidence of drunkenness helps to explain why the Indian murder and suicide rates are three to four times as high as among whites.

If the Indian is staging a revival, he clearly has a long way to go.

And yet, although much devastation, dilution, and assimilation have taken place, and the classic culture of the Indian has been everywhere eroded, something of value still remains.

Many of the Indian pow-wows, dances, and rituals that are celebrated today are bogus and meretricious. Except for the annual ceremonials of the Pueblos, and some of those of the Northwest, their original meaning has become obscured or forgotten. They are often vulgar, even ridiculous. Nevertheless, they bestow on their participants a sense of identity and solidarity, and bolster tribal morale.

In the sphere of art, the situation is different. It is in his art and in the revival of his handicrafts that the inner life of the Indian seems to express itself most forcefully and effectively. There is a quality about Indian art that is not always present in his re-vamped rituals, which too often give the impression of being prettied up for tourists and smack of Disneyland. It is as if the Indian artist and craftsman executes his or her paintings, sculptures, jewelry, textiles, and basketry with a confidence born of the admiration and interest with which a thoughtful public regards it. Into them he pours his heart and soul. Similarly, the volume of Indian poetry, fiction and drama is constantly increasing. The voice of the Indian writer is vivid and distinctive, and his subject-matter possesses a mysterious and elevated quality that is already acting as a leaven in the American and Canadian literature in which it is embedded.

The Indian's new-found confidence also extends into his material and political worlds. Groups of Indians throughout America are today asserting themselves in a manner that would have been inconceivable only a few years ago. Who would ever have anticipated that the Wampanoag, whom we encountered at the very beginning of this chapter, would today be suing the State of Massachussetts for the return of their lands? They are citing as their authority an ancient copy of an Indian Nonintercourse Act of 1790, unearthed by chance, which prohibited the transfer of Indian lands without federal government approval. This obscure piece of legislation the white man, having thoroughly suppressed the Indian, had somehow neglected to repeal. The action of the Wampanoag has thrown the white man into a financial panic, and the Wampanoag have regained a tract of land on Martha's Vineyard.

Nearby, the Penobscot and Passamaquoddy have also taken to the legal warpath. They have sent the State of Maine into an economic tizzy. Under the Indian Nonintercourse Act, they are laying claim to two-thirds of the State, worth an estimated 25 billion dollars. They are asking 300 million dollars damages for 180 years of illegal occupation. The sale of municipal bonds and the progress of construction and house and land sales in the State have been seriously affected. In Rhode Island, the Narraganset have laid claim to over 3000 acres in the town of Charlestown; in Connecticut, the Shaghticoke and Western Pequot are filing for property in the towns of Kent and Ledyard; and in New York State the Oneida are demanding ownership of 300,000 acres between Syracuse and Utica.

In Illinois, Kansas, Missouri, and Iowa, a number of tribes have combined to wrest a six-million-dollar settlement of a land-claim. The Sioux are arguing before the United States Supreme Court that the boundaries of their Rosebud Reservation in South Dakota were improperly determined and are invalid. In Michigan, the State's Supreme Court has upheld the right of the Chippewa to fish in Lake Superior free from state restrictions, and in Minnesota the same tribe has won exemption from local and state taxes. In northern California, the Yurok Indians have ousted white fishing and logging companies, have combated white tourist agents, and are asserting that land-claims in and around the town of Klamath are fraudulent. Their example has stirred other tribes to seek similar redress. A century ago, such audacity would have resulted in the Yurok being shot or transported.

Indian and white man recognize, of course, that there is no possibility, in the end, of the Indian regaining more than a tithe of his ancient domains. As a result of his legal manoeuvring he may, however, extract large sums in compensation. He might even secure a revision of some of the oil, coal and natural gas leases which work to the advantage of commercial companies and not to his own. In the meantime, it is amusing to watch the Indian turning against the white man the weapons which the white man once employed so unscrupulously against him. He may ultimately obtain, if not his pound, then at least his ounce of flesh. In that respect, he is truly learning the white man's ways.

Sadly, the white American does not seem to comprehend the depth of the Indian's anger. The prospects for any rapid rapprochement between the white man and the red man are not favourable. The principal stumbling block is the fact that the white man cannot recognize and acknowledge the enormity of what he has done. The twentieth-century American regards himself as a benevolent, amiable, freedom-loving fellow, a friend to all mankind. He has always possessed a remarkable capacity for turning a blind eye to his own shortcomings. Dr. Johnson, in his *Taxation No Tyranny*, had a point when he asked: 'How is it that we hear the loudest *yelps* for liberty among the drivers of negroes?' The American Indian might equally ask: 'How is it that we hear the loudest *yelps* for liberty among the drivers of Indians?'

The Indian is still being driven. He may therefore be pardoned if he greets the ardour for human rights expressed by American Presidents, Senators and Congressmen with a snicker or an outright horse-laugh. He knows too well what American Presidents, Senators and Congressmen have done to him in the immediate past, and are doing to him today. He holds a poor opinion of their credentials as the champions of liberty and justice.

The white American is bewildered and hurt by what he regards as this harsh and unforgiving attitude. He has forgiven the Indian – so why cannot the Indian forgive him? He overlooks the fact that the Indian may have too much to forgive. Henry Steele Commager once put his finger squarely on this cheerful propensity of the white American to forgive himself his own sins.

> Even in the nineteenth century, perhaps even in the twentieth century, Americans developed the habit of brushing aside whatever was embarrassing that still characterizes them, the habit of taking for granted a double standard of history and morality. There were, to be sure, awkward things in our history, but somehow they were not to be held against us, somehow they didn't count. . . The conquest and decimation of the Indian didn't count – after all, the Indians were heathens – and when that argument lost its force, there was the undeniable charge that they got in the way of progress.

The Indian episode is one of those 'awkward things' in American history.

247

The Indian nation is not disposed to allow the American to 'brush it aside' and pretend it 'does not count'. What is more, the Indian has a very long memory. He broods over his wrongs. And he is extremely patient.

Perhaps the white American is right: perhaps it is futile and damaging to continue to nurse an ancient grudge. The better course may be to forgive. But forgiveness must take a long time: and in the meantime it would be foolish to ignore the fact, which any conversation with an Indian or any visit to a reservation will confirm, that Indian resentments have in no whit diminished. The truth of the matter is that the Indian chapter in American history is not closed, though the white American might wish or even think it so. Many years must pass before the Indian's wounds have healed, and before a genuine reconciliation between the two races can take place.

Bibliography

The following books are intended for the general reader. Specialized studies of individual tribes and culture areas are unfortunately too numerous to attempt a listing. For these, consult the bibliographies in the books below. All are published in New York unless otherwise indicated.

Alexander, Hartley Burr, *The World's Rim, Great Mysteries of The North American Indian*, University of Nebraska Press, Lincoln, Nebraska, 1935.

Association on Indian American Affairs, Inc., *Indian Affairs* and *American Indian*, Periodically published.

Brandon, William, *The American Heritage Book of Indians*, American Heritage Publishing Company, 1961.

Brophy, William A., and Aberle, Sophie D., *The Indian, America's Unfinished Business*, University of Oklahoma Press, Norman, Oklahoma, 1966.

Collier, John, *Indians of the Americas*, W. W. Norton, 1947.

Driver, Harold E., *Indians of North America*, University of Chicago Press, Chicago, Illinois, 1961.

Eggan, F. (ed.), *Social Organization of North American Tribes*, University of Chicago Press, Chicago, Illinois, 1955.

Fitting, James E. (ed.), *The Development of North American Archaeology*, Anchor Books, Doubleday, 1973.

Folsom, Franklin, *America's Ancient Treasures, A Travel Guide to Archaeological Sites and Museums of Indian Lore*, Rand McNally, 1974.

Hagan, William T., *American Indians*, University of Chicago Press, Chicago, Illinois, 1961.

Hassrick, Royal B., *North American Indians*, Octopus Books, London, 1974.

Highwater, Jamake (ed.), *Fodor's Guide to Indian America*, David McKay, 1975.

Jennings, Jesse D., *Prehistory of North America*, McGraw Hill, 1974.

Josephy, Alvin M., Jr., *The Indian Heritage of America*, Alfred A. Knopf, 1968.

Josephy, Alvin M., Jr., *The Patriot Chiefs*, Viking Press, 1961.

Kroeber, A. L., *Anthropology*, Harcourt Brace, 1948.

Kroeber, Theodora, *Ishi*, University of California Press, Berkeley and Los Angeles, 1961.

La Farge, Oliver, *A Pictorial History of the American Indian*, Crown Publishers, 1956.

Marquis, Arnold, *A Guide to America's Indians: Ceremonials, Reservations and Museums*, University of Oklahoma Press, Norman, Oklahoma, 1975.

Meggers, Betty J., *Prehistoric America*, Aldine Atherton, 1972.

Spencer, Robert F., and Jennings, Jesse D., *The Native Americans*, Harper & Row, 1965.

Steiner, Stan, *The New Indians*, Harper & Row, 1968.

Sterling, Mathew, *Indians of the Americas*, National Geographic Society, Washington, D.C., 1957.

Underhill, Ruth M., *Red Man's America*, University of Chicago Press, Chicago, Illinois, 1953.

U.S. Bureau of Indian Affairs, *Where To Learn More About Indians*, Government Printing Office, Washington, D.C., 1970.

White, Jon Manchip, *A World Elsewhere*, Thomas Y. Crowell, 1975.

Whiteford, Andrew Hunter, and Zim, Herbert S., *North American Indian Arts*, Golden Press, 1970.

Wissler, Clark, *Indians of the United States*, Revised edition by Lucy Wales Kluckhohn, Anchor Books, Doubleday, 1966.

Index

Figures in **bold type** refer to the page numbers of illustrations

251